MW01614322

100 Notorious Organized Crime Figures Around The World

Mafia Bosses, Cartel Leaders, and Criminal Empires Worldwide

By Alexander Gambino

Copyright Page

Copyright © 2025 by Alexander Gambino

All rights reserved. No part of this publication may be reproduced, stored in a retrieval system, or transmitted in any form or by any means, electronic or mechanical, without permission in writing from the author.

This is a work of nonfiction. All information has been compiled from publicly available sources and is believed to be accurate at the time of publication.

This book is available in eBook and paperback formats.

Published by Alexander Gambino

Contents

Introduction

This book is meant to be a journey into the criminal underworld, an exploration of the figures who have ruled cities, influenced governments, and built empires not with laws, but with fear, blood, and money. Across continents and generations, organized crime has evolved from back-alley rackets into sprawling, multinational networks that rival legitimate industries in wealth and reach.

These are the men, and sometimes women, who've commanded loyalty, orchestrated violence, and evaded justice for decades. From the mafia dons of New York and the narco-kings of Colombia, to the yakuza lieutenants of Japan and the oligarch-backed mafias of Eastern Europe, each figure profiled in this volume shaped not just the criminal world, but the political, economic, and social fabric of their time.

The book is divided by region, tracing the rise of syndicate leaders within the unique historical and cultural conditions that birthed them. Yet despite their differences, a common thread emerges: organized crime is not merely about illegal enterprise, it is about control. It thrives in vacuums of governance, festers in inequality, and often walks hand-in-hand with the very institutions meant to stop it.

This is not a collection of folklore or gangster glorification. It is a forensic look at the real histories behind the myths. Every profile is built on thorough research, not rumor. These stories are more than criminal biographies. They are windows into how power works when it answers to no one.

North-American Organized Crime

Organized crime in North America has deep roots, stretching back to colonial-era smuggling and piracy. Over time, it became a forceful shadow economy, one that exploited prohibition, poverty, and institutional weaknesses. In the early 20th century, loosely organized street gangs and ethnic criminal factions, notably the Italian-American "Black Hand," laid the groundwork for what would become more structured mafias.

The Prohibition era (1920–1933) transformed American criminality. Once illicit entrepreneurs gained unprecedented profits from bootleg liquor, catalyzing rapid market consolidation. Clans led by figures like Al Capone in Chicago and Lucky Luciano in New York matured into disciplined, hierarchical syndicates, ushering in the era of the American Mafia. Their operations soon expanded into gambling, labor racketeering, loan sharking, and narcotics trafficking following repeal.

Chicago's Outfit and the Five Families in New York epitomized this evolution. These organizations refined the concept of a crime "family," a formalized, syndicate-based framework structured around control, territory, and loyalty, under the oversight of bodies like the Mafia Commission.

With growing wealth, organized crime diversified into both illegal and legitimate spheres. By mid-century, families infiltrated public institutions. Using extortion and graft to own labor unions, construction projects, and even public contracts, they effectively blurred the line between legitimate enterprise and criminal enterprise.

Across the U.S., ethnic and regional criminal groups thrived alongside the Italians. Irish gangs in Boston and

Chicago, Jewish and Polish syndicates, and regional outfits like the New Orleans Crime Family mirrored the Italian-American model, demonstrating that organized crime was a pan-ethnic phenomenon responding to similar structural opportunities.

By the late 20th century, North American crime syndicates had transformed into transnational networks. They forged alliances with Latin American drug cartels, Hong Kong triads, and Balkan mafias, facilitated by globalization. Meanwhile, legal innovations like the RICO Act shifted the balance, enabling federal authorities to prosecute entire organizations, not only individuals.

Today, traditional mafias are diminished, fractured by prosecution, internal betrayals, and adaptation. However, they are not extinct. Figures like the remaining Chicago Outfit or remnants of the Five Families continue to operate discreetly. Furthermore, newer criminal enterprises like cyber syndicates, street gangs, and organized immigrant crime often replicate Mafia structures: hierarchical leadership, diversified revenue channels, and political infiltration.

Charles "Lucky" Luciano

Charlie "Lucky" Luciano began his journey into organized crime after immigrating from Sicily to New York City in 1906 around the age of eight to ten. Growing up on Manhattan's Lower East Side, he was already engaged in petty crimes like shoplifting and extortion by his early teens. His rise to power accelerated through strategic alliances, particularly with Jewish mobsters Meyer Lansky and Bugsy Siegel, bridging ethnic divisions that had long separated criminal factions. In 1931, Luciano orchestrated the murders of rival mafia bosses Joe Masseria and Salvatore Maranzano, effectively ending the Castellammarese War and positioning himself as the dominant Mafia leader in New York. He solidified his hold on power by forming key relationships with figures like Frank Costello and Vito Genovese, while simultaneously betraying former mentors to modernize and restructure the Mafia into a more business-like organization.

Luciano's criminal operations were vast, spanning bootlegging during Prohibition, illegal gambling, racketeering, prostitution, and drug trafficking. He established the National Crime Syndicate, which coordinated criminal activities across the United States and implemented a corporate structure within the Mafia. This innovation boosted both efficiency and profits, allowing him to build an expansive and powerful criminal empire.

Publicly, Luciano projected the image of a refined businessman. He was often seen in tailored suits and took up residence in luxury hotels like the Waldorf-Astoria. Behind closed doors, however, he was a calculating and ruthless strategist who prioritized profits over tradition and did not hesitate to eliminate rivals to preserve his control. His reputation as a business-oriented leader helped transform the Mafia into a modern criminal enterprise.

One of the most notable episodes in Luciano's life was his 1936 conviction on compulsory prostitution charges, which resulted in a 30 to 50-year prison sentence. Yet, even from prison, he managed to retain influence over organized crime. During World War II, he played a covert role in helping the U.S. Navy prevent sabotage on the docks by leveraging his control over the longshoremen's unions. This cooperation led to his sentence being commuted in 1946.

Throughout his career, Luciano accumulated significant wealth through his illegal enterprises, although the exact figures remain unknown due to the secretive nature of his operations. Thanks to the coordinated structures he put in place, his influence extended deeply into organized crime circles across the country. These efforts were often supported by his connections with corrupt law enforcement officials and local government figures, particularly in New York City, who enabled his activities through bribes and mutual benefit.

Luciano's downfall began with his 1936 conviction, and his power diminished further following his deportation to Italy in 1946. This move effectively removed him from the center of American organized crime and curtailed his direct involvement. He died of a heart attack on January 26, 1962, at Naples International Airport in Italy, where he had gone to meet with a Hollywood movie producer. Though exiled, he remained a symbolic figure within the world of organized crime, and his death marked the end of an era. Still, the organizational structures he created continued to define the Mafia long after he was gone.

Luciano's legacy is immense. He founded The Commission and helped establish the Five Families, setting a precedent for how organized crime would operate in America. Often referred to as the "father of modern organized crime," his life has been the subject of countless books, films, and academic research.

Funded by his ruthless criminal endeavors, Luciano had a taste for the finer things in life, reportedly owning a Patek Philippe watch and frequently indulging in luxury clothing and jewelry. Perhaps most interestingly, his cooperation with the U.S. government during World War

II in protecting the docks from foreign sabotage demonstrates the complex and often paradoxical relationship between crime and politics during that time.

Meyer "Mob's Accountant" Lansky

Meyer Lansky began his path into organized crime after immigrating from Grodno, then part of the Russian Empire, now Belarus, to New York City in 1911 at the age of nine. Settling in Manhattan's Lower East Side, Lansky quickly became involved in petty crimes and formed a lifelong friendship with Bugsy Siegel. The two would go on to co-found the "Bugs and Meyer Mob," a gang known for its violent enforcement tactics. Lansky later partnered with Charles "Lucky" Luciano to form the National Crime Syndicate, a groundbreaking move that united various ethnic crime groups under a cooperative framework. His alliances with figures like Luciano and Siegel were instrumental in bridging Jewish and Italian organized crime factions. Lansky also played a role in the betrayal and elimination of rival boss Salvatore Maranzano, a move that helped establish The Commission, a governing body for the mafia in the United States.

Lansky was involved in a wide range of criminal activities, including bootlegging during Prohibition, illegal gambling, racketeering, and money laundering. He was a driving force behind the development and management of casinos in Las Vegas, Cuba, and the Bahamas. Using his sharp financial acumen, he built an empire by constructing a sophisticated network for laundering money through offshore banks and legitimate businesses. His mastery of financial operations earned him the nickname "Mob's Accountant," and he became a central figure in the monetary engine behind organized crime.

Known for his reserved and intelligent demeanor, Lansky maintained a public image that avoided the flamboyance typical of other mobsters. Privately, he was a highly strategic thinker with a strict adherence to agreements, and his calculating, discreet approach allowed him to maintain significant influence while avoiding excessive law enforcement attention. He preferred to operate from the shadows, focusing on financial control rather than open displays of power or violence.

Throughout his life, Lansky was implicated in numerous illegal gambling operations, but he managed to evade major convictions. One of the most notable episodes in his later years came in 1970, when he fled to Israel to avoid indictment, seeking citizenship under the Law of Return. He was denied, however, and forced to return to the United States, where charges were eventually dropped due to his deteriorating health. Like several other crime figures of his era, Lansky also played a covert role in aiding the U.S. Navy during World War II. Through his influence over the docks, he helped prevent sabotage in a collaboration known as Operation Underworld.

Lansky accumulated vast wealth through his criminal enterprises, with estimates suggesting he had over $300 million hidden in offshore accounts. Although these claims were never conclusively proven, the belief in his financial power was widespread. His influence extended beyond U.S. borders into Cuba and the Bahamas, where his gambling and financial operations cemented his reach as an international figure in organized crime.

He maintained long-standing connections with corrupt officials and law enforcement personnel, secured through bribes and mutual benefit. These relationships allowed him to operate with impunity, especially in key locations like Havana and Las Vegas, where his gambling enterprises flourished. His ability to navigate political and legal systems was a key component of his lasting power.

Though eventually indicted, Lansky managed to avoid any significant prison sentence. His failed attempt to secure Israeli citizenship to escape prosecution marked the beginning of his final decline. Increased law enforcement pressure and a shifting organized crime landscape that no longer favored his traditional methods diminished his influence in his later years.

Lansky died of lung cancer on January 15, 1983, in Miami Beach, Florida, at the age of 80. Despite decades of investigations, authorities were never able to locate the vast fortune he was rumored to have hidden. This has fueled ongoing speculation that either he had successfully hidden his wealth or that it never existed to the degree people believed.

He left behind a lasting legacy, having pioneered money laundering techniques and demonstrating the immense power of financial control within organized crime. Today, Lansky is remembered as a master strategist and financial architect of the criminal underworld. His life has inspired numerous portrayals in popular culture, including the character Hyman Roth in *The Godfather Part II*.

Despite his role in global crime, Lansky had a personal side few knew, he had a deep love of history and philosophy and often engaged in thoughtful discussions on these subjects. He also reportedly possessed compromising photographs of FBI Director J. Edgar Hoover with his long-time aide Clyde Tolson, allegedly using them to blackmail Hoover and keep the FBI from investigating his criminal activities.

Arnold "The Big Bankroll" Rothstein

Arnold Rothstein was born into a prosperous Jewish family in New York City. His father, Abraham Rothstein, known as "Abe the Just," was a respected businessman who hoped his son would follow a conventional path. But Arnold had different ambitions. He dropped out of school at sixteen and dove headfirst into the world of gambling. With a sharp mathematical mind and an uncanny ability to read people, Rothstein quickly rose through the ranks of New York's underground gambling scene. By the 1910s, he had become a key figure in the city's criminal underworld, gaining a reputation as a brilliant bookmaker and strategist.

Rothstein's criminal empire was vast and varied. He ran high-stakes gambling operations, financed bootlegging enterprises during Prohibition, and took part in narcotics trafficking, most notably the distribution of heroin. He was also a loan shark, offering high-interest loans to the desperate, and a key player in fixing sporting events. His most notorious involvement was the 1919 Black Sox Scandal, where eight players from the Chicago White Sox were accused of intentionally losing the World Series. While Rothstein was never formally convicted, he was widely believed to have financed the fix, operating through intermediaries to shield himself from legal consequences. Rothstein's brilliance lay in staying behind the scenes, he meticulously planned operations while letting others carry out the riskier aspects of the work.

He cultivated a cool, composed persona, often described as calm and calculating. Rothstein dressed impeccably and avoided the spotlight, preferring to manipulate events from the shadows. His mind worked like a chess master's, always a few moves ahead. He treated crime as a business and emphasized structure, efficiency, and long-term profit. His demeanor and tactics stood in stark contrast to the more volatile gangsters of his era.

In addition to the Black Sox Scandal, Rothstein was linked to another controversial event: the 1921 Travers Stakes horse race. His horse, Sporting Blood, won under suspicious circumstances after Rothstein placed a large bet following the sudden withdrawal of the race's favorite due to injury. This prompted speculation that Rothstein had insider knowledge or had manipulated the situation entirely.

Financially, Rothstein was among the wealthiest figures in organized crime during his time. Though estimates vary, he was known for carrying large amounts of cash and was nicknamed "The Big Bankroll." His deep pockets gave him considerable leverage. He used his wealth to influence politicians, law enforcement, and even rival criminals, helping him cement his position as one of the most powerful men in New York's underworld.

He also developed close ties with political operators, including connections to Tammany Hall, New York's infamous Democratic political machine. These relationships provided a buffer between Rothstein and law enforcement, offering him a layer of protection that few others enjoyed. Bribes and backroom deals were instrumental in shielding his operations from scrutiny.

Rothstein's downfall, however, came not from federal agents or a rival gang, but from a dispute over a poker game. In 1928, after losing a significant sum during a high-stakes match, Rothstein refused to pay, alleging the game had been rigged. On November 4 of that year, he was shot at the Park Central Hotel in Manhattan. He died two days later, on November 6, at the age of 46. His murder remains unsolved, with theories ranging from unpaid debts to retribution from betrayed partners in crime.

Despite his relatively short life, Rothstein left an indelible mark on organized crime. He is credited with professionalizing criminal enterprises and laying the foundation for the syndicates that followed. His mentorship of figures like Charles "Lucky" Luciano, Meyer Lansky, and Frank Costello directly shaped the structure of the American Mafia. His legacy also extended into culture and literature. most famously as the inspiration for Meyer Wolfsheim in F. Scott Fitzgerald's *The Great Gatsby*. He has also been portrayed in modern media, including the series *Boardwalk Empire*, where his character captures the cunning and power Rothstein wielded.

Rothstein's strategic mind and business instincts were ahead of his time. He was among the first to recognize the immense profit potential of Prohibition, pouring money into bootlegging operations long before others followed suit. His life, legacy, and mysterious death continue to captivate historians and storytellers alike, offering a glimpse into the origins of modern organized crime.

Louis "Lepke" Buchalter

Louis "Lepke" Buchalter was born on Manhattan's Lower East Side into a large Ashkenazi Jewish family. His mother affectionately called him "Lepke," Yiddish for "Little Louis," a nickname that stuck with him for life. After his father died in 1909, Buchalter's life veered toward crime. By his early twenties, he had been incarcerated multiple times for petty offenses. Upon his release in 1922, he joined forces with his childhood friend Jacob "Gurrah" Shapiro, and together they built a criminal enterprise centered around labor racketeering. They focused on New York's garment industry, where they gained control over key unions and used them to extort businesses. Their grip on labor gave them both immense power and wealth, marking the start of Buchalter's rise in organized crime.

Buchalter's criminal activities expanded well beyond labor racketeering. He and Shapiro ran extortion schemes and loan-sharking operations, offering high-interest loans to desperate borrowers. During Prohibition and beyond, Buchalter also entered the narcotics trade, playing a role in the distribution of heroin and other illegal substances. But his most infamous contribution to organized crime was the establishment of Murder, Inc., a nationwide network of contract killers who carried out assassinations on behalf of the National Crime Syndicate. Operating quietly and efficiently, Murder, Inc. eliminated informants, rivals, and anyone who posed a threat to Syndicate interests. Under Buchalter's leadership, the group became a feared enforcement arm of the underworld.

Despite his violent empire, Buchalter was known for his calm and calculated demeanor. He was not the type to court attention or public spectacle. Instead, he preferred to remain behind the scenes, quietly orchestrating operations through trusted lieutenants. Those loyal to him were often rewarded with gifts, vacations, and nights out, gestures that earned him loyalty and helped shield his identity from the spotlight. His low public profile allowed him to avoid major law enforcement scrutiny for years, despite the scale and brutality of his operations.

One of the most consequential events tied to Buchalter was the 1935 assassination of fellow gangster Dutch Schultz. Schultz had become a liability after proposing the murder of prosecutor Thomas Dewey, a move that alarmed other Syndicate leaders who feared the backlash it would provoke. To prevent this unauthorized and dangerous act, the Syndicate decided Schultz had to be eliminated. Buchalter was tasked with overseeing the hit, and Schultz was gunned down shortly thereafter. The episode highlighted Buchalter's central role in enforcing the Syndicate's internal rules and protecting its long-term interests.

At the height of his power, Buchalter's criminal operations generated millions of dollars each year. His control over the garment industry's unions, combined with the enforcement capabilities of Murder, Inc., made him one of the most powerful mob bosses of his era. But as his influence grew, so did law enforcement attention, particularly from Thomas Dewey, the same prosecutor Schultz had targeted. Buchalter's operations came under increasing pressure, and his name began appearing more frequently in federal investigations.

His downfall began in 1936 when he ordered the murder of Joseph Rosen, a former trucker and union man he suspected of cooperating with authorities. That murder would later become a centerpiece of the government's case against him. As the legal pressure mounted, Buchalter surrendered to federal authorities in 1939, under the mistaken belief that he had secured a deal that would spare him from execution. While he was initially tried on federal charges, he was ultimately convicted for Rosen's murder in state court.

On March 4, 1944, after exhausting all appeals, Buchalter was executed in the electric chair at Sing Sing Prison. His execution marked a significant moment in American criminal history, he remains the only major organized crime boss in the United States to be put to death by the state. The government's successful prosecution and execution of Buchalter sent shockwaves through the underworld and demonstrated the expanding reach of law enforcement.

Buchalter's legacy in organized crime is defined by both innovation and brutality. He introduced a new, systematic model for contract killings through Murder, Inc., a concept that would influence organized crime for decades. His death also served as a cautionary tale for other mob leaders, proving that no amount of power could guarantee immunity from justice.

Outside the criminal world, Buchalter left his mark on American culture. His life was dramatized in the 1975 film *Lepke*, starring Tony Curtis, and he has appeared in various television portrayals, including *The Untouchables*. He was also immortalized in literature, poet Robert Lowell referenced Buchalter in his work *Memories of West Street and Lepke*, reflecting on their time together in prison. Despite his violent career, the nickname his mother gave him, "Little Louis," endured, a strangely humanizing touch to the life of a man who engineered some of the most chilling crimes in American history.

Al "Scarface" Capone

Al Capone began his criminal career in Brooklyn, New York, where he was born in 1899 to Italian immigrant parents. As a teenager, he became involved with several street gangs, including the notorious Five Points Gang. He also worked as a bouncer at the Harvard Inn, where he earned the nickname "Scarface" after being slashed across the face during a barroom fight. In the early 1920s, Capone moved to Chicago to work under the influential crime boss Johnny Torrio. Following an assassination attempt that left Torrio wounded and led to his retirement, Capone assumed control of his operations. He quickly expanded the organization, capitalizing on Prohibition to build a vast and profitable criminal empire.

Capone's rise to power was supported by his strong ties to corrupt politicians and law enforcement officials, which allowed him to operate with near impunity. He also cultivated a loyal network of gang members who enforced his rule and eliminated rivals. His criminal activities included bootlegging, illegal gambling, prostitution, and racketeering. Capone's organization controlled numerous speakeasies, gambling dens, and brothels throughout Chicago, supplying illegal alcohol during Prohibition and generating enormous profits. He used violence and intimidation to eliminate competition and relied on bribery to shield himself from prosecution, making him one of the wealthiest gangsters of his time.

Capone carefully cultivated a public image as a generous and charitable figure. He donated to various causes and opened soup kitchens during the Great Depression, which helped him gain favor with some segments of the public. Behind the scenes, however, he was known for his ruthless nature and willingness to use violence to achieve his goals. He had a flamboyant personality and was often seen wearing expensive suits and flashy jewelry. His charisma and public relations efforts further enhanced his popularity, despite the brutal reality of his criminal operations.

One of the most notorious events associated with Capone was the St. Valentine's Day Massacre on February 14, 1929, in which seven members of a rival gang were gunned down in a Chicago garage. Although Capone was in Florida at the time and was never charged, the massacre shocked the nation and increased public demand for his arrest. In 1931, he was finally brought to justice, not for murder or racketeering, but for tax evasion. He was convicted and sentenced to 11 years in federal prison, serving time in several facilities, including the infamous Alcatraz. While incarcerated, Capone's health began to deteriorate due to untreated syphilis, which progressively impaired both his mental and physical condition.

At the height of his power, Capone's net worth was estimated to be around $100 million, which would be equivalent to more than $1.5 billion today. His wealth gave him immense influence over Chicago's political landscape and law enforcement agencies, particularly in cities like Chicago and Cicero, where his operations were centered. Through a combination of bribes and intimidation, Capone effectively ensured protection for his criminal enterprises.

Despite his conviction, Capone continued to appeal his sentence without success. His health continued to decline rapidly during his time in prison, and his influence on organized crime diminished significantly. His eventual downfall was driven by relentless law enforcement pressure and his inability to function as his illness worsened. Capone was released in 1939 and spent his final years in isolation, far removed from the criminal empire he once commanded.

He died of cardiac arrest on January 25, 1947, at his estate in Palm Island, Florida, at the age of 48. Although he had become a shadow of his former self, his death marked the symbolic end of an era in organized crime. Al Capone remains one of the most infamous crime figures in American history, a name synonymous with the gangster era of the 1920s and 1930s.

Capone's impact on organized crime was profound. He demonstrated the immense profitability of criminal enterprise during Prohibition and the importance of cultivating political connections. His methods and organizational structure influenced countless crime groups that followed. Today, he is remembered as a cultural icon, with his life and crimes serving as inspiration for numerous books, films, and television shows.

Despite his violent legacy, Capone had a softer side that surprised many. While incarcerated at Alcatraz, he played the banjo in the prison band and found solace in music. In fact, he allegedly was such a lover of jazz that he once kidnapped jazz pianist Fats Weller at gunpoint, only to lavish him food, drinks, and cash while Weller played at Capone's birthday party. During the Great Depression, he opened one of the first soup kitchens in Chicago, serving meals to thousands of unemployed citizens. These gestures helped humanize him in the eyes of the public, adding layers of complexity to one of America's most notorious criminals.

Benjamin "Bugsy" Siegel

Benjamin "Bugsy" Siegel was born in Brooklyn, New York, to Russian-Jewish immigrant parents. From an early age, he gravitated toward crime, finding his footing in the rough neighborhoods of New York as a teenage hoodlum. He rose to prominence by forming the "Bug and Meyer Mob" with his lifelong friend Meyer Lansky. The two operated as bootleggers and racketeers during the Prohibition era, gaining a fearsome reputation for their effectiveness and brutality. Siegel's combination of charisma and volatility helped him rise through the ranks of organized crime, ultimately becoming a key member of the National Crime Syndicate, the powerful criminal confederation uniting various ethnic crime groups across the country.

Siegel's criminal activities spanned a wide array of enterprises. He began with bootlegging and gambling but soon branched into extortion and murder. As his stature grew, Siegel expanded the Syndicate's reach to the West Coast, spearheading operations in California. There, he established gambling and narcotics rackets, building a criminal empire that extended from New York to Los Angeles. His ability to forge new territory and manage illicit business ventures made him an indispensable figure within the national crime network.

Although he was feared for his violent nature, Siegel also cultivated a glamorous public image. Known for his tailored suits, expensive tastes, and effortless charm, he often mingled with Hollywood's elite. He formed friendships with actors like George Raft and Cary Grant, and even attempted to break into film production himself. Siegel relished the celebrity lifestyle, but his ambitions went beyond notoriety. He dreamed of becoming a legitimate businessman and saw Las Vegas as the perfect canvas for his vision. His most famous, and ultimately fatal, business venture was the Flamingo Hotel, a luxury resort he hoped would transform the Nevada desert into a mecca for upscale gambling.

The construction of the Flamingo Hotel would become Siegel's most infamous project. Initially budgeted at $1 million, the project's costs ballooned to over $6 million amid delays, lavish spending, and alleged mismanagement. The initial launch in December 1946 was a disaster, plagued by unfinished construction and low turnout. The hotel was forced to shut down shortly after opening. However, Siegel pushed forward, and the Flamingo reopened in March 1947 with greater success. Still, the suspicions surrounding the missing funds had already strained his relationships with East Coast mob bosses. Many believed Siegel had embezzled money from the project, and his assurances were no longer enough to calm tensions.

Though exact numbers are unclear, Siegel accumulated substantial wealth over the course of his criminal career. The Flamingo was intended as a way to both grow and legitimize his fortune, establishing a foothold in the newly emerging Las Vegas casino industry. He envisioned a city where gambling, luxury, and entertainment would converge, and the Flamingo's opulent design reflected his vision. Its architectural style set a new standard for what a casino resort could be and inspired future developments on the Las Vegas Strip.

Siegel maintained connections with political figures and law enforcement officials, often using bribes to protect his interests. But his fame and increasingly visible lifestyle brought more scrutiny than protection. Federal authorities began to investigate his activities more aggressively, and his position within the Syndicate became increasingly unstable.

On June 20, 1947, Siegel was assassinated in the living room of his girlfriend Virginia Hill's Beverly Hills home. He was shot multiple times through a window in a carefully orchestrated hit. Though his murder remains officially unsolved, it is widely believed that the order came from mob leaders who had grown tired of the financial chaos surrounding the Flamingo project. His death was swift, brutal, and marked the end of one of organized crime's most flamboyant figures.

Siegel's assassination allowed other mob leaders to step in and assume control of the Flamingo, which went on to become a major success. His original dream of turning Las Vegas into a luxurious gambling destination was ultimately realized—not by him, but through the very organization that had him killed. His legacy, however, remains intact. Siegel is widely credited with helping to lay the foundation for modern Las Vegas, and his life has been dramatized in numerous books and films, securing his place in the lore of American organized crime.

Despite his dislike for the nickname "Bugsy," which referred to his volatile behavior, the media embraced it, and it became synonymous with his legacy. His ties to Hollywood added another layer to his mythos, blending celebrity with criminality. Even his design of the Flamingo helped define the visual identity of Las Vegas, turning Siegel into a cultural icon whose influence still echoes today.

Carlo "The Godfather" Gambino

Carlo Gambino began his life in crime in Sicily, where he was born on August 24, 1902, into a family with established Mafia connections. At the age of 19, he illegally immigrated to the United States in 1921, settling in Brooklyn and quickly immersing himself in the criminal underworld. His ascent in organized crime was gradual but steady, marked by strategic alignments with influential figures like Joe Masseria and later Salvatore Maranzano. After Maranzano's assassination in 1931, Gambino continued to rise, eventually becoming underboss to the powerful Albert Anastasia. His calculated nature and growing influence laid the groundwork for his eventual takeover.

In 1957, Gambino orchestrated Anastasia's murder, a high-profile assassination carried out in a Manhattan hotel barbershop. This brazen act shocked the public but eliminated a major obstacle to his rise. After seizing control of the crime family, it was later renamed in his honor. Gambino also formed strong alliances with key figures such as Vito Genovese and Meyer Lansky, enhancing his power and influence across organized crime factions. Under his leadership, the family grew into the most dominant of New York's Five Families.

Gambino's criminal operations were extensive, encompassing extortion, loan sharking, illegal gambling, and labor racketeering. He infiltrated labor unions and secured control over major industries like construction and trucking, using his position to extract money through kickbacks and contract manipulation. These ventures also provided cover through legitimate businesses, allowing illicit activities to flourish under a respectable facade.

He projected a public image of modesty, choosing to live in a simple Brooklyn home and avoiding the limelight.

Known for his strategic mind and preference for diplomacy over violence, Gambino earned the nickname "The Quiet Don." His understated leadership style made him an elusive target for law enforcement and allowed him to operate undisturbed for decades. Privately, he was calculating and deliberate, building one of the most effective and enduring criminal empires in American history.

Gambino's reign included several notorious incidents. Most famously, he orchestrated the murder of Albert Anastasia in 1957, a pivotal moment that shocked both the Mafia and the general public. That same year, he attended the infamous Apalachin Meeting, a gathering of Mafia leaders from across the country. When the meeting was raided by law enforcement, Gambino managed to evade capture, further bolstering his reputation for caution and skillful evasion.

His financial success was immense. At the time of his death, his net worth was estimated at $70 million, equivalent to over $400 million today. He led the most powerful of New York's Five Families and held significant influence over The Commission, the Mafia's governing body. His reach extended across the United States, solidifying his place at the top of the organized crime hierarchy.

Gambino maintained longstanding connections with corrupt officials and law enforcement officers, using bribes and shared interests to ensure protection for his operations. His influence reached into local governments, particularly in New York City, where much of his activity was based. These connections were instrumental in maintaining the security and longevity of his criminal enterprises.

Unlike many of his contemporaries, Gambino was never convicted of any major crimes besides a brief imprisonment of 22 months for tax evasion in his earlier years. His decline did not come through legal troubles or betrayal, but through natural causes. He retained control over his empire until the very end, evading the fate that had brought down so many other mob bosses.

Carlo Gambino died of a heart attack on October 15, 1976, at his home in Massapequa, Long Island, at the age of 74. His funeral, while subdued in comparison to the scale of his power, was attended by hundreds, including law enforcement officials who observed the proceedings closely. His quiet death mirrored his discreet approach to power.

Gambino left a lasting legacy in the world of organized crime. He demonstrated the effectiveness of a low-profile leadership style and became a model for future Mafia bosses who sought to avoid the media spotlight. He is remembered as one of the most successful and powerful figures in American Mafia history, with his life frequently portrayed in books, films, and television shows.

Beyond crime, Gambino had a personal passion for baseball. He was an avid fan of the New York Yankees and was known to follow games regularly. In fact, he reportedly died while watching a Yankees game, a fitting end for a man whose love for the sport remained with him until his final moments.

Frank "The Prime Minister of the Underworld" Costello

Frank Costello entered the world of organized crime after immigrating from Calabria, Italy, to East Harlem, New York, at the age of four. By his teenage years, he was already involved in petty crimes and had joined local gangs. His rise to power accelerated during Prohibition when he aligned himself with major figures like Lucky Luciano and Meyer Lansky. The trio engaged in large-scale bootlegging operations, and Costello's sharp political instincts and ability to form strategic alliances helped him distinguish himself from his peers. His close partnership with Luciano proved particularly important, eventually leading to Costello's position as consigliere and later acting boss of the Luciano crime family.

Costello was heavily involved in illegal activities such as bootlegging, gambling, and racketeering. His criminal enterprises expanded into slot machines, bookmaking, and casino operations across Louisiana and Florida. Unlike many of his contemporaries who thrived on violence, Costello built his empire by exploiting political connections and emphasizing stability and financial growth. He favored ventures that generated consistent profit with minimal conflict, which allowed him to develop a reputation as one of the more business-minded leaders in the Mafia.

Publicly, Costello projected the image of a respectable businessman. He was often seen wearing tailored suits and mingling with members of high society. Behind the scenes, he was known for his calm demeanor, calculated decision-making, and preference for negotiation over bloodshed. His charisma and diplomacy earned him the nickname "The Prime Minister of the Underworld," a reflection of his ability to straddle the line between the criminal and legitimate worlds. His capacity to navigate both spheres set him apart from many of his peers.

Costello's influence and notoriety peaked in the 1950s when he was called to testify during the widely publicized Kefauver Hearings, which aimed to expose the extent of organized crime in America. His televised refusal to answer key questions led to a conviction for contempt of Congress, drawing national attention to his operations. In 1957, he narrowly survived an assassination attempt ordered by rival mobster Vito Genovese. Though the attempt failed, it signaled the waning of his power. Following the attack, Costello stepped down from his position, allowing Genovese to take control.

Through his control of gambling operations and legitimate fronts, Costello accumulated immense wealth, with some estimates placing his net worth at around $1 billion at the time of his death. He held tremendous influence over politicians, judges, and law enforcement officials, and he routinely used bribes and behind-the-scenes deals to protect and expand his criminal enterprises. His reach extended from local to national politics, and he was known to have direct connections with powerful figures such as New York City Mayor Fiorello La Guardia and Police Commissioner Lewis J. Valentine.

Despite his ability to operate in the shadows for many years, Costello was eventually caught and convicted on charges of contempt of Congress and tax evasion during the 1950s. He served time in prison, and his influence within the Mafia declined as law enforcement scrutiny intensified and internal power struggles, particularly with Genovese, took their toll.

Costello died of a heart attack on February 18, 1973, at the age of 82, in his Manhattan home. Unlike many of his contemporaries who met violent ends, Costello managed to live out his final years in relative peace, his death closing the chapter on one of the most intellectually formidable and politically savvy figures in American organized crime.

His legacy lives on as a model for those in the underworld who value strategy and diplomacy over brute force. Costello demonstrated the enormous value of political connections and the effectiveness of a less violent approach to organized crime. His influence is said to have inspired fictional characters such as Don Vito Corleone in *The Godfather*, further embedding his legacy in popular culture.

Costello was also known for his personal quirks. He reportedly never carried a gun, choosing instead to rely on his intellect and extensive network to maintain control and solve problems. In his later years, he developed a passion for gardening and spent much of his time cultivating flowers and participating in horticultural shows, a quiet hobby that stood in stark contrast to his life at the center of the American Mafia.

Vito Genovese

Vito Genovese began his life in organized crime after immigrating from Risigliano, Italy, to New York City at the age of 15. Settling in Manhattan's Little Italy, he became involved in petty crimes as a teenager and joined local gangs. His early criminal career led him to work under Giuseppe "Joe the Boss" Masseria during the Prohibition era. Genovese made a major move toward power by aligning himself with Charles "Lucky" Luciano. Together, they orchestrated the assassinations of both Masseria and Salvatore Maranzano in 1931, dismantling the old Mafia hierarchy and laying the foundation for The Commission, a governing body that would oversee organized crime throughout the country.

Genovese forged important alliances with influential figures like Luciano and Meyer Lansky. His partnership with Luciano was a key factor in his rise, eventually earning him leadership roles within the Mafia. However, his ambition eventually brought him into conflict with Frank Costello. In 1957, Genovese ordered a failed assassination attempt on Costello. Although Costello survived, he chose to step down from leadership, allowing Genovese to assume control of the family, which would later bear his name.

Throughout his career, Genovese engaged in a wide range of criminal activities, including drug trafficking, extortion, loan sharking, illegal gambling, and murder. He played a pivotal role in expanding the family's operations into narcotics, establishing international heroin distribution networks. By leveraging strategic connections and eliminating rivals, Genovese consolidated his control over the organization and extended its influence well beyond New York, making the Genovese family one of the most powerful in the United States.

While he publicly maintained the image of a respectable businessman, Genovese was feared privately for his ruthlessness and readiness to use violence. He was known for his aggressive pursuit of power and his manipulative tactics, often resorting to murder and intimidation to assert dominance and enforce loyalty. His reputation as a power-hungry and violent figure earned him respect and fear throughout the criminal underworld.

Genovese was involved in several high-profile scandals that drew the attention of law enforcement and the public. One of the most notable was the 1957 Apalachin Meeting, a gathering of Mafia leaders in upstate New York. The meeting was raided by police, resulting in numerous arrests and exposing the national scale of organized crime. Genovese's role in the failed assassination attempt on Frank Costello further intensified public scrutiny and confirmed his determination to dominate the Mafia.

Though exact figures are unknown, Genovese amassed significant wealth through his control of the family's criminal enterprises. Under his leadership, the Genovese family grew into a national force within organized crime. His ambition extended beyond his own family; he sought to become the "boss of all bosses," using his position to assert influence across various Mafia factions and criminal enterprises throughout the country.

To protect his operations, Genovese maintained relationships with corrupt officials and law enforcement officers, secured through bribes and mutual interests. His influence reached into local government, especially in New York City, where many of his operations were based. These connections were instrumental in shielding his criminal network from investigation and prosecution for many years.

Eventually, Genovese's luck ran out. In 1959, he was convicted on narcotics trafficking charges and sentenced to 15 years in prison. The conviction was made possible by testimony from informants within his organization. His downfall was further accelerated by internal betrayals, most notably by Joe Valachi, a former associate who became a government witness and exposed the inner workings of the Mafia for the first time in public history.

Vito Genovese died of a heart attack on February 14, 1969, while serving his prison sentence at the United States Medical Center for Federal Prisoners in Springfield, Missouri. His death marked the end of an era for the Genovese crime family. Although the family continued under new leadership, it never regained the same level of dominance that it held during his reign.

Genovese left behind a legacy defined by ambition, violence, and strategic cunning. His rise and subsequent fall highlighted the power, and the peril, of seeking control within the volatile world of organized crime. His life became the subject of numerous films and documentaries, reinforcing his image as one of the most feared and influential mob bosses in American history.

Despite his expansive criminal empire, Genovese died with minimal assets, leaving only a modest inheritance to his family. In a surprising twist to his story, he once fled to Italy to avoid prosecution and aligned himself with Benito Mussolini's Fascist regime, only to later assist the U.S. Army during World War II. These contradictions underscored the complex and often paradoxical life of a man who embodied both the heights of power and the depths of criminal desperation.

Mickey Cohen

Mickey Cohen, born Meyer Harris Cohen on September 4, 1913, in Brooklyn, New York, relocated to Los Angeles with his family as a child. He began his criminal path in his teens through petty theft, eventually transitioning into professional boxing during the 1930s. His time in the ring brought him into contact with figures from the Chicago Outfit, including associates of Al Capone. During Prohibition, Cohen worked as an enforcer for Capone's organization, gaining a reputation for violence. In the late 1930s, he was sent to Los Angeles to support Bugsy Siegel in expanding organized crime on the West Coast. Following Siegel's assassination in 1947, Cohen quickly took over his operations, securing his place as a powerful crime boss in Los Angeles.

Cohen's criminal activities were wide-ranging, covering illegal gambling, loan sharking, extortion, and racketeering. He also ran legitimate businesses, like florists and nightclubs, which doubled as fronts for his illicit operations. His influence extended into the Hollywood scene, where he was notorious for blackmail schemes involving celebrities and studio executives. Known for surviving multiple assassination attempts, Cohen enforced his operations with a mixture of violence and intimidation.

Despite his criminal empire, Cohen carefully crafted a public persona rooted in luxury and charisma. He dressed in expensive, custom-made suits, drove luxury cars, and dined in elite restaurants. He courted the press and maintained high-profile relationships with celebrities, presenting himself as a "celebrity gangster." His flamboyant lifestyle and media savvy made him a unique fixture in Los Angeles culture.

One of the most infamous chapters in Cohen's life was his role in the aftermath of Bugsy Siegel's murder. While rumors circulated about revenge, Cohen ultimately solidified control over Siegel's criminal operations without provoking a gang war. Another major scandal emerged from his indirect link to the death of Johnny Stompanato, Cohen's associate and the lover of actress Lana Turner. When Turner's daughter fatally stabbed Stompanato in 1958, the incident garnered massive media coverage and again placed Cohen in the public spotlight.

At the height of his influence, Cohen's empire generated immense wealth, allowing him to live extravagantly and hold sway over elements of the political and law enforcement apparatus in Los Angeles. Though some officials were complicit, others pursued Cohen relentlessly, resulting in several high-profile convictions.

In 1951, Cohen was convicted of tax evasion and served four years in prison. A second tax evasion conviction in 1961 led to a 15-year sentence. While incarcerated, first in Alcatraz, then in Atlanta, Cohen survived an assassination attempt by a fellow inmate. After his release in 1972, he lived more quietly until his death from stomach cancer on July 29, 1976. He was buried at Hillside Memorial Park Cemetery in Culver City, California.

Cohen's legacy endures as one of America's most colorful organized crime figures. His life has been depicted in numerous films, books, and television series, offering a glimpse into the entanglement of organized crime with media, celebrity, and politics in mid-20th-century Los Angeles. Despite. or perhaps because of, his criminal notoriety, he remains a fascinating emblem of the American gangster era.

Among the many oddities of his life, Cohen was known to own over 200 tailored suits, underscoring his obsession with image and luxury. He managed to maintain a public reputation as a businessman and philanthropist, occasionally donating to local charities. His armored Cadillac, once a symbol of his paranoid need for protection, is now displayed in the Southward Car Museum in New Zealand.

Joseph "Joe Bananas" Bonanno

Joseph Bonanno, born on January 18, 1905, in Castellammare del Golfo, Sicily, immigrated to the United States in 1924 to escape Benito Mussolini's crackdown on the Sicilian Mafia. Settling in Brooklyn, Bonanno became involved in organized crime and aligned himself with Salvatore Maranzano during the Castellammarese War, a violent struggle for control among rival Mafia factions in New York. After Maranzano's assassination in 1931, the 26-year-old Bonanno assumed leadership of the crime family that would eventually bear his name, making him one of the youngest bosses among New York's Five Families.

As the head of the Bonanno family, he oversaw a wide array of criminal enterprises, including loan-sharking, narcotics trafficking, prostitution, and gambling. His influence extended to the formation of The Commission; a governing body created to manage disputes and ensure cooperation among the Mafia's ruling families. Bonanno was one of its founding members, further solidifying his place in the upper echelons of organized crime.

Bonanno distinguished himself from his more flamboyant peers with a quiet and reserved leadership style. He adhered strongly to traditional Sicilian values such as honor, loyalty, and family, and he avoided unnecessary publicity. His autobiography, *A Man of Honor*, presents him as a man of principles trying to navigate a treacherous underworld, a self-image that shaped public perception of him in later years.

One of the most dramatic episodes in Bonanno's criminal career came in the early 1960s when he attempted to eliminate rivals Carlo Gambino and Tommy Lucchese in a bid to consolidate power. The conspiracy failed, and Bonanno mysteriously vanished in 1964, an event that ignited a violent internal conflict known as the "Banana War." He resurfaced in 1966 and officially retired from the Mafia in 1968, relocating to Arizona in an attempt to live quietly outside the Mafia spotlight.

Bonanno's criminal empire made him immensely wealthy and influential. He controlled lucrative rackets in New York while also expanding operations into California and Arizona. Through various legitimate business investments, he was able to launder illicit profits and build a vast financial network that extended well beyond the traditional Mafia strongholds.

Although Bonanno managed to avoid major convictions for most of his life, his criminal activities inevitably intersected with political and law enforcement domains. While direct ties to officials remain unconfirmed, his ability to operate with relative impunity for decades suggests a degree of political or institutional protection behind the scenes.

His downfall began after the failed assassination plot and internal strife eroded his power. Despite retiring, he remained on law enforcement's radar. In 1985, Bonanno was sentenced to 14 months in prison for contempt after refusing to testify in a federal racketeering case. This marked the last chapter of his direct involvement with organized crime.

Joseph Bonanno died of heart failure on May 11, 2002, in Tucson, Arizona, at the age of 97. He was one of the last surviving original bosses of New York's Five Families and lived long enough to witness the decline of the very Mafia system he had helped build and define.

Bonanno's life has been extensively chronicled in books and films, most notably in his own memoir and in the television movie *Bonanno: A Godfather's Story*. His insistence on traditional values and his decades-long leadership made him a central figure in the history of American organized crime.

Despite his fierce reputation, Bonanno detested the media-given nickname "Joe Bananas," which he found demeaning. He also claimed to have been kidnapped during his 1964 disappearance, though many believe he staged it to escape brewing conflict. In his final years, Bonanno lived a surprisingly peaceful life, even participating in community events in Tucson, a sharp contrast to his violent past.

Tommy "Three Finger Brown" Lucchese

Tommy Lucchese, born Gaetano Lucchese on December 1, 1899, in Palermo, Sicily, immigrated to the United States with his family in 1911. A childhood work accident left him missing two fingers, earning him the nickname "Three Finger Brown." During Prohibition, he became involved in organized crime and aligned himself with Gaetano Reina's gang. When Reina was murdered in 1930, Lucchese backed Tommy Gagliano in the power struggle that followed, helping him become boss of the renamed Gagliano family. Lucchese remained underboss for over two decades, quietly building his influence, until he officially took control of the family in 1951 following Gagliano's death.

As boss, Lucchese significantly expanded his family's criminal empire. He directed operations across multiple rackets, including extortion, loan-sharking, illegal gambling, and labor racketeering. He particularly focused on infiltrating the garment industry and trucking unions, which he leveraged for both financial gain and power. These ventures not only brought in massive revenue but also extended the family's influence into legitimate sectors of New York's economy.

Lucchese was widely respected for his strategic mind and calm, diplomatic leadership style. Unlike some of his more flamboyant contemporaries, he avoided the spotlight and preferred to work behind the scenes. His ability to maintain peace within his family and build influential alliances set him apart as a stabilizing force in the often chaotic world of organized crime.

One of the more dramatic moments in Lucchese's career came in the early 1960s when Joseph Bonanno, in a bid to seize power, targeted him and other members of The Commission in a failed assassination plot. The plan unraveled, leading to Bonanno's temporary disappearance and a major reshuffling of Mafia leadership. Lucchese's survival during this period further cemented his reputation as a savvy and unshakeable leader.

Lucchese's dominance over key industries and labor unions brought his family immense wealth. His partnership with Carlo Gambino was especially significant, forming a power bloc that influenced much of the Mafia's direction during the mid-20th century. These strategic alliances, combined with his steady leadership, made the Lucchese family one of the most powerful in New York.

Part of Lucchese's success can be attributed to the political connections he cultivated over the years. He reportedly maintained relationships with figures in New York City politics, including several mayors, using these ties to shield his operations from intense law enforcement scrutiny. These relationships helped to insulate his family from major legal trouble and allowed their enterprises to flourish with minimal interference.

Despite a life steeped in crime, Lucchese managed to avoid major convictions. In his later years, however, his health began to deteriorate due to heart disease and a brain tumor. These health issues gradually sidelined him from day-to-day operations, marking the beginning of his decline.

Tommy Lucchese died on July 13, 1967, from a brain tumor at his home in Lido Beach, Long Island. His funeral was a major event, drawing over a thousand attendees, including influential figures from both the underworld and legitimate society. Law enforcement monitored the ceremony closely, a testament to his prominence in the criminal world.

Lucchese's legacy is defined by stability, strategic growth, and enduring influence. His tenure as boss brought about a period of prosperity and reduced violence within his family. His name lives on through the Lucchese crime family, which remains one of the most well-known Mafia organizations in the United States.

Despite his involvement in organized crime, Lucchese was known to have a personal passion for horse racing and reportedly placed large bets on races. He also maintained a reputation as a devoted family man and was said to be involved in charitable activities within his community, further complicating the public's perception of one of the Mafia's most calculated and enduring leaders.

Dutch Schultz

Dutch Schultz, born Arthur Simon Flegenheimeron August 6, 1902, in the Bronx to German-Jewish immigrants, began his criminal ascent through petty thefts and burglaries. After serving time for burglary, he adopted the name "Dutch Schultz" and entered the lucrative world of bootlegging during Prohibition. Partnering with Joey Noe, Schultz established a wide network of speakeasies and breweries throughout the Bronx. He quickly gained a reputation for ruthlessness, using violence and intimidation to eliminate competitors and enforce his growing empire.

As his criminal enterprise expanded, Schultz moved beyond bootlegging into illegal gambling, extortion, and control of the Harlem numbers racket. His gang became notorious for using extreme violence, including torture and murder, to maintain dominance. Schultz was a central figure in several brutal gang wars, clashing with rivals like Legs Diamond and Vincent "Mad Dog" Coll, both of whom met violent ends.

Temperamental and paranoid, Schultz was feared even among his own associates. He was known to lash out unpredictably and often took matters into his own hands. Still, he attempted to mask his violent reputation by cultivating the image of a legitimate businessman, investing in real estate and dressing impeccably. His efforts to appear respectable never erased the stain of his brutality.

One of the most infamous episodes in Schultz's life involved his obsession with killing U.S. Attorney Thomas Dewey, who had begun a high-profile campaign against organized crime. Schultz sought approval from the National Crime Syndicate to eliminate Dewey, but the request was denied due to concerns about the potential backlash of killing a federal prosecutor. Schultz, defiant and reckless, decided to proceed anyway. In response, the Syndicate ordered his assassination to protect their broader interests.

At his peak, Schultz's operations pulled in millions of dollars annually. His hold over Harlem's numbers game alone was immensely profitable. Despite his wealth, Schultz remained distrustful and miserly, often hiding large sums of cash in secret locations to evade law enforcement and tax collectors. His paranoia extended to those around him, further isolating him as pressure from authorities mounted.

Schultz used bribery and intimidation to influence local officials and police. But his violent and high-profile tactics made him a target for federal prosecutors, particularly Dewey, and earned him national notoriety. As the noose tightened, Schultz's desperation grew, culminating in his fatal miscalculation regarding Dewey.

On October 23, 1935, Schultz was dining at the Palace Chop House in Newark, New Jersey, when hitmen from Murder, Inc., the Syndicate's enforcement wing, stormed in and opened fire. He was struck multiple times and taken to a hospital, where he underwent emergency surgery. Despite initial hopes he might survive, Schultz died the following day from peritonitis caused by his injuries.

In his final hours, Schultz delivered a bizarre, rambling statement to law enforcement, a delirious monologue filled with cryptic phrases that has since become the subject of speculation and legend. His death marked the violent end of one of Prohibition's most notorious crime bosses.

Schultz's legacy is one of unchecked ambition and violent excess. His rise and fall have been immortalized in books, films, and television, serving as a cautionary tale from one of America's most lawless eras. His story epitomizes the dangers of organized crime when loyalty, fear, and ego collide.

Among the most enduring legends surrounding Schultz is that of a hidden treasure: before his death, he is rumored to have buried a fortune estimated at $7 million somewhere in the Catskill Mountains. Despite countless searches over the decades, the treasure has never been found, further mythologizing Schultz's place in gangster lore. Some even believe his final, delirious words may contain clues to the treasure's location—a mystery that continues to captivate amateur sleuths and treasure hunters to this day.

Joseph Colombo

Joseph Colombo was born on June 16, 1923, in Brooklyn, New York, into a family already deeply connected to organized crime. His father, Anthony Colombo, was an early member of the Profaci crime family, setting the stage for Joseph's eventual immersion in the underworld. After serving in the U.S. Coast Guard during World War II, Colombo returned to civilian life and held a variety of jobs before committing fully to a criminal career. He quickly rose through the ranks of the Profaci family and, in 1963, secured his place at the top by exposing a plot by boss Joseph Magliocco to assassinate rival Mafia leaders. This revelation earned him favor with the Mafia Commission, which rewarded his loyalty by granting him control of the family. In recognition of his leadership, the organization was renamed the Colombo crime family.

Under Colombo's direction, the family remained deeply involved in traditional Mafia rackets. These included extortion, loan-sharking, illegal gambling, and labor racketeering. Colombo capitalized on his influence over labor unions, especially in the construction and trucking sectors. This control provided the family with a steady stream of income and a powerful grip on crucial facets of New York City's infrastructure and economy.

Colombo's personality stood in stark contrast to the typically secretive demeanor of his fellow mob bosses. He was charismatic, bold, and unusually public-facing. Rather than shun the spotlight, Colombo embraced it, establishing himself as a media-savvy figure who sought attention beyond the confines of organized crime. This approach was especially evident in his Italian civil rights activism, where he styled himself as a defender of Italian-American identity. His public persona made him both influential and divisive, not just among the public, but also within the Mafia itself.

In 1970, Colombo founded the Italian-American Civil Rights League, a move that would catapult him into national prominence. The organization aimed to combat negative stereotypes and discrimination against Italian-Americans but also served to boost Colombo's visibility and influence. The League garnered significant attention and even succeeded in pressuring the producers of *The Godfather* to remove the words "Mafia" and "Cosa Nostra" from the film's script. While this bolstered Colombo's image among some Italian-Americans, it simultaneously attracted unwanted scrutiny from law enforcement and resentment from other mob leaders who feared his openness could jeopardize their secrecy.

Colombo's empire brought considerable wealth to the family. His control over key labor unions and lucrative rackets allowed him to accumulate substantial income and expand into legitimate business fronts. Under his leadership, the Colombo family maintained a strong position within New York's Mafia hierarchy and extended its influence across the city.

Colombo's activism through the Civil Rights League earned him political visibility, but it also came at a steep cost. His high-profile campaigns drew the attention of government agencies and law enforcement officials, including the FBI. More critically, his visibility caused friction with other Mafia bosses who preferred to operate in the shadows. The tension between Colombo's public persona and the Mafia's traditional secrecy created a dangerous imbalance.

That danger came to a head on June 28, 1971, during the second Italian Unity Day rally at Columbus Circle, a public event Colombo himself had organized. As he addressed the crowd, he was shot three times by Jerome A. Johnson, who was immediately gunned down by Colombo's bodyguards. Colombo survived the assassination attempt but was left permanently paralyzed, effectively ending his leadership within the Mafia.

Joseph Colombo remained in a vegetative state for nearly seven years following the shooting. He died on May 22, 1978, from cardiac arrest related to his injuries. He was just 54 years old. His incapacitation marked the end of an unprecedented chapter in Mafia history, one defined by public activism, controversy, and high-stakes power plays.

Colombo's legacy is as complex as it is unique. He is remembered not only as a Mafia boss but also, ironically, as a civil rights advocate who challenged the portrayal of Italian-Americans as criminals in media and society. His creation of the Italian-American Civil Rights League and its influence on the cultural conversation around ethnicity and crime left an indelible mark. Colombo's story has since been portrayed in multiple forms of media, including the television series *The Offer* and *Godfather of Harlem*.

Among the more surprising aspects of Colombo's life is the fact that he was able to influence the iconic *Godfather* film by having key Mafia terms removed from the script. Despite being a mob boss, he positioned himself as a civil rights leader, an approach that no other figure in the Mafia had taken before or has attempted since. His shooting at a rally he organized himself stands as a stark reminder of the volatility and risk that came with blending criminal power and public attention.

Albert "The Mad Hatter" Anastasia

Albert Anastasia, born Umberto Anastasio on September 26, 1902, in Calabria, Italy, immigrated to New York City in 1919 and began his criminal career as a longshoreman on the Brooklyn waterfront. His exposure to the gritty underbelly of the docks led him quickly into organized crime. By the 1920s, Anastasia had joined the crew of Giuseppe "Joe the Boss" Masseria, rising rapidly through the ranks due to his violent enforcement style and loyalty. He played a central role in the 1931 assassination of Masseria, aligning himself with Charles "Lucky" Luciano's plan to modernize and restructure the Mafia into a more efficient, corporate-style syndicate.

Anastasia soon became instrumental in establishing and co-leading Murder, Inc., the enforcement wing of the National Crime Syndicate. This shadowy group was tasked with carrying out contract killings, enforcing order within the underworld, and eliminating rivals. Under Anastasia's direction, Murder, Inc. carried out numerous assassinations during the 1930s and early 1940s. His rise continued, and in 1951, he became the boss of what would eventually be known as the Gambino crime family. His operations expanded into extortion, racketeering, and tight control over the New York waterfront, granting him both enormous influence and access to vast illicit wealth.

Known by the nicknames "The Mad Hatter" and "Lord High Executioner," Anastasia was feared for his ruthless and impulsive use of violence. He was infamous for enforcing Mafia rules without mercy, and his volatile temperament made him one of the most intimidating figures in organized crime. Though not one for flamboyance or publicity, his brutal methods and unpredictable behavior gave him a legendary status within criminal circles.

One of the most infamous incidents linked to Anastasia was the 1952 murder of Arnold Schuster, a Brooklyn shoe salesman who had assisted in capturing the notorious bank robber Willie Sutton. After seeing Schuster on television, Anastasia allegedly ordered his murder on a whim, despite the Mafia's unspoken rule against killing civilians. The brazen act drew national attention and law enforcement scrutiny, leading many within the underworld to question Anastasia's judgment and volatility.

Through his control of the docks and unions, Anastasia accumulated significant wealth and wielded substantial power. His reach extended into legitimate labor unions, giving him sway over the shipping and construction industries. This leverage translated into indirect political influence, as many local officials and businessmen found themselves dependent on union cooperation, which Anastasia could manipulate at will.

Though hard evidence of direct political ties is limited, Anastasia's ability to operate so freely for so long suggests some degree of protection or influence. However, his high-profile murders and erratic decisions ultimately isolated him from other Mafia leaders, particularly Vito Genovese, who sought to consolidate his own power. Genovese conspired with Anastasia's underboss, Carlo Gambino, to remove him permanently.

On October 25, 1957, Albert Anastasia was gunned down while seated in a barber's chair at the Park Sheraton Hotel in Manhattan. Masked gunmen entered the shop and shot him multiple times, killing him instantly. His assassination marked a major turning point in Mafia power dynamics and paved the way for Carlo Gambino to assume leadership of the crime family, which would later bear his name.

Anastasia's violent death symbolized the end of an era in which brutal enforcers held top positions in the Mafia. Despite his ignoble end, his legacy lives on in popular culture and historical accounts of organized crime. He is remembered as one of the most feared and controversial mob bosses in American history, and his role in founding Murder, Inc. cemented his place in the criminal hall of fame.

Though he was one of the most ruthless mobsters of his time, Anastasia once served in the U.S. Army during World War II and received an honorable discharge, a fact that helped him secure American citizenship. Surprisingly, despite his notoriety, he maintained a relatively low public profile during his life, and only a few photographs of him are known to exist.

Vincent "The Chin" Gigante

Vincent Louis Gigante was born on March 29, 1928, in Manhattan's Greenwich Village to Italian immigrant parents. Before rising to power in the underworld, he briefly pursued a career as a professional boxer, competing in 25 matches between 1944 and 1947. His transition to organized crime began when he became a protégé of Vito Genovese, serving as both his chauffeur and bodyguard. In 1957, Gigante made a name for himself by attempting to assassinate Genovese's rival, Frank Costello. Though the attempt failed, it solidified his standing within the Mafia. By 1981, Gigante had risen to the top, becoming boss of the Genovese crime family, one of New York's notorious Five Families.

Under Gigante's leadership, the Genovese family expanded its criminal reach across a range of illicit enterprises. These included extortion, loan-sharking, illegal gambling, and labor racketeering. One of the most notable operations during his tenure was the infamous "Windows Case," a bid-rigging scheme that manipulated contracts for installing windows in New York City housing projects. The scam involved both the Genovese and Colombo families and generated millions of dollars in fraudulent profits.

Nicknamed "The Chin," a shortened version of "Vincenzo" as pronounced by his Italian mother, Gigante was infamous for his eccentric behavior and secrecy. He became widely known for pretending to suffer from severe mental illness. For years, he wandered the streets of Greenwich Village in a bathrobe and slippers, muttering to himself, and avoiding direct communication with most people. This elaborate act earned him the nickname "The Oddfather" and allowed him to sidestep prosecution for decades, as courts and investigators struggled to determine whether he was mentally fit to stand trial.

Gigante's most notorious act of deception was his long-running feigned insanity. Between 1969 and 1995, he was hospitalized 20 times for psychiatric evaluations. This elaborate ruse successfully delayed legal proceedings and baffled law enforcement. Despite the mounting suspicion that his behavior was a calculated strategy, it wasn't until 1997 that he was finally convicted of racketeering and conspiracy. In 2003, in a plea deal on obstruction of justice charges, Gigante admitted that his mental illness had been a fraud all along, confirming what prosecutors had believed for years.

As the head of the Genovese family, Gigante wielded tremendous power and accumulated substantial wealth. He oversaw a wide range of criminal activities and extended the family's influence into legitimate industries, particularly construction and labor unions. His leadership helped maintain the Genovese family's reputation as one of the most stable and powerful criminal organizations in the United States.

Although Gigante avoided overt political involvement, his family's infiltration of labor unions and legitimate business sectors allowed for indirect political leverage. His ability to manipulate the legal system through his prolonged deception further demonstrated his strategic thinking and the degree of influence he held over institutional processes.

Eventually, Gigante's charade unraveled. He was deemed competent to stand trial and, in 1997, was convicted of racketeering and sentenced to 12 years in federal prison. In 2003, already incarcerated, he faced new charges and pleaded guilty to obstruction of justice, formally admitting that his insanity had been an act intended to avoid prosecution.

Vincent Gigante died of heart disease on December 19, 2005, at the U.S. Medical Center for Federal Prisoners in Springfield, Missouri, at the age of 77. His death marked the end of one of the most unusual and cunning reigns in Mafia history.

Gigante's legacy endures in the lore of organized crime. His bizarre deception and methodical leadership style have made him one of the most memorable figures in Mafia history. His life has been portrayed in various forms of media, most notably in the television series *Godfather of Harlem*, where he is played by actor Vincent D'Onofrio.

One surprising fact about Gigante's life is that his brother, Louis Gigante, was a Catholic priest and a New York City councilman, illustrating the stark contrast between their life paths. Despite his criminal empire, Gigante maintained two separate families: one with his wife Olympia Grippa, and another with his mistress Olympia Esposito, fathering eight children in total. His dual domestic life further underscores the contradictions and complexity of one of the underworld's most enigmatic leaders.

Sam "Momo" Giancana

Sam Giancana, born Gilormo Giangana on May 24, 1908, in Chicago's Little Italy, began his path to organized crime through the notorious 42 Gang, a group known for its violent tendencies and criminal ambition. As a skilled getaway driver and enforcer, Giancana earned a reputation for efficiency and brutality, eventually catching the attention of Al Capone's Chicago Outfit. His talents quickly found a home in the Outfit, and by the late 1930s, he was fully integrated into its ranks. Over the next two decades, Giancana climbed steadily through the hierarchy. In 1957, when Tony Accardo stepped down from daily leadership, Giancana officially assumed control, becoming the new acting boss of the Chicago Outfit.

Under Giancana's command, the Outfit broadened its reach and deepened its grip on multiple rackets. He was pivotal in taking control of Chicago's African American lottery payout system, a move that dramatically boosted the organization's revenue. He also oversaw the Outfit's operations in illegal gambling and liquor distribution and expanded political racketeering efforts, particularly in Louisiana. Beyond domestic borders, Giancana diversified the Outfit's income streams by investing in offshore casinos located in Iran, the Caribbean, and Great Britain, positioning himself as a truly international crime boss.

Nicknamed "Momo," short for "Mooney," a reference to his erratic and often explosive behavior, Giancana was feared within the organization for his temper and ruthless methods. However, he also had a penchant for the glamorous. He socialized with entertainers and political figures, regularly appearing in the company of singer Frank Sinatra and his lover, Phyllis McGuire of the McGuire Sisters. This duality of brutality and charm gave

Giancana a high profile uncommon for mob leaders of the era.

One of the most enduring and controversial stories tied to Giancana is his alleged role in the 1960 U.S. presidential election. It has long been claimed that he used his political influence and control over union votes to help John F. Kennedy secure the presidency. Further entwining him with American political history, Giancana was reportedly recruited by the CIA to aid in a covert plan to assassinate Cuban leader Fidel Castro, offering a rare glimpse into the murky intersections between organized crime and government intelligence operations.

Giancana's power and wealth grew steadily throughout his tenure. He held considerable sway over operations not only in Chicago but also in Las Vegas and Havana. The Outfit's dominance over casinos, bookmaking, and political corruption turned Giancana into one of the most formidable crime bosses in the country. His lavish lifestyle and international ventures were a testament to the vast reach and profitability of his criminal empire.

His relationships also extended into political circles, with rumored ties to the Kennedy family. His close friendship with Frank Sinatra reportedly opened doors to prominent politicians, further entrenching his influence. However, these associations eventually backfired, as they invited closer scrutiny from law enforcement. Attorney General Robert F. Kennedy, in particular, became fixated on Giancana, subjecting him to intense investigations and surveillance.

In 1965, Giancana's refusal to testify before a grand jury earned him a one-year sentence for contempt of court. Upon release, he fled to Mexico to escape further legal trouble, only returning in 1974 after being deported to the U.S. He was subpoenaed to testify before the Church

Committee investigating collusion between the CIA and the Mafia. Just days before he was scheduled to testify, on June 19, 1975, Giancana was assassinated in the basement kitchen of his Oak Park, Illinois home, shot multiple times in the head and neck while cooking. His murder remains unsolved, with theories ranging from CIA silencing to retribution by the Outfit for his perceived disloyalty.

Giancana's legacy remains a subject of public fascination. His life has inspired numerous books and films, and his daughter, Antoinette Giancana, co-authored *Mafia Princess*, a memoir offering an intimate portrayal of her father's dual identity as a feared mob boss and family man. His flamboyant lifestyle and rumored political entanglements continue to captivate organized crime historians and the general public alike.

Among the lesser-known facts about Giancana is his romantic relationship with singer Phyllis McGuire, a union that attracted significant media attention at the time. He also had a strong interest in astrology and often sought guidance from astrologers before making important personal or business decisions. Despite being suspected of numerous murders throughout his criminal career, Giancana was never formally convicted of any homicide, further enhancing the mystique surrounding his reign and ultimate demise.

Anthony "Tony Ducks" Corallo

Anthony Corallo, born on February 12, 1913, in East Harlem, New York City, began his criminal career in the 1920s as a member of the 107th Street Gang. By 1935, he had joined the Gagliano crime family, which would later be known as the Lucchese family. Corallo quickly climbed the ranks, becoming a caporegime by 1943 and shifting his base of operations to Queens. Known for his keen intellect and connections in organized labor, he became deeply involved in labor racketeering and developed a close working relationship with Teamsters president Jimmy Hoffa during the 1940s and 1950s. His growing influence within the family culminated in his ascension to boss in 1974, following the incarceration of Carmine Tramunti.

Under Corallo's leadership, the Lucchese family entered a period of exceptional prosperity. He maintained control over numerous illicit enterprises, including illegal gambling, narcotics trafficking, and labor racketeering. Corallo's most notable strength lay in his manipulation of labor unions. He had deep ties to the Painters and Decorators Union, the Conduit Workers Union, and the United Textile Workers Union, leveraging these positions for both profit and power. His business acumen and connections allowed the Lucchese family to operate with relative impunity and expand its grip on the underworld economy.

Nicknamed "Tony Ducks" for his uncanny ability to evade criminal convictions, Corallo was a cautious and calculating leader. He was known for his low profile and strategic thinking, rarely discussing business during in-person meetings due to fear of FBI surveillance. Instead, he famously used the car phone in his Jaguar to conduct conversations, while being chauffeured around New York City. This unorthodox method of communication reflected both his paranoia and his adaptability in a changing law enforcement landscape.

Corallo's most infamous moment came in the early 1980s when the FBI successfully planted a listening device in his Jaguar. The bug captured hours of incriminating conversations in which Corallo discussed a range of mob affairs, including illegal gambling, drug trafficking, labor racketeering, and even murder. These recordings provided critical evidence that would later be used in the landmark Mafia Commission Trial, which targeted the leadership of several New York crime families.

The wealth Corallo accumulated during his criminal career was substantial. His investments and control over powerful unions translated into immense financial gain. He lived in a luxurious, multi-million-dollar ranch-style home in Oyster Bay Cove, New York, a far cry from the streets where he began. By the height of his power, he was considered one of the most influential mob bosses in America, and his decisions had ripple effects throughout the entire Mafia network.

Although his direct political connections remain largely undocumented, Corallo's grip on various labor unions afforded him indirect political leverage. His control over unions gave him influence over both local businesses and political figures who depended on union support, helping him insulate his operations from external threats. This strategic advantage contributed to his long period of dominance and his ability to avoid conviction for many years.

Corallo's downfall came as a result of the very surveillance he tried so hard to avoid. The FBI's recordings of his car conversations provided the basis for a sweeping indictment in the Mafia Commission Trial, a prosecution that aimed to dismantle the upper echelon of organized crime leadership in New York. In 1986, he was convicted on racketeering charges and sentenced to 100 years in federal prison.

He spent his final years at the Federal Medical Center for prisoners in Springfield, Missouri. On August 23, 2000, Anthony Corallo died of natural causes at the age of 87. His death marked the end of an era for the Lucchese family and the old-school brand of Mafia leadership he had epitomized.

Corallo is remembered as one of the most powerful and cautious Mafia bosses in American history. His tenure was characterized by expansion, strategic growth, and a meticulous approach to avoiding law enforcement detection. Under his rule, the Lucchese family solidified its status as a dominant force in organized crime, and his legacy endures through the organization that still bears his influence.

Stefano "The Undertaker" Magaddino

Stefano Magaddino was born in Castellammare del Golfo, Sicily, and immigrated to the United States in 1909, eventually settling in Brooklyn, New York. He became involved with a group of fellow Sicilian mafiosi known as "The Good Killers," a faction engaged in a deadly vendetta against the rival Buccellato clan. In 1921, after being implicated in a revenge killing in New Jersey, Magaddino fled to Buffalo, where he aligned himself with local mobster Angelo Palmeri. Following Palmeri's death in 1922, Magaddino assumed control of the Buffalo crime family, establishing what would become one of the most discreet yet enduring Mafia organizations in the country.

As boss of the Buffalo crime family, Magaddino oversaw a wide array of criminal activities, including bootlegging during Prohibition, illegal gambling, loan sharking, extortion, and narcotics trafficking. Under his leadership, the family's influence extended well beyond Western New York, reaching into Southern Ontario and Montreal in Canada, as well as areas of Ohio and Pennsylvania. His empire thrived in part due to his calculated decision to keep operations low-key. While many Mafia families drew attention with lavish spending and violence, Magaddino's organization moved quietly, which allowed them to operate under the radar for decades.

Nicknamed "The Undertaker," Magaddino earned this moniker from his legitimate business—the Magaddino Memorial Chapel, a funeral home in Niagara Falls. He was known for his frugality and austere demeanor, traits that set him apart from more ostentatious mob bosses. Magaddino valued discipline and secrecy, expecting the same from his men. His modest personal lifestyle and quiet authority made him a respected and feared figure within La Cosa Nostra, and his long-standing presence in organized crime earned him a reputation as a cautious and calculated leader.

Despite his discretion, Magaddino's life was not without violence. In 1936, a bomb meant for him killed his sister instead, and in 1958, a grenade was thrown into his home but failed to explode. These attacks underscored the dangers that even the most reserved mob bosses faced. Tensions rose again in the early 1960s when his cousin, Joseph Bonanno, allegedly plotted to kill him along with other Commission members. In response, Magaddino's faction reportedly retaliated by orchestrating Bonanno's kidnapping in 1964, an event that shifted power dynamics within the American Mafia and fueled internal strife.

Magaddino's criminal network generated substantial wealth, but his refusal to share generously led to growing dissatisfaction within his ranks. In 1968, a police raid on his son's home revealed $500,000 in hidden cash, sparking outrage among his lieutenants who had long suspected him of hoarding profits. The discovery intensified resentment and confirmed their suspicions, contributing to a major rift within the organization. That breach would become the catalyst for his downfall.

While his specific political ties remain undocumented, Magaddino's long reign suggests a working relationship with local authorities. His discreet style and the geographic isolation of his territory may have allowed him to avoid the level of scrutiny faced by Mafia families in New York City or Chicago. Nevertheless, by the late 1960s, internal fractures began to undermine his authority. The exposure of his hidden fortune prompted top lieutenants to break away, forming rival factions and accelerating the decline of the once-unified Buffalo family.

Stefano Magaddino died of a heart attack on July 19, 1974, at the age of 82. He passed away at Mount Saint Mary's Hospital in Lewiston, New York, and was buried in St. Joseph's Cemetery in Niagara Falls. His death marked the end of an era for the Buffalo crime family, which never fully regained the stability or prominence it had enjoyed under his command.

Magaddino's legacy in organized crime is undeniable. As one of the original Commission members, he helped shape the national structure of the American Mafia. His emphasis on discretion, discipline, and regional autonomy influenced the way many mid-tier families operated. Though less flamboyant than many of his contemporaries, his longevity and strategic insight made him a pillar of Mafia leadership for more than half a century.

Early in his criminal career, Magaddino's involvement with "The Good Killers" reflected the deeply personal nature of Sicilian vendettas that often fueled early Mafia violence. His participation in the infamous 1957 Apalachin Meeting, a gathering of top Mafia leaders that was famously raided by law enforcement, brought national attention to organized crime's inner workings. The funeral home he operated served as a legitimate front for his illicit empire, reinforcing his image as "The Undertaker." His 50-year reign makes him one of the longest-serving Mafia bosses in American history, and his story remains a key chapter in the evolution of organized crime in North America.

Paul "Big Paul" Castellano

Paul Castellano was born in Brooklyn, New York, the son of a butcher, and became involved in organized crime early in life. His familial ties to the Mafia were strong, he was both a cousin and brother-in-law to Carlo Gambino, the influential boss of the Gambino crime family. These connections helped pave the way for his rise within the organization. After Gambino's death in 1976, Castellano was appointed as his successor, a decision that sparked significant internal dissent. By bypassing underboss Aniello Dellacroce, Castellano alienated a faction of the family that remained loyal to Dellacroce, planting the seeds of a future power struggle.

Under Castellano's leadership, the Gambino family expanded its reach into legitimate industries, most notably construction, meat distribution, and labor unions. He played a critical role in establishing the family's dominance over New York City's concrete industry, forming a syndicate known as the "Concrete Club," which extracted kickbacks from contractors on major building projects. While Castellano was more interested in white-collar crimes and the financial side of operations, the family still engaged in traditional criminal activities such as gambling, loan-sharking, and extortion. His dual focus on legitimate business fronts and illegal rackets made the Gambino family one of the most financially formidable crime organizations in the country.

Castellano earned the nickname "The Howard Hughes of the Mob" due to his preference for business over bloodshed and his focus on sophisticated operations rather than street-level violence. He lived in opulence, residing in a Staten Island mansion designed to resemble the White House, a symbol of both his power and taste for the extravagant. However, this aloof lifestyle and his detachment from the daily workings of the family created a growing divide between himself and traditional mobsters. Many resented his elitism and believed he lacked the street credibility required of a Mafia boss.

That internal resentment came to a head in the wake of a controversial decision in 1985. When Aniello Dellacroce died, Castellano chose to appoint Thomas Bilotti, a loyal but unpopular figure, as his new underboss. The move alienated key members of the family who had expected a more respected figure to assume the role. Castellano's leadership style, combined with his ongoing indictment on federal racketeering charges, made him a vulnerable target. On December 16, 1985, he and Bilotti were gunned down outside Sparks Steak House in Manhattan. The unsanctioned hit was orchestrated by John Gotti, a rising capo in the family who subsequently assumed control of the Gambino organization.

At the peak of his influence in the early 1980s, Castellano's net worth was estimated at $20 million, approximately $50 million in today's dollars. His wealth was derived from a combination of legitimate enterprises and illicit operations. Through control of key unions and business sectors, Castellano positioned himself as one of the most powerful and financially savvy mob bosses of his generation. While there is limited documentation of specific political ties, his deep integration into labor and construction networks suggests a degree of influence with local officials and the ability to minimize scrutiny from law enforcement.

Despite his calculated approach, Castellano's downfall was rooted in his own leadership missteps. His failure to maintain unity within the family, his perceived arrogance, and his prioritization of white-collar crime over traditional Mafia values all contributed to the loss of support from his capos. His murder by Gotti marked one of the most dramatic power shifts in modern Mafia history, signaling the end of Castellano's white-collar reign and the rise of a more flamboyant and violent era under Gotti's command.

Castellano's assassination shocked the public and underscored the brutal realities of organized crime leadership. His execution in broad daylight outside a popular Manhattan steakhouse became one of the most notorious mob hits in American history. His death effectively ended his vision for a more business-focused Mafia and set the tone for a more aggressive leadership style under Gotti.

Despite his controversial legacy, Castellano left a lasting mark on the Gambino family and organized crime as a whole. His efforts to legitimize the family's revenue streams reshaped its operations, while his dramatic fall highlighted the inherent instability of Mafia power structures. His life and death have been portrayed in numerous films and documentaries, including the 2019 film "The Irishman," reflecting his historical significance within the underworld.

Castellano's Staten Island mansion, modeled after the White House, became a symbol of his extravagant taste and was listed for $18 million in 2024, potentially setting a new real estate record for the borough. Though he never abandoned his criminal roots, Castellano was widely recognized for his business acumen and ability to integrate legitimate enterprises into the family's operations. His media portrayals continue to reinforce the duality of his legacy, a man who sought to run the Mafia like a Fortune 500 company but ultimately fell victim to its oldest traditions of blood, loyalty, and revenge.

John "The Teflon Don" Gotti

John Gotti began his criminal career in the East New York neighborhood of Brooklyn, in the state where he was born in 1940 to Italian immigrant parents. He became involved with local street gangs at an early age, including the Fulton-Rockaway Boys, and by his late teens, he was working for the Gambino crime family at the Bergin Hunt and Fish Club under caporegime Carmine Fatico. Gotti's rise within the organization was marked by ambition and a capacity for violence. His most decisive move came in December 1985, when he orchestrated the assassination of Gambino boss Paul Castellano outside Sparks Steak House in Manhattan. The bold hit shocked both the underworld and the public, and it allowed Gotti to seize control of the Gambino family, which was considered the most powerful Mafia family in New York at the time.

To consolidate power, Gotti formed alliances with key figures such as underboss Salvatore "Sammy the Bull" Gravano, whose loyalty proved instrumental during Gotti's initial years as boss. Gotti's leadership was characterized by a blend of charisma, ruthlessness, and strategic networking. However, this alliance would later become his undoing when Gravano turned state's evidence and testified against him. Gotti's criminal empire spanned multiple states and involved a wide range of illegal activities, including murder, loan sharking, gambling, drug trafficking, and extortion. His reputation for enforcing discipline through violence, combined with his ability to intimidate rivals and law enforcement alike, cemented his position as a formidable figure in organized crime.

He cultivated a public image that contrasted with the traditional mob boss persona. Nicknamed the "Dapper Don," Gotti was frequently seen in expensive suits and carried himself with a polished, charismatic demeanor.

Privately, he was known for his explosive temper and a strict, often brutal enforcement of the mob's rules. He also stood out for his willingness to court media attention, a rare trait in the Mafia world. His flamboyant and media-savvy style earned him both admiration and resentment within organized crime circles and contributed to his reputation as one of the most recognizable figures of his era.

Gotti's most notorious act was the public execution of Paul Castellano, a move that defied the Mafia's code of discretion and sparked outrage across the country. In the years that followed, Gotti gained the nickname "The Teflon Don" for repeatedly escaping conviction despite being charged in multiple trials. His streak came to an end in 1992 when his former underboss, Sammy Gravano, turned against him and revealed extensive details about the Gambino family's operations. Gotti was convicted on charges including murder and racketeering, finally bringing his reign to a close.

At the height of his power, Gotti's net worth was estimated at around $30 million. He wielded substantial influence across New York's underworld, and under his leadership, the Gambino family reached new heights of profitability and prominence. Gotti maintained strong connections with corrupt politicians and law enforcement officials, using bribery and mutual interests to ensure the smooth operation of his criminal enterprises. His reach extended deep into local government structures in areas like New York City, where his operations were based.

Despite his outward confidence, Gotti's position became increasingly precarious. The attention he attracted, combined with internal betrayals and intensifying law enforcement pressure, gradually led to his downfall. His conviction in 1992 marked the end of an era for the Gambino family. He was sentenced to life in prison without the possibility of parole and was incarcerated in several federal facilities. His health began to decline during his time in prison, and he ultimately died of throat cancer on June 10, 2002, at the United States Medical Center for Federal Prisoners in Springfield, Missouri, at the age of 61.

Gotti's death marked a symbolic turning point in organized crime. Despite his criminal record, he remains one of the most infamous figures in American history and a cultural icon of the Mafia era. His influence extended beyond his own organization, with future crime figures taking cues from his ability to manipulate the media and maintain a powerful personal brand. His leadership style, blending fear, loyalty, and publicity, continues to spark debate among both law enforcement and organized crime historians.

Beyond his criminal reputation, Gotti had a personal side that reflected his fascination with Mafia mythology. He reportedly loved *The Godfather* films and modeled aspects of his image and demeanor after characters in the series. During his incarceration, he shared a prison cell with Philadelphia drug trafficker George Martorano, who described Gotti as both charismatic and feared. Even behind bars, Gotti's duality. his charm and menace, remained intact, cementing his legacy as one of the most captivating and controversial mob bosses in American history.

Raymond Patriarca

Raymond Patriarca was born on March 17, 1908, in Worcester, Massachusetts, and moved with his family to Providence, Rhode Island, when he was just four years old. Leaving school at an early age, he gravitated toward a life of crime, engaging in hijackings, armed robberies, and bootlegging during Prohibition. His rise through the underworld was steady and calculated. By 1954, following the retirement of Philip Buccola, Patriarca assumed full control of the New England crime family. He centralized operations in Providence, running his empire from a vending machine business called Coin-O-Matic Distributors, which operated as a front for his sprawling criminal enterprise.

Under his leadership, the Patriarca crime family became one of the most disciplined and profitable in the United States. Patriarca maintained tight control over all operations, demanding a cut from any criminal activity conducted within his territory. His illicit ventures included gambling, loan sharking, extortion, narcotics trafficking, and contract killings. He was also respected among Mafia circles for his ability to resolve disputes between rival factions, which helped preserve peace and stability in the broader American Mafia network.

Patriarca was a firm believer in keeping a low profile. He avoided public attention, preferred working from the shadows, and enforced a strict code of discipline within his ranks. Despite his understated public demeanor, he was feared behind closed doors for his willingness to use lethal violence when necessary. His rules were absolute, and those who defied them often paid with their lives.

Among the darker stories tied to Patriarca's reign was an alleged order for an elderly mobster to kill his own son following a failed business deal. When the father refused,

Patriarca reportedly expelled him from the organization. In another chilling instance, he is believed to have sanctioned the murder of his own brother after an FBI bug was discovered in his office, an oversight deemed unforgivable in his tightly run syndicate.

Financially, Patriarca's criminal empire brought him significant wealth. His revenue streams were bolstered by investments in legitimate businesses, including a stake in the Dunes hotel and casino in Las Vegas. Like many mob bosses of his time, he profited from casino skimming operations while projecting an image of modesty, often dressing plainly and driving unassuming cars.

His sway extended into politics and law enforcement. In 1938, he was released from a five-year prison sentence after serving just four months, aided by a falsified parole petition. The scandal led to the impeachment of a state official and exposed the depth of Patriarca's influence in political and legal circles.

Patriarca's downfall began in 1970, when he was convicted of conspiracy to commit murder and sentenced to ten years in prison. Yet, even from behind bars, he maintained command over his organization. Paroled in 1975, he continued to face legal troubles. In 1980, he was arrested again for allegedly orchestrating two murders, though his deteriorating health prevented him from standing trial.

Suffering from heart disease and diabetes in his later years, Patriarca died of a heart attack on July 11, 1984, at the age of 76. He was buried at Gate of Heaven Cemetery in East Providence, Rhode Island. His death marked the end of an era, but not the end of his family's name. His son, Raymond Patriarca Jr., took over the organization, though he never commanded the same respect or control as his father, leading to a gradual weakening of the family's power.

Patriarca's legacy remains firmly entrenched in American organized crime history. Over three decades, he built and maintained one of the most disciplined and enduring Mafia syndicates in the country. The New England crime family continues to be referred to as the Patriarca family, a testament to the mark he left on the underworld.

Few mob bosses managed to balance power and subtlety as effectively as Patriarca. He ran a deadly and highly profitable criminal organization from the front office of a vending machine company and lived modestly despite his fortune. His story stands as a powerful example of the quiet, methodical leadership style that can wield influence for generations, both in crime and in legend.

Kenny "The Boss" Gallo

Kenny Gallo's descent into the criminal underworld began at a remarkably young age. By the age of 14, he was already involved in cocaine smuggling, working alongside figures such as Joey Avila. His early ventures expanded quickly, connecting him with powerful criminal organizations including Pablo Escobar's Medellín Cartel, the Los Angeles Milano Mafia Family, and New York's Colombo Mafia Family. Gallo's criminal portfolio came to encompass drug trafficking, credit fraud, and extortion, and he operated with increasing sophistication as his reputation within the underworld grew.

Gallo's criminal enterprises were diverse and far-reaching. He led a narcotics crew affiliated with the Medellín Cartel, rising to prominence as one of the most prolific cocaine smugglers on the West Coast. He also became deeply entrenched in the adult film industry, directing 29 adult films between the late 1980s and early 2000s and marrying adult film star Tabitha Stevens. These ventures, both legal and illicit, helped him build wealth and notoriety. In parallel, he served as an associate of the Colombo crime family, contributing to their operations through extortion, gambling, and additional underworld dealings.

Known for his assertiveness and adaptability, Gallo developed a reputation for being able to move fluidly between the criminal world and legitimate enterprises. His charisma and sharp instincts made him a valuable asset in both domains. These traits would later serve him well in a radically different phase of his life, when he began working with federal authorities.

One of the most significant chapters in Gallo's story was his time as a government informant. Codenamed "Breakshot" by the FBI, he wore a wire for eight years, gathering intelligence on key operations within the Colombo and Lucchese crime families. His undercover work was instrumental in facilitating several major arrests and convictions, striking serious blows to the leadership and structure of these powerful organizations.

Gallo amassed significant wealth through his criminal exploits, once owning a nightclub in Palm Springs before reaching the legal drinking age. His involvement in the adult film industry and connections to organized crime generated large profits and elevated his status among both criminal associates and social circles. Despite his outward flash, Gallo's internal conflict eventually led him to cooperate with law enforcement.

His most consequential connection to law enforcement came through his decision to turn informant. Faced with the dangers of mob life and growing personal disillusionment, Gallo agreed to work with federal agents, effectively ending his criminal career and contributing to the dismantling of the very syndicates he had once served.

Following his decision to cooperate, Gallo entered the Witness Protection Program. As of the latest public information, he remains alive under a new identity. He has focused his post-crime life on writing, media work, and activism, becoming a vocal advocate for change in the same communities he once exploited.

Gallo's memoir, *Breakshot: A Life in the 21st Century American Mafia*, co-written with Matthew Randazzo V, offers an unvarnished account of his life in organized crime and his journey toward redemption. The book has received praise for its raw honesty and insight into modern-day mafia operations, and it has played a role in educating the public about the inner workings of the criminal underworld.

A colorful figure with many contradictions, Gallo has made several notable media appearances, including on *Flipped: A Mobster Tells All* and Spike TV's *Deadliest Warrior*, where he served as an expert on the Medellín Cartel. In 2009, he launched "Street Tolerance," an initiative promoting LGBTQ+ acceptance in traditionally hostile subcultures, marking his shift from mobster to social advocate. His personal life has also attracted attention; he was married to adult film star Tabitha Stevens and later to filmmaker Anne Kaneko. Gallo's story, marked by violence, reinvention, and transformation, stands as one of the most compelling modern narratives of life within, and beyond, the American mafia.

Frank Lucas

Frank Lucas was born in La Grange, North Carolina, and moved to Harlem, New York, during his youth. He would later claim to have been mentored by the influential Harlem crime boss Ellsworth "Bumpy" Johnson, although this relationship remains disputed by some historians. Regardless of the exact nature of their association, Lucas sought to fill the power vacuum following Johnson's death in 1968. Ambitious and business-minded, Lucas set out to build a heroin empire of his own. His strategy was simple but revolutionary: cut out the Italian Mafia and other intermediaries by sourcing heroin directly from Southeast Asia, thereby increasing purity and reducing cost. It was a move that would make him one of the most notorious drug lords in American history.

Lucas built his operation around heroin imported from the Golden Triangle region, an area where the borders of Thailand, Laos, and Myanmar converge. He branded his product "Blue Magic" and quickly gained a reputation for offering high-quality heroin at prices competitors couldn't match. Allegedly, he used U.S. military planes and, more controversially, the coffins of deceased American servicemen to smuggle drugs back to the United States during the Vietnam War. Though he later retracted the coffin claim, the story helped cement his legend. By removing middlemen, Lucas retained higher profits and tighter control, enabling him to dominate Harlem's heroin trade throughout the early 1970s.

Known for his discipline and strategic approach, Lucas often avoided the flamboyance that characterized other gangsters of his era. He dressed modestly and kept a low profile, believing that attention was bad for business. However, there were moments when he indulged in luxury. One such instance came in 1971, when he attended the Muhammad Ali vs. Joe Frazier fight at Madison Square Garden wearing a $125,000 chinchilla coat and matching hat. The extravagant outfit caught the eye of law enforcement agents and triggered increased surveillance, setting off a chain of events that would eventually bring down his empire.

That coat became infamous, especially after Lucas's arrest in 1975. During a raid on his New Jersey estate, authorities seized $584,000 in cash, though Lucas insisted they had confiscated over $11 million and failed to report the full amount. The raid exposed the extent of his operation and ended his reign atop New York's heroin hierarchy. His rise and fall mirrored the volatility of the drug trade: meteoric, violent, and ultimately unsustainable.

Lucas claimed at his peak to have earned up to $1 million a day from heroin sales, though this figure is likely exaggerated. Nevertheless, his wealth was undeniable. He invested in real estate across the country, purchasing properties in Miami, Detroit, and North Carolina. He also owned a ranch stocked with 300 Black Angus cattle, a personal indulgence that symbolized both his rural roots and financial power. His fortune bought him security, influence, and loyalty but it also brought attention from the very authorities he worked to avoid.

Corruption played a key role in sustaining Lucas's enterprise. He bribed law enforcement officers and public officials to protect his operations and ensure shipments went unimpeded. Ironically, it was this network of corrupt contacts that unraveled during his prosecution. Facing decades behind bars, Lucas chose to cooperate with authorities. His testimony led to over 100 convictions, including those of dirty cops and rival traffickers. In exchange, his 70-year sentence was reduced, and he was released in 1981. However, his return to crime led to a second arrest in 1984, and he served additional time until his release in 1991.

Lucas spent his later years largely out of the spotlight. A car accident left him wheelchair-bound, and he lived a quieter life until his death on May 30, 2019, in Cedar Grove, New Jersey, at the age of 88. Though he had once been at the center of one of the most lucrative drug operations in U.S. history, his final years were defined by reflection, reduced mobility, and attempts at rehabilitation.

His legacy is both celebrated and condemned. Lucas's life was dramatized in the 2007 film *American Gangster*, with Denzel Washington portraying him. The film introduced his story to a broader audience but also reignited debates about the glamorization of criminal figures. Lucas's narrative remains a study in ambition, brutality, and redemption, a complex portrait of a man who both destroyed and inspired lives.

Lucas famously trusted only his family, specifically relatives from North Carolina, to handle his heroin operation. He believed that blood loyalty offered more security than fear or money ever could. After turning informant, he and his family entered the Witness Protection Program. He later co-authored a memoir, *Original Gangster*, detailing his life, rise, and eventual fall; an insider account of one of America's most notorious drug empires.

Ellsworth "Bumpy" Johnson

Ellsworth "Bumpy" Johnson was born in Charleston, South Carolina, and moved to Harlem in 1919, where he would eventually rise to become one of the most influential figures in the neighborhood's criminal and cultural history. His underworld journey began in the numbers racket, a popular form of illegal gambling that thrived in Harlem. Johnson became the principal lieutenant to Madame Stephanie St. Clair, famously known as the "Queen of Numbers." Their partnership soon drew them into conflict with Dutch Schultz, a mobster seeking control over Harlem's lucrative gambling operations. The resulting turf war in the 1930s was marked by violence, threats, and strategic maneuvering. After Schultz's murder, Johnson shifted his approach and forged an alliance with the Italian Mafia, negotiating a degree of autonomy for Harlem's criminal enterprises. This diplomatic move secured his place as a dominant force in Harlem's underworld for decades.

Johnson's criminal enterprises extended well beyond gambling. He was involved in extortion and narcotics trafficking, including heroin distribution. His influence on Harlem's illegal economy was considerable, and by the 1950s, his reputation had reached national attention. In 1952, he was convicted of a heroin-related drug conspiracy and sentenced to 15 years in prison. He served the majority of his sentence at Alcatraz, one of the most notorious prisons in the United States. After serving over a decade behind bars, he was released on parole in 1963.

Despite his criminal background, Johnson was widely respected for his intellect and charisma. Known for his sharp mind and interest in literature, he earned the nickname "The Professor." He was also a skilled chess player, often engaging in matches with accomplished opponents. Johnson's personality blended sophistication with streetwise grit. He could be both ruthless in business and generous in his personal dealings. His intelligence and composed demeanor made him a unique figure in the criminal world, one who commanded respect in both underground and community circles.

In 1965, Johnson made headlines again when he staged a sit-in at a Harlem police station to protest what he viewed as constant and unjust surveillance by law enforcement. Refusing to leave the station, he was arrested for "refusal to leave a police station," though he was later acquitted. The incident was a rare public act of protest by a crime figure and highlighted the ongoing tension between Johnson and the authorities. It also reinforced his status in the community as someone willing to stand up to power, even in unconventional ways.

Johnson's wealth, though never officially documented, was evident in his lifestyle and influence. He controlled large swaths of Harlem's illegal activity and invested in legitimate business ventures as well. But unlike many gangsters, he was known for giving back to his neighborhood. He helped locals pay rent, covered funeral costs, and provided financial support to struggling families. This earned him a reputation as a protector of Harlem, blurring the line between criminality and community leadership.

Throughout his life, Johnson maintained a complicated relationship with law enforcement. He was regularly surveilled and arrested yet managed to avoid long-term convictions after his release from Alcatraz. His network of connections and his strategic alliances with Mafia families and influential figures likely contributed to his ability to evade further serious legal consequences. Though his criminal activities never fully ceased, he remained free until his death.

Johnson died of a heart attack on July 7, 1968, at the age of 62, while dining at Wells Restaurant in Harlem. At the time of his death, he was under federal indictment for another drug conspiracy charge. Despite the indictment, he spent his final years in Harlem, continuing to exert influence and maintain relationships with those he had supported for decades.

His legacy has endured through film, television, and cultural lore. Johnson has been portrayed in multiple productions, most notably in *American Gangster* and the series *Godfather of Harlem*, where his character is brought to life as both a feared crime boss and a complex community figure. His life has become emblematic of the blurred lines between power, respect, and criminality in 20th-century urban America.

Bumpy Johnson's nickname came from a physical bump on the back of his head, a small feature that belied the formidable reputation he would later earn. He was a passionate chess player and regularly faced off against strong opponents, using strategy and intellect as tools both on the board and in the streets. Despite a life built on illegal enterprises, Johnson was deeply rooted in his community, offering protection, financial aid, and a measure of stability in an era of social and economic upheaval.

Nicky "Mr. Untouchable" Barnes

Nicky Barnes, born in Harlem, New York City, endured a violent childhood with an abusive, alcoholic father and left home at an early age. He was first imprisoned in 1965 for heroin possession, where he came under the influence of prominent figures like "Crazy" Joe Gallo of the Colombo crime family and Matthew Madonna of the Lucchese family. These associations refined his outlook on organized crime and laid the groundwork for his rise. After his release, Barnes returned to Harlem and began building a tightly controlled heroin trafficking operation that would eventually make him one of the most notorious drug lords in American history.

Barnes founded a vast heroin distribution network across Harlem, characterized by its organization and discipline. In 1972, he co-founded "The Council," a seven-man syndicate that operated like a corporate board to oversee Harlem's heroin trade. The Council regulated prices, resolved disputes, and enforced order among hundreds of street-level dealers. This model of governance allowed Barnes to dominate the heroin market in New York City and shield himself from prosecution for years despite heavy law enforcement scrutiny.

Charismatic and flashy, Barnes projected an image of supreme confidence and invulnerability. He was frequently seen in custom-tailored suits, luxury cars, and high-end nightclubs. This carefully curated persona earned him the nickname "Mr. Untouchable," a label that symbolized both his success and his seeming immunity to the justice system. His swagger and brazenness caught national attention, culminating in a 1977 *New York Times Magazine* cover story that depicted him as the face of the urban drug empire.

That article proved to be a turning point. President Jimmy Carter, outraged by the glorification of Barnes, instructed the Justice Department to make his prosecution a top priority. In 1978, Barnes was convicted on federal drug trafficking charges and sentenced to life in prison without the possibility of parole. The conviction marked the collapse of one of the most powerful drug empires in American history.

At his peak, Barnes's enterprise stretched across multiple states and even into Canada. He controlled hundreds of dealers, moved thousands of kilos of heroin annually, and was worth an estimated $50 million. His wealth funded a lifestyle of extravagance, and his influence extended deep into criminal and street culture. While there's no evidence of formal ties to law enforcement or political figures, his ability to operate for so long without serious consequence suggests the likelihood of inside connections or corrupted contacts.

Barnes's fall from grace accelerated behind bars. While serving his life sentence, he learned that members of The Council had betrayed him, mismanaging his finances, sleeping with his mistress, and breaking the rules he had set. Enraged, Barnes turned informant in 1982. His testimony led to the indictment and conviction of 44 individuals, including top Council members, effectively dismantling the very organization he helped build.

In recognition of his cooperation, Barnes's sentence was commuted, and he was released from prison in 1998 under the federal witness protection program. He lived out the rest of his life under an assumed identity. His death from cancer occurred on June 18, 2012, but it was kept secret and not publicly revealed until seven years later in 2019.

Barnes's life remains a defining narrative in the history of American organized crime. His autobiography, *Mr. Untouchable: My Crimes and Punishments*, co-written with Tom Folsom, and a 2007 documentary of the same name offer a candid account of his rise, fall, and transformation. His story is frequently cited in discussions about the intersection of crime, media, and justice in late 20th-century America.

A number of surprising facts surround Barnes's life. While in prison, he won a national poetry contest for federal inmates and earned a college diploma with honors. He was portrayed by Cuba Gooding Jr. in *American Gangster* (2007), which dramatized his rivalry with fellow drug kingpin Frank Lucas. His cooperation with federal authorities remains one of the most prominent examples of a major drug trafficker turning state's evidence and disappearing into the witness protection system.

Russell "The Quiet Don" Bufalino

Russell Bufalino was born in Montedoro, Sicily, and immigrated to the United States in 1906, eventually settling in Buffalo, New York. From a young age, he became involved in organized crime and developed close ties with influential mafiosi. During the 1920s, he began working with Joseph Barbara, a prominent underworld figure based in Pennsylvania. By 1940, Barbara had appointed Bufalino as underboss of the Pittston crime family. When Barbara died in 1959, Bufalino assumed leadership of the organization, which came to be known as the Bufalino crime family. His rise to power marked the beginning of one of the most enduring reigns in American Mafia history.

Under Bufalino's leadership, the family operated a wide range of criminal enterprises, including loan sharking, extortion, illegal gambling, and labor racketeering. His influence extended throughout Pennsylvania and into parts of New York and New Jersey. The organization's quiet, calculated presence allowed it to avoid the media attention and law enforcement pressure that plagued flashier crime families in major cities. This low-profile strategy became a defining feature of Bufalino's leadership style, enabling the family to conduct its affairs with relative impunity for decades.

Bufalino was famously discreet, earning him nicknames such as "The Quiet Don" and "McGee." He rarely drew attention to himself and avoided the lavish displays of wealth common among other mob bosses. His calculating demeanor, emphasis on secrecy, and focus on loyalty made him both respected and feared within La Cosa Nostra. Subordinates were expected to follow his disciplined lead, and he maintained tight control over the family's activities. This quiet strength gave him longevity in a world where many others were brought down by hubris or betrayal.

One of the most significant events in Bufalino's criminal career was his involvement in the infamous Apalachin meeting in 1957. Alongside Joseph Barbara, Bufalino played a role in organizing the summit, which brought together over 100 mafiosi from across the United States, Italy, and Cuba. The meeting was intended to solidify national alliances and coordinate operations, but it was raided by law enforcement, resulting in the arrest of many attendees. The event blew the lid off what had previously been widely denied: the existence of a nationwide Mafia network. Bufalino's role in the Apalachin meeting placed him firmly within the upper echelon of organized crime.

Despite his understated lifestyle, Bufalino accumulated significant wealth through his various rackets. However, his stinginess was a point of contention among some subordinates who felt undercompensated. Still, he managed to maintain control over the family for decades, using fear, respect, and strategic alliances rather than brute force. His quiet efficiency allowed him to operate with minimal disruption, even as larger crime families drew heat from the FBI and federal prosecutors.

Though there is little concrete evidence of high-level political connections, Bufalino's long reign hints at a degree of cooperation or influence within local law enforcement. The family's relatively rural geographic base likely shielded them from the same level of surveillance seen in urban centers. His ability to remain largely untouched by legal scrutiny for so long suggests that he either maintained useful relationships or knew how to stay a step ahead of investigations.

By the late 1970s and early 1980s, Bufalino's legal troubles began to catch up with him. He faced convictions for extortion and conspiracy to kill a witness, which resulted in several years of incarceration. Despite these setbacks, Bufalino continued to hold power over his organization, guiding operations from behind bars and remaining a respected figure until his final days.

Russell Bufalino died of natural causes on February 25, 1994, at the age of 90. He passed away at Nesbitt Memorial Hospital in Kingston, Pennsylvania, and was buried in Denison Cemetery in nearby Swoyersville. His death marked the end of one of the most stable and quiet tenures in American Mafia history.

Bufalino's legacy is that of a master strategist who avoided the fate that befell so many of his contemporaries. By operating in the shadows and steering clear of the media spotlight, he preserved the longevity of his crime family well into the late 20th century. His life and criminal career were depicted in the 2019 film "The Irishman," where he was portrayed by Joe Pesci, further cementing his role in the annals of Mafia history.

Bufalino's understated image belied his powerful influence. He was rumored to have been recruited by the CIA for covert operations, including alleged plots to assassinate Fidel Castro, though such claims remain unconfirmed. Perhaps most famously, he was a close associate of Teamsters boss Jimmy Hoffa and is widely suspected of having played a role in Hoffa's mysterious 1975 disappearance. Though never charged in connection with the case, Bufalino's name remains one of the most frequently mentioned in theories surrounding Hoffa's fate—a chilling reminder of the reach and quiet power of "The Quiet Don."

Vito Rizzuto

Vito Rizzuto was born on February 21, 1946, in Cattolica Eraclea, Sicily, and immigrated to Canada with his family in 1954. His father, Nicolo Rizzuto, gradually carved out a position in Montreal's criminal underworld, ultimately taking control from the Calabrian-led Cotroni crime family. Vito became actively involved in the family's affairs and, by the 1980s, had assumed leadership. His ascension solidified the Rizzuto family's dominance over Montreal's organized crime landscape, marking the beginning of an era in which they would become Canada's most powerful Mafia organization.

Under Rizzuto's leadership, the family's criminal enterprises were vast and international. They were deeply involved in drug trafficking, illegal gambling, loan sharking, money laundering, and contract killings. The Rizzutos maintained strong ties to the Bonanno crime family in New York and had far-reaching connections to criminal organizations in South America and Europe, making their influence truly global. Vito operated a complex and far-reaching network that extended well beyond Canada's borders.

Known for his diplomatic nature, Rizzuto was widely respected for his ability to mediate disputes between rival factions. Unlike many mob bosses who governed with fear and overt violence, he preferred to negotiate and build consensus. His emphasis on diplomacy and behind-the-scenes control allowed him to avoid the kind of attention that brought down many of his contemporaries. His measured leadership earned him a reputation as a shrewd, calculated figure within international organized crime circles.

One of the most infamous episodes in Rizzuto's criminal career was his role in the 1981 murders of three Bonanno captains in New York, an event aimed at resolving an internal power struggle within the American Mafia. Though the crime went unsolved for years, Rizzuto was arrested in 2004 and extradited to the United States in 2006. He pleaded guilty in 2007 and was sentenced to ten years in prison. His imprisonment created a power vacuum in Montreal, igniting a wave of violence and retribution. Several members of his family, including his father and son, were murdered during this chaotic period.

The Rizzuto crime family controlled a lucrative empire, earning millions through drug trafficking and various illicit enterprises. Their wealth was supplemented by interests in legitimate businesses, including the construction industry, which provided both money laundering opportunities and additional influence. Rizzuto's economic reach strengthened his power and allowed the organization to maintain its dominance for decades.

While concrete evidence of direct political influence is limited, the Rizzuto family's sustained ability to operate with minimal interference from law enforcement for years indicates a degree of protection or strategic discretion. Their involvement in construction and related industries likely brought them into contact with public officials and business leaders, further insulating their operations.

Rizzuto's arrest and incarceration marked the beginning of his family's decline. The leadership vacuum and rise of rival factions led to an era of instability and bloodshed within Montreal's underworld. Upon his release in 2012, Rizzuto attempted to regain control, but the damage was done. His once-unified empire had been fractured by years of violence and betrayal.

On December 23, 2013, Vito Rizzuto died in Montreal of complications from lung cancer. His death, just a year after being released from prison, brought a definitive end to his reign and symbolized the closing chapter of one of Canada's most powerful criminal dynasties. The news sent ripples through both the underworld and the public, as one of the last great Mafia bosses passed away.

Rizzuto's story has become emblematic of the rise and fall of modern organized crime in North America. His leadership style, international reach, and complex criminal network have been chronicled in numerous books and television series, most notably *Bad Blood*, which dramatized his life and legacy. He is remembered as a master strategist whose ability to maintain a powerful syndicate for decades left an indelible mark on Canadian and global crime history.

Nicknamed "Montreal's Teflon Don," Rizzuto earned his reputation for eluding law enforcement for much of his criminal career, mirroring the American mobster John Gotti. Despite his role at the top of a vast criminal empire, Rizzuto managed to maintain a low public profile, which contributed significantly to his longevity. His life and operations continue to fascinate the public and media, with the story of the Rizzuto family standing as one of the most compelling sagas in organized crime.

Angelo "The Gentle Don" Bruno

Angelo Bruno was born in Villalba, Sicily, and immigrated to the United States as a child, settling in the South Philadelphia neighborhood that would later become his stronghold. From a young age, he immersed himself in the world of organized crime, gradually earning influence through his connections and strategic thinking. By 1959, he had emerged as the boss of the Philadelphia crime family, following a successful power struggle with then-leader Antonio Pollina. His rise marked a turning point for the organization, ushering in a period of calm after internal conflict.

As head of the Philadelphia mob, Bruno maintained the family's traditional Cosa Nostra operations, including illegal gambling, loan sharking, and extortion. However, he drew a hard line against drug trafficking, forbidding his members from getting involved in the narcotics trade. Despite this, he allowed outside criminal groups to sell drugs within Philadelphia's borders, provided they paid him a cut of the profits. This hands-off but lucrative arrangement highlighted Bruno's pragmatic approach to business and his focus on long-term organizational stability over short-term gain.

Known for his composed demeanor and diplomatic leadership, Bruno earned the nickname "The Gentle Don." In stark contrast to the blood-soaked reputations of many of his contemporaries, he favored quiet negotiation and compromise over murder and intimidation. His ability to keep the peace, both within his own ranks and with other families, was rare in the volatile world of organized crime. This nonviolent stance did not make him weak—on the contrary, it enhanced his stature as a calm but powerful figure who ran a tight, disciplined operation.

Still, not everyone in his organization shared his vision. Tensions began to simmer beneath the surface as younger and more aggressive members chafed under Bruno's restrictions. particularly his refusal to let them participate in the booming drug trade. By the late 1970s, dissatisfaction was mounting among ambitious lieutenants eager for more autonomy and faster profits. Bruno's decision to allow outside traffickers to operate in Philadelphia while denying the same opportunities to his own men created deep resentment and planted the seeds of betrayal.

On March 21, 1980, that betrayal culminated in Bruno's assassination. While sitting in his car outside his South Philadelphia home, he was shot in the back of the head with a shotgun. The hit had been ordered by his consigliere, Antonio Caponigro, who believed eliminating Bruno would elevate his own position within the organization. However, the murder had not been sanctioned by the Mafia Commission, a violation of protocol with deadly consequences. Shortly after the assassination, Caponigro was found dead, stuffed into the trunk of a car, with cash crammed into his mouth and rectum—a symbolic message from the Commission condemning his greed and unauthorized actions.

Bruno's murder unleashed chaos within the Philadelphia mob. The stable, relatively peaceful regime he had maintained for over two decades gave way to a bloody and prolonged power struggle. Successors rose and fell with alarming speed as internal violence escalated, fracturing the family and drawing intense law enforcement scrutiny. What had once been one of the most orderly Mafia factions quickly descended into instability and decline.

Despite the violent end to his reign, Bruno's legacy is remembered as a rare example of leadership guided by restraint. His era is often described as a golden age for the Philadelphia mob, prosperous, discreet, and relatively peaceful. His story, marked by a commitment to diplomacy in a world defined by brutality, continues to be referenced in studies of Mafia history and in popular portrayals of organized crime.

Though he built his reputation in the shadows, Bruno maintained a legitimate front through several business ventures. He owned an extermination company in Trenton, New Jersey, and held interests in both an aluminum products firm in Florida and the Plaza Hotel in Havana, Cuba. These enterprises helped him blend his criminal activities with lawful income streams, further solidifying his low-profile image.

Bruno was not born with that name. He originally went by Angelo Annaloro but adopted his paternal grandmother's maiden name, Bruno, as a way to distance himself from his birth identity, perhaps a symbolic gesture to mark his entry into the underworld. His life and death were eventually immortalized on screen, with actor Harvey Keitel portraying him in Martin Scorsese's 2019 film *The Irishman*, a fitting nod to a mobster who stood apart for his calm in a world of chaos.

James "Whitey" Bulger

James "Whitey" Bulger was born in Dorchester, Massachusetts, and raised in the South Boston housing projects known as Mary Ellen McCormack. His striking blond hair earned him the nickname "Whitey," a name he reportedly disliked. After early involvement in street gangs, he joined the U.S. Air Force but was later dishonorably discharged. In the 1950s, he served time for armed robbery and other offenses, including a stint in Alcatraz. Upon release, Bulger became affiliated with the Winter Hill Gang, an Irish-American criminal organization operating out of Boston. By the 1970s, he had risen to leadership, asserting control over organized crime in the region.

As head of the Winter Hill Gang, Bulger ran a vast criminal enterprise that included drug trafficking, loan sharking, extortion, and murder. He was eventually implicated in 19 murders and convicted in connection with 11 of them. His influence extended beyond Boston into other parts of New England. Known for his brutal enforcement tactics, he eliminated rivals and kept subordinates in check through fear and calculated violence.

Despite his violent reputation, Bulger cultivated a public image as a sort of Robin Hood figure in South Boston, claiming to shield the community from outside criminals. In reality, this was largely a facade. Behind closed doors, Bulger proved himself a master manipulator, most infamously through his covert relationship with the FBI. Beginning in 1975, he served as an informant, supplying intelligence on rival Mafia groups in exchange for protection. Corrupt FBI agents, most notably John Connolly, shielded him from investigation, allowing his criminal empire to flourish unchecked for years. This collusion became one of the most scandalous episodes in

FBI history, ultimately leading to multiple convictions within the Bureau.

Bulger amassed considerable wealth through his criminal activities, though the exact scale remains uncertain. At the height of his reign, he was one of the most dangerous and influential mob bosses in the United States. His power reached beyond Boston's underworld, and he maintained contacts with other criminal organizations nationwide.

His ties to law enforcement were not limited to the FBI. His brother, William "Billy" Bulger, served as President of the Massachusetts State Senate and later as president of the University of Massachusetts. Though there is no direct evidence of Billy's involvement in criminal activity, his political stature drew added scrutiny to the Bulger family.

In 1994, after learning of an impending indictment from his FBI handler, Bulger fled Boston and disappeared. He remained a fugitive for 16 years, during which time he was added to the FBI's Ten Most Wanted Fugitives list, second only to Osama bin Laden. In 2011, he was finally captured in Santa Monica, California, where he had been living quietly under an alias with his longtime partner, Catherine Greig.

Bulger's time as a fugitive came to a brutal end. On October 30, 2018, less than 24 hours after being transferred to the United States Penitentiary in Hazelton, West Virginia, he was found beaten to death in his cell. The attack was swift and violent, and widely believed to be an act of retribution for his years as an informant. His death underscored the enduring dangers of prison life for known cooperators.

Bulger's life has left a lasting mark on American criminal history and pop culture. His story has inspired documentaries, books, and films, most notably the 2015 film *Black Mass*, with Johnny Depp portraying him. His betrayal of law enforcement trust and manipulation of the FBI remain cautionary tales about institutional corruption and the blurry line between justice and complicity.

Among the many strange chapters of his life, one of the most surprising was his involvement in the CIA's MK-Ultra experiments during his 1950s incarceration, where he was subjected to LSD-based mind-control research. Despite his violent career, he maintained a strong interest in reading, and during his time on the run, he reportedly kept a personal library. The $2 million reward placed on his head made him one of the most sought-after fugitives in the world.

Maurice "Mom" Boucher

Maurice "Mom" Boucher was born on June 21, 1953, in Causapscal, Quebec. His early years were marked by petty crime and multiple stints in prison, laying the foundation for a life entrenched in the criminal underworld. In the early 1980s, he joined the white supremacist motorcycle gang SS, where his leadership potential first became evident. By 1987, Boucher had become a full-patch member of the Hells Angels' Montreal chapter. His rapid ascent through the organization culminated in the founding of the elite Nomads chapter in 1995. Driven by ambition and strategic ruthlessness, Boucher sought to monopolize Quebec's lucrative drug trade, a move that ignited a violent and prolonged conflict with rival gangs.

Under Boucher's leadership, the Hells Angels evolved into a formidable criminal enterprise, engaging in large-scale drug trafficking, extortion, and contract killings. He orchestrated a brutal campaign to eliminate rival groups, particularly during the Quebec Biker War, which saw waves of violence and bloodshed. The war would claim many lives and entrench Boucher's reputation as one of Canada's most dangerous crime bosses.

Boucher was known for his charismatic yet fearsome personality. He often appeared before the media with a smile, cultivating an image of composed defiance. Within the gang, he ruled through intimidation and strategic decisiveness, earning the respect and fear of those around him. His control over the Hells Angels was both meticulous and unyielding, reinforcing his moniker "Mom," a darkly ironic reference to his micromanaging and controlling leadership style.

Among the most shocking moments during his reign was the 1995 car bombing that killed 11-year-old Daniel

Desrochers, a tragic incident that galvanized public outrage. Although not directly linked to Boucher, the event intensified scrutiny on biker gangs and led to increased pressure from Canadian law enforcement. The murder of innocent civilians, particularly a child, marked a turning point in public sentiment and government resolve to crack down on organized crime.

By the late 1990s, Boucher had amassed considerable wealth from his criminal enterprises. He owned luxury properties, including a mansion in Montreal and real estate holdings in Mexico. His influence extended beyond the Hells Angels, touching various aspects of both criminal and legitimate business circles. Despite his wealth and power, he remained a high-priority target for law enforcement.

Boucher's connections to other organized crime groups, including the Rizzuto crime family, further complicated efforts to dismantle his operations. However, unlike many of his underworld counterparts, Boucher had an openly combative relationship with law enforcement. He was at the center of numerous investigations and operations aimed at eradicating organized crime in Quebec.

His criminal empire began to unravel in 2002, when he was convicted of ordering the murders of two prison guards. The conviction led to a life sentence without the possibility of parole for 25 years. It was a major victory for Canadian authorities and marked the downfall of one of the country's most feared underworld figures.

While serving his sentence at the Archambault prison, Boucher was diagnosed with throat cancer. He died on July 10, 2022, at the age of 69, while receiving palliative care. His death closed the chapter on a life defined by crime, violence, and ruthless ambition.

Boucher's legacy remains one of brutal dominance. He played a central role in the Quebec Biker War, which claimed over 160 lives and fundamentally reshaped the landscape of organized crime in Canada. His influence on the structure and tactics of criminal organizations remains a topic of continued interest and concern.

In spite of his criminal persona, Boucher had surprising personal quirks. He enjoyed opera and was particularly fond of Luciano Pavarotti's performances. His nickname, "Mom," was a sardonic nod to his obsessive control over his gang's operations, likening his behavior to that of an overbearing mother. Even during his incarceration, Boucher remained active in the organization, with his daughter, Alexandra Mongeau, acting as a trusted intermediary and messenger between him and his associates.

Sonny Barger

Sonny Barger was born on October 8, 1938, in Modesto, California, and raised in Oakland. In 1957, he co-founded the Oakland chapter of the Hells Angels Motorcycle Club, which would go on to become the organization's central power base. Barger's leadership was pivotal in unifying the various Hells Angels chapters, transforming them into a cohesive national and eventually international force. His role in shaping the club's identity and expanding its reach made him one of the most influential figures in outlaw motorcycle culture.

Under Barger's command, the Hells Angels became widely associated with criminal enterprises, including drug trafficking, weapons violations, and violent crimes. Barger himself had a long history of legal troubles. He was convicted of assault with intent to murder in 1965, possession of narcotics with intent to distribute in 1973, and conspiracy to transport and receive explosives in interstate commerce with the intent to kill and damage buildings in 1988. These convictions underscored his deep involvement in the club's more illicit activities.

Known for his charismatic presence and unwavering authority, Barger carefully cultivated the image of the rugged, rebellious outlaw biker. He was often seen as the face of the Hells Angels and was admired within the biker community for his loyalty, leadership, and unapologetic dedication to the lifestyle. His commanding yet strategic style helped maintain the club's internal discipline and public mystique, contributing to its enduring cultural impact.

One of the most infamous moments tied to Barger and the Hells Angels was the 1969 Altamont Free Concert, where the club had been hired to provide security. The event descended into chaos and violence, culminating in the stabbing death of concertgoer Meredith Hunter by a Hells Angels member. The incident, immortalized in the documentary *Gimme Shelter*, remains a defining moment in the history of 1960s counterculture and served to solidify the Hells Angels' fearsome reputation.

Although exact financial details remain unclear, Barger's leadership position within the Hells Angels, along with his work as a published author and public figure, contributed to his wealth and power. His autobiography and several other books were commercially successful, further amplifying his notoriety and public influence.

Barger's relationship with law enforcement was marked by continuous hostility. He was the subject of numerous investigations and prosecutions over the decades. Despite this, his high-profile status meant he was frequently brought into the legal spotlight, where his trials often garnered significant media attention and stirred public debate over the Hells Angels' role in society.

His criminal exploits led to several prison terms, most notably his 1988 conviction for conspiracy to transport explosives with intent to kill and destroy property, for which he served 57 months. Even while incarcerated, Barger remained a dominant figure within the Hells Angels, continuing to shape the club's culture and reputation.

On June 29, 2022, Sonny Barger passed away at the age of 83 after a long battle with cancer. His death marked the end of an era not only for the Hells Angels but for the larger outlaw biker movement, where he had long been a towering presence.

Barger's legacy is complex. He is remembered as the architect of the modern Hells Angels and as a living embodiment of the outlaw biker image. Through his books and media appearances, he contributed significantly to the mythologizing of biker culture and became a symbol of rebellion and countercultural identity.

Despite his criminal record, Barger appeared in the television series *Sons of Anarchy*, portraying Lenny "The Pimp" Janowitz, a role that paid homage to his real-life persona. He was also a bestselling author, with his books offering both an inside look at biker life and reflections on his personal philosophy. After undergoing a laryngectomy in the early 1980s due to throat cancer, Barger learned to speak using esophageal speech, further reinforcing his image as a hardened survivor and unrelenting figure of the outlaw world.

Italian Organized Crime

Italian organized crime, often encapsulated by the term *"Mafia,"* traces its origins to mid-19th century Sicily. Born amid the violence and instability following Italy's unification, it began as a clandestine system of informal protection and honor among rural landowners, an illicit substitute for unreliable official institutions. The Sicilian word *mafiusu*, meaning "swagger" or "boldness," reflected this culture of fierce local control and vigilante justice.

By the late 1800s, Sicily was awash in socio-political upheaval. The collapse of feudal structures, mass migration, and weak law enforcement created fertile ground for mafiosi to emerge as community enforcers; regulators of land disputes, vote manipulators, and overseers of informal justice . These early clans cultivated a secretive code of loyalty and silence (*omertà*), imbuing the organization with both social influence and protective legitimacy.

Following World War II, the Mafia adapted to new opportunities. Palermo's postwar building boom became a lucrative venture; mafiosi seized public construction contracts, cementing their integration into Italy's legitimate economy while expanding their power. Violent internal conflicts, like the First and Second Mafia Wars in the 1960s–80s, further transformed the landscape, culminating in the brutal Corleonesi domination under Salvatore Riina.

Comparative Italian syndicates followed similar trajectories. The Camorra in Naples, with its loose but violent network, emerged from 19th-century prison gangs and thrived by infiltrating politics, construction, and later the drug trade, even sponsoring candidates before Mussolini temporarily suppressed them. Meanwhile,

Calabria's 'Ndrangheta, traditionally family-based and horizontally structured, rose over the late 20th century to dominate European cocaine trafficking, controlling as much as 80% of shipments through Gioia Tauro.

In the face of economic hardship and political instability, many Italians emigrated to North America in the early 20th century, bringing the Mafia overseas. Among them emerged the American Mafia or *Cosa Nostra*, which crystallized in the 1920s and '30s. Prohibition-era smuggling offered immense profits, prompting figures like Lucky Luciano, Salvatore Maranzano, and members of the Sicilian diaspora to forge enduring crime families .

Luciano, in particular, masterminded a groundbreaking reorganization: he abolished the "boss of all bosses" model and established the Mafia Commission, composed of representatives from the Five Families of New York and allied syndicates, to mediate disputes and coordinate national criminal enterprises. This governance model allowed for hierarchical structure and centralized control, facilitating Mafia dominance over illicit economies and unionized industries for decades.

After the repeal of Prohibition, organized crime diversified into gambling, narcotics, labor racketeering, construction, and international trafficking. Labor unions, unions like the Teamsters, and municipal public works became Mafia strongholds, powerful devices for crowding out competition through extortion, corruption, and violence .

The Camorra, in particular, capitalized on regional crises such as Naples' 1980 earthquake by exploiting relief funds and construction contracts, later branching into drug smuggling, waste management, and cigarette counterfeiting, fueling immense wealth and political ties.

The 1970s and '80s marked a turning point. Italy witnessed major anti-mafia judicial campaigns following high-profile assassinations of judges and journalists (Falcone and Borsellino in 1992), which triggered sweeping legal reforms. In the U.S., the RICO Act (1970) enabled prosecutors to pursue entire criminal organizations. The first wave of convictions came in 1980, with the heads of all Five Families receiving life sentences combined for 100-plus years.

Despite these pressures, the Mafia endured, crumbling in public but adapting underground. High-security 41-bis prison regimes aimed to neutralize leadership, while "pentiti" (collaborators) filled the state with vital intel.

Today, Italian organized crime remains quiet yet entrenched. *Cosa Nostra*, though significantly weakened, survives in pockets of Palermo and the U.S. Camorra clans continue to thrive through diversified crimes, from waste management and falsified olive oil exports to extortion and violence. Their decentralized structure enables resilience and regeneration .

The 'Ndrangheta now ranks among the wealthiest criminal groups globally, leveraging cocaine logistics and financial doctrines throughout Europe, Australia, and North America. While each syndicate differs in structure, they share a blend of violence, corruption, and corporate mimicry, effectively operating like criminal multinationals.

Michele Navarra

Michele Navarra began his rise in Corleone, Sicily, not with a gun, but with a medical degree. Born on January 5, 1905, Navarra was both a trained engineer and a licensed physician, educated at the University of Palermo. After serving as a captain in the Royal Italian Army, he returned to his hometown and became director of the local hospital. But beneath his public image as a respected doctor, Navarra quietly assumed control of the Corleone Mafia in 1943, following the ousting of Calogero Lo Bue. His ascent marked the beginning of a new era in which criminal power was blended seamlessly with civic respectability.

Navarra's reign coincided with a time of political upheaval and reconstruction in postwar Sicily, and he exploited these circumstances to tighten his grip on power. He used his medical credentials to issue false certificates that influenced election results and manipulated public institutions to further the Mafia's control. He also served as a medical consultant for the State Railways, using this position to grant favors, assign contracts, and distribute jobs to allies. By embedding himself into Sicily's bureaucratic infrastructure, Navarra transformed the Corleone clan into an arm of the local establishment.

Though he maintained a facade of professionalism and composure, Navarra ruled with ruthless efficiency. Between 1944 and 1948, Corleone experienced a surge in Mafia-related killings, with at least 57 murders attributed to internal feuds and enforcement of the clan's interests. One of the most high-profile killings was that of socialist labor leader Placido Rizzotto in 1948, a vocal opponent of Mafia influence in agricultural unions. Navarra ordered Rizzotto's assassination and, according to reports, had 11-year-old Giuseppe Letizia, who had witnessed the abduction, silenced with a fatal injection while under hospital care. The calculated cruelty of the act revealed the doctor's chilling capacity for violence disguised as medical aid.

Navarra preferred to delegate enforcement to loyal underlings, one of whom was the ambitious and violent Luciano Leggio. Initially a subordinate, Leggio grew powerful through his own cattle-rustling operations and quickly began to challenge Navarra's authority. Their relationship deteriorated, and in 1958, Navarra attempted to eliminate Leggio by orchestrating a hit. The attempt failed. On August 2, 1958, Navarra and a colleague, Dr. Giovanni Russo, were ambushed and killed in a hail of automatic gunfire on a rural road outside Corleone. Over 120 bullets were fired. The assassination, carried out by Leggio's men, marked a dramatic and bloody end to Navarra's reign.

Navarra's leadership style stood in stark contrast to the violence that defined his successors. He presented himself as cultured, orderly, and pragmatic, an archetype of the "respectable" mafioso who preferred manipulation and patronage over public displays of brutality. His administration of power through institutions like hospitals, railways, and municipal offices allowed him to operate with impunity, building a legacy that blurred the line between organized crime and state authority.

During his tenure, Navarra steered the Corleone clan into lucrative rackets involving land disputes, public construction, and transportation. His control over trucking routes, job placements, and contract bidding made him one of the most influential figures in rural Sicily. Though not flashy or ostentatious, Navarra held quiet sway over key sectors of the local economy and was a trusted intermediary between Cosa Nostra and political interests, particularly the Christian Democratic Party, which he supported from 1948 onward after initially backing Sicilian separatists.

His assassination triggered a period of chaos and transformation for the Mafia in Corleone. The resulting power vacuum was quickly filled by Leggio, whose brutal methods ushered in a new generation of mafiosi, including Salvatore Riina and Bernardo Provenzano, who would later plunge Sicily into the most violent Mafia wars in its history. Navarra's era, by contrast, came to be remembered as one of calculated, institutionalized criminality rather than reckless bloodshed.

Despite his deep influence on the modern Cosa Nostra, Navarra remains a relatively shadowy figure compared to his successors. He left no vast estate, and many of his financial dealings remain undocumented. Yet his innovations, particularly his use of public authority to serve criminal ends, created a blueprint for Mafia infiltration of state systems that endured long after his death.

Michele Navarra's legacy is that of a pioneer in white-collar organized crime. He refined the Mafia's ability to mask coercion with respectability, setting the stage for decades of systemic corruption in Sicilian politics and business. Though ultimately overthrown by younger, more violent men, his impact on the structure and strategy of the Sicilian Mafia was lasting. In Corleone and beyond, he remains a symbol of how power, when hidden behind a doctor's coat, can become far more insidious.

Salvatore "Toto" Riina

Salvatore "Toto" Riina began his path into organized crime after being born on November 16, 1930, in Corleone, Sicily, into a poor family. At the age of 19, he committed his first murder in order to gain entry into the local Mafia. His ascent within Cosa Nostra accelerated when he aligned with Luciano Leggio and Bernardo Provenzano to form the powerful Corleonesi faction. During the Second Mafia War in the early 1980s, Riina and his allies systematically eliminated rival clans, enabling him to rise to the top and become the undisputed "boss of bosses" of the Sicilian Mafia. His ascent was built on calculated betrayal as much as alliance, often forming partnerships with other Mafia families only to later turn on them in pursuit of greater power.

Riina's criminal empire spanned a wide range of illegal activities, including drug trafficking, extortion, murder, and large-scale bombings. He was instrumental in expanding Cosa Nostra's reach into international heroin trafficking and orchestrated countless assassinations to secure and maintain control. His leadership was marked by an unrelenting campaign of violence, not just within the Mafia, but also against the Italian government, as he sought to control Sicily and influence national politics through fear and intimidation.

Publicly, Riina maintained the image of a simple, humble farmer from Corleone. Privately, however, he was known for extraordinary brutality and a complete lack of remorse. Feared and loathed even among his peers, he earned the nickname "The Beast" for his ruthless methods. His leadership style was defined by extreme violence, cold calculation, and an unyielding willingness to kill anyone who posed even a minor threat to his rule.

Riina's reign came to international attention through a series of infamous acts. Most notably, in 1992 he orchestrated the assassinations of two prominent anti-Mafia judges, Giovanni Falcone and Paolo Borsellino. Their murders shocked the nation and triggered an unprecedented crackdown on organized crime in Italy. The following year, in 1993, Riina ordered a wave of bombings across mainland Italy, targeting cultural landmarks and killing civilians in a desperate effort to coerce the government into submission. These acts marked one of the bloodiest chapters in Italy's fight against the Mafia.

Through control of the heroin trade and extortion rackets, Riina amassed considerable wealth and turned Cosa Nostra into one of the most powerful criminal organizations in the world. He unified previously rival Mafia factions under his brutal leadership and managed operations from hiding for more than two decades. His influence reached into the political sphere as well. Riina was believed to have maintained ties with corrupt politicians and officials, including allegations of connections to former Italian Prime Minister Giulio Andreotti, although Andreotti denied any involvement. In Sicily, Riina exerted significant control over local governments through bribery and intimidation, shaping political decisions and obstructing law enforcement efforts.

After 23 years on the run, Riina was finally captured in 1993 near his home in Palermo. His downfall was driven by intensified law enforcement campaigns and the testimonies of Mafia informants who provided crucial information about his operations and whereabouts. The arrest marked a turning point in Italy's war on organized crime.

Riina died of cancer on November 17, 2017, in the prison wing of a hospital in Parma, Italy, just one day after his 87th birthday. At the time of his death, he was serving 26 life sentences for numerous murders and other crimes. His passing marked the end of one of the darkest and most violent eras in the history of the Sicilian Mafia.

His legacy remains one of fear and infamy. Riina influenced future crime groups by demonstrating how sheer violence and terror could be used to seize and maintain control, though his approach also provoked stronger government crackdowns and public backlash. He is remembered as one of the most brutal Mafia bosses in history, with his life story inspiring a range of books and films that attempt to capture the horror of his reign.

Even in prison, Riina reportedly never expressed remorse for his actions. A surprisingly humanizing detail about his secretive life was his fondness for gardening, during his years in hiding, he often spent time tending to plants, a quiet hobby that stood in jarring contrast to his savage legacy.

Bernardo "The Tractor" Provenzano

Bernardo Provenzano began his criminal career in his late teens by joining the Corleone Mafia under boss Luciano Leggio during the 1950s. Alongside Salvatore "Toto" Riina, Provenzano earned a reputation as a ruthless enforcer. His cold and systematic execution of rivals led to his nickname, "The Tractor." A pivotal moment in his rise came with his participation in the 1958 assassination of Michele Navarra, a move that enabled Leggio to take control of the Corleonesi clan. Provenzano's continued involvement in purges throughout the Second Mafia War of the 1980s further cemented his position within the Mafia's upper hierarchy, ultimately placing him among its most powerful figures.

Throughout his criminal career, Provenzano was deeply involved in a variety of illegal activities, including murder, extortion, drug trafficking, and corruption. He was linked to numerous killings during the violent Mafia wars and played a significant role in the 1992 assassinations of anti-Mafia judges Giovanni Falcone and Paolo Borsellino. These murders sparked national outrage and brought intense scrutiny to Cosa Nostra. In response to the law enforcement crackdown that followed Riina's arrest in 1993, Provenzano transitioned the organization from a strategy of open violence to one of discretion and calculated financial expansion. He focused on infiltrating public contracts and legitimate businesses, steering Cosa Nostra into lower-profile yet highly profitable ventures.

Provenzano presented himself to the public as a reclusive and modest individual, avoiding the flamboyant lifestyle favored by many of his predecessors. Privately, he was known for his strategic mind and absolute commitment to secrecy. He communicated through handwritten notes known as "pizzini," avoiding phones and digital communication to reduce the risk of surveillance. This methodical and calculated approach allowed him to remain a fugitive for more than four decades. His style of leadership emphasized pragmatism, diplomacy, and long-term planning, earning him quiet respect within the Mafia's ranks.

Provenzano's name became associated with some of the most infamous events in recent Mafia history. He was implicated in the 1992 assassinations of judges Falcone and Borsellino, acts that marked a turning point in Italy's war on organized crime. He was also involved in the 1993 bombings in Rome, Milan, and Florence, which targeted cultural landmarks and killed civilians in an attempt to intimidate the Italian government into relaxing its anti-Mafia efforts. These attacks intensified the crackdown on organized crime and made Provenzano one of the most wanted men in Italy.

Despite his secretive nature, Provenzano amassed considerable wealth through his control of public works contracts and the Mafia's infiltration into legitimate businesses. Though the full extent of his financial holdings remains unknown, his influence over the Sicilian Mafia was substantial. He successfully unified various factions under his leadership and redirected Cosa Nostra toward a more sustainable and less visible model of criminal enterprise focused on financial gain and survival.

To maintain this control, Provenzano relied on deep-rooted connections with corrupt politicians and public officials. Through bribery and blackmail, he ensured that Cosa Nostra's interests were protected at the highest levels. His influence over local governments in Sicily allowed him to manipulate public contracts and political appointments, further embedding the Mafia into the region's infrastructure.

After 43 years on the run, Provenzano was finally captured in 2006 at a farmhouse near Corleone, Sicily. His arrest marked the culmination of a sustained law enforcement campaign that involved advanced surveillance techniques and the cooperation of informants. The fall of Provenzano signaled a major victory in Italy's long-standing battle against the Mafia.

He died of cancer on July 13, 2016, at the age of 83, in a prison hospital in Milan. At the time of his death, he was serving multiple life sentences for crimes that included murder and Mafia association. His passing closed the chapter on one of the most enigmatic and enduring figures in Cosa Nostra's history.

Provenzano's legacy is that of a master strategist who reshaped the Mafia into a modern, low-profile enterprise. He influenced future crime groups by proving that discretion, not violence, could be a more effective tool for longevity and power. His methods continue to be studied by law enforcement and scholars as a blueprint for understanding the evolution of organized crime.

Even amid his notoriety, Provenzano displayed unusual quirks. He reportedly never used mobile phones or computers, relying entirely on handwritten notes to communicate, which helped him avoid capture for decades. In one particularly brazen move, he underwent prostate surgery at a French hospital under a false identity and even billed the Italian national health service for the procedure, an act that typified his ability to manipulate systems while hiding in plain sight.

Salvatore "The Baron" Lo Piccolo

Salvatore Lo Piccolo began his ascent through the ranks of the Sicilian Mafia as a driver and bodyguard for Palermo boss Rosario Riccobono. When Riccobono was eliminated during the Second Mafia War of the early 1980s, Lo Piccolo aligned himself with the victorious Corleonesi faction led by Salvatore Riina and Bernardo Provenzano. His loyalty and ability to survive the brutal internal purges earned him the trust of the new leadership. By the early 1990s, he had risen to become the capomandamento of San Lorenzo, a powerful district covering several neighborhoods in Palermo. Quietly but steadily, he expanded his influence, setting the stage for a career defined by discretion, strategic planning, and an emphasis on minimizing exposure.

Lo Piccolo's criminal empire was diverse and highly profitable. He played a major role in international cocaine trafficking, while also orchestrating extortion operations that collected the traditional Mafia "pizzo" from businesses across Palermo. He manipulated public contracts and skimmed funds from public works projects, redirecting a significant portion of these illicit earnings into real estate investments. His financial reach extended beyond Sicily, with assets in Northern Italy and suspected ties to American Mafia families. Lo Piccolo understood the value of economic control over brute force, and he built his empire accordingly.

Adopting a leadership style reminiscent of Bernardo Provenzano, Lo Piccolo prioritized discretion and internal order. He avoided flashy displays of power, preferring instead to settle disputes through quiet arbitration. His calculated avoidance of public violence helped the Mafia maintain a lower profile during a time when authorities were increasingly focused on dismantling the organization. This approach allowed him to operate in the shadows for over two decades, becoming one of the most elusive and influential Mafia figures of his generation.

One of the most revealing moments of Lo Piccolo's career came after his arrest, when police uncovered a document titled the "Ten Commandments" of the Mafia. The list laid out strict behavioral rules for members, such as prohibitions against looking at a friend's wife, avoiding bars and clubs, and always prioritizing the organization, even over personal family events. The discovery provided a rare and illuminating glimpse into the internal code of conduct within Cosa Nostra, reinforcing the notion that discipline and loyalty were central to Lo Piccolo's leadership philosophy.

At the peak of his power, Lo Piccolo was widely considered a top contender to succeed Provenzano as the new "boss of bosses" following Provenzano's arrest in 2006. His extensive network, financial clout, and reputation for stability positioned him as a natural heir to the Mafia's highest position. Much of his wealth came from narcotics trafficking and extortion, but he also invested shrewdly in real estate across Italy and possibly beyond. These ventures helped launder illicit profits and solidified his financial base of power.

Although detailed records of political alliances remain scarce, Lo Piccolo's prolonged evasion of law enforcement suggested he enjoyed some degree of protection or support within local institutions. His understated leadership and focus on financial gain rather than open violence made him a difficult target, as he avoided many of the mistakes that led to the downfall of flashier and more aggressive bosses.

His luck ran out on November 5, 2007. After 24 years as a fugitive, Lo Piccolo was arrested near Palermo during a police raid on a villa where he was meeting with other top Mafia members. The operation was made possible by intelligence from a cooperating witness and marked a major blow to the leadership of the Sicilian Mafia. Among those arrested was his son, Sandro Lo Piccolo, who had become deeply involved in his father's criminal operations and was being groomed to continue the family's legacy.

Following his arrest, Lo Piccolo was sentenced to life imprisonment on multiple charges, including murder and Mafia association. He remains incarcerated under the 41-bis prison regime, an especially restrictive form of imprisonment designed to prevent Mafia bosses from maintaining influence while behind bars. His detention effectively ended his direct involvement in organized crime, though his long career left a significant mark on Cosa Nostra's modern evolution.

Lo Piccolo's era was defined not by bloodshed, but by a calculated shift toward financial consolidation and reduced visibility. His tenure emphasized economic control, strategic restraint, and internal discipline, principles that allowed the Mafia to persist with less public scrutiny. His downfall, combined with the arrest of other senior figures, severely weakened the Sicilian Mafia's upper echelons and intensified law enforcement pressure throughout the region.

The "Ten Commandments" found at the time of his arrest remain one of the most discussed artifacts of modern Mafia history, revealing an internal culture shaped by control and hierarchy. His family was deeply enmeshed in the criminal world, Sandro's arrest occurred alongside his father, while another son, Calogero, was captured in a separate anti-Mafia operation in 2008. Lo Piccolo's influence extended well beyond Sicily, with connections to the American Mafia and operations in Northern Italy, underscoring Cosa Nostra's international reach during his reign.

Pasquale "The Accountant" Condello

Pasquale Condello's ascent within the 'Ndrangheta began under the tutelage of Paolo De Stefano, one of Calabria's most powerful mafia bosses. Early in his criminal career, Condello made a name for himself by participating in the 1975 assassination of Antonio Macrì, a pivotal event that intensified internal rivalries and reshaped the power dynamics within the organization. This high-profile murder marked him as a rising enforcer, and over the following decades, he evolved from a loyal soldier into one of the most influential figures in the Calabrian underworld. His standing solidified after the 2004 arrest of Giuseppe Morabito, at which point Condello was widely recognized as the de facto head of the 'Ndrangheta.

Throughout his criminal career, Condello was involved in a wide range of illegal enterprises, including drug trafficking, extortion, and the manipulation of public contracts. He was instrumental in expanding the 'Ndrangheta's reach beyond southern Italy, forging relationships with Colombian cartels and positioning the organization as a dominant force in international cocaine trafficking. These connections helped funnel narcotics from South America into Europe, generating vast profits and further entrenching the 'Ndrangheta's position as a global criminal powerhouse.

Condello was known for his strategic thinking and quiet authority. Unlike more flamboyant mafia figures, he operated behind the scenes and maintained a calm, reserved exterior. His low-profile approach and long periods of invisibility drew frequent comparisons to Bernardo Provenzano of the Sicilian Mafia. Both men prioritized discretion over notoriety, and Condello, much like Provenzano, cultivated a reputation as a calculating leader who relied on complex networks rather than public displays of power.

One of the most notorious incidents associated with Condello was his alleged role in the assassination of Lodovico Ligato, a former president of the Italian State Railways. Ligato was gunned down in 1989 in a killing linked to disputes over public contracts. His death exposed the depth of the 'Ndrangheta's infiltration into legitimate sectors of Italian society and highlighted how the mafia's grip extended well beyond extortion and narcotics. It was a stark reminder of the group's influence over politics and business, particularly in southern Italy.

Over the years, Condello accumulated immense wealth. His earnings came not only from narcotics but also from skimming profits off lucrative public works contracts. The financial influence of his clan extended well into Northern Italy and even beyond national borders. While exact figures remain elusive, his empire was built on both raw criminal power and shrewd economic maneuvering.

Though little has been confirmed publicly, Condello's ability to operate freely for nearly two decades despite being one of Italy's most wanted men suggests he benefited from a web of protection. His apparent success in evading justice for so long points to potential collusion with political allies or compromised law enforcement officials, an all-too-common phenomenon in regions with deep mafia roots. The manipulation of public contracts further indicates that the reach of his network likely extended into bureaucratic or administrative corridors.

After eighteen years on the run, Condello's freedom came to an end on February 18, 2008. Police arrested him in a residence in Reggio Calabria, bringing one of Italy's longest and most frustrating manhunts to a close. Though he was armed at the time, he chose not to resist, surrendering without incident. His arrest marked a symbolic victory for Italian law enforcement and dealt a significant blow to the 'Ndrangheta's leadership structure.

Condello was later sentenced to multiple life terms for his crimes. He remains incarcerated under Italy's harsh 41-bis prison regime, a strict form of solitary confinement intended to sever communication between imprisoned mafia bosses and their external networks. As of the latest available reports, he continues to serve his sentence under these conditions.

Condello's reign as a mafia leader represented a turning point in the evolution of the 'Ndrangheta. His strategic approach to crime emphasized global expansion, business infiltration, and operational secrecy. Law enforcement officials and academics have since studied his methods in an effort to better understand how the Calabrian mafia transformed into one of the most dangerous and financially successful criminal organizations in the world.

His legacy is underscored by the nickname "Il Supremo," a reflection of the reverence he commanded within the organization. Investigators also dubbed him "the Provenzano of Calabria," drawing comparisons to the notorious Sicilian boss due to their similar leadership styles. Despite being one of the most dangerous fugitives in Italian history, his arrest concluded not with violence but with silent compliance, an ending befitting a man who ruled from the shadows.

Giuseppe "The Straight Shooter" Morabito

Giuseppe Morabito began his criminal career in the early 1950s in Africo, Calabria, engaging in illegal activities that included unauthorized occupation of property, illegal possession of weapons, and violent offenses. As a young man, he became deeply involved in the criminal world of the 'Ndrangheta and eventually rose to lead the Morabito clan. His power was solidified through his leadership during internal conflicts, notably the "Faida di Motticella" in the 1980s, which allowed him to assert dominance within the organization. By forging strategic alliances with other 'Ndrangheta families, Morabito expanded his clan's influence throughout Calabria and beyond.

His partnerships with prominent clans such as the Bruzzaniti and Palamara further cemented his authority. In addition to these intra-organization ties, Morabito also maintained a strong relationship with the Sicilian Mafia. He notably provided shelter to Cosa Nostra boss Totò Riina during Riina's years as a fugitive, reinforcing the link between the 'Ndrangheta and Cosa Nostra and enabling cooperative criminal operations between the groups.

Morabito engaged in a wide array of criminal activities, including international drug trafficking, arms smuggling, extortion, and money laundering. He orchestrated complex cocaine and heroin trafficking routes in collaboration with criminal networks in South America and the Balkans. His empire was built on a vast infrastructure of global drug smuggling, which he combined with the infiltration of legitimate businesses to launder illicit profits. This approach allowed him to expand the reach of the 'Ndrangheta across Europe and into South America, positioning his clan as a key player in the international narcotics trade.

Publicly, Morabito cultivated a low-profile image, appearing as a traditional patriarch from a remote region of Italy. Privately, he ruled with an iron grip and was feared for his ruthless control over the clan's operations. He earned the nickname "u tiradrittu," or "the straight shooter," for his decisive leadership style and his reputation for swift, uncompromising decisions. He was calculating, authoritative, and known for maintaining order and discipline within the often-fragmented structure of the 'Ndrangheta.

His name was tied to several high-profile incidents. In 1967, he was implicated in the "Strage di Locri," in which three members of a rival clan were killed. Although he was acquitted in 1971 due to a lack of evidence, the incident highlighted the violent feuds that plagued the 'Ndrangheta. Another major scandal involved the University of Messina, where Morabito's clan infiltrated the institution and exerted control over academic appointments and degrees. This influence remained largely unchecked until police conducted a major crackdown in 2001.

Morabito accumulated substantial wealth through his control of international drug trafficking and money laundering operations. Under his leadership, the Morabito clan became one of the most powerful factions within the 'Ndrangheta. His authority extended to other clans and was reinforced by strong connections with the Sicilian Mafia, enabling coordinated criminal efforts across Italy and beyond. His ability to unify and manage criminal enterprises on a large scale made him a central figure in Italian organized crime.

To maintain and expand this power, Morabito developed relationships with corrupt politicians and officials. Allegations even surfaced about his interactions with elements of Italian intelligence services during the 1970s.

He used bribery and intimidation to control local governments in Calabria, manipulating public contracts and neutralizing opposition to his criminal operations.

After 12 years as a fugitive, Morabito was captured on February 18, 2004. He was found hiding in a rural bunker near Cardeto, Calabria, during a joint operation by the Carabinieri's Special Operations Group and the Calabria Hunters Squadron. His arrest followed intensified law enforcement activity and the deployment of advanced surveillance techniques that eventually led authorities to his secret hideout.

He is currently serving a life sentence in an Italian prison under the strict 41-bis regime, a special detention protocol designed to isolate high-ranking Mafia members from their networks and prevent them from continuing to operate from prison. His capture and imprisonment marked a major success in Italy's campaign against organized crime, particularly the powerful and secretive 'Ndrangheta.

Morabito's influence continues to shape the way organized crime is studied and understood. He demonstrated the power of strategic alliances, economic infiltration, and low-profile leadership in expanding a criminal enterprise. His methods became a model for subsequent generations of 'Ndrangheta leaders, and his long evasion of capture only added to his legend. Today, he is remembered as one of the most powerful and elusive bosses in the history of the 'Ndrangheta.

Among the more surprising aspects of his story is that he reportedly continued to receive a state pension during his years as a fugitive, illustrating the difficulty Italian authorities faced in dismantling entrenched criminal networks. Additionally, he is the grandfather of Giuseppe Sculli, a former professional footballer who played for clubs such as Juventus and Lazio. Sculli's career was occasionally overshadowed by his familial ties to the 'Ndrangheta, adding a public and controversial dimension to Morabito's legacy.

Luigi Mancuso

Luigi Mancuso rose to prominence within the 'Ndrangheta during the 1980s and 1990s, ultimately becoming the leader of the Mancuso 'ndrina, based in the Vibo Valentia province of Calabria. His rise was marked by strategic alliances and a keen understanding of the criminal underworld, allowing him to expand the clan's influence beyond its local territory. Under Mancuso's guidance, the Mancuso clan emerged as one of the most dominant criminal organizations in the region, with its tentacles reaching into national and international territories. His leadership not only consolidated power within Vibo Valentia but also positioned the clan as a major player within the broader structure of the 'Ndrangheta.

Under Mancuso's leadership, the clan engaged in a wide range of criminal activities that brought immense financial rewards. These included drug trafficking, extortion, money laundering, and the manipulation of public contracts. Through strategic partnerships with international drug cartels, Mancuso's organization played a key role in the importation and distribution of narcotics across Europe. The scope and complexity of these operations reflected a high level of coordination and sophistication, reinforcing the clan's standing within the criminal hierarchy. The profits generated through these enterprises were further laundered through legitimate businesses, giving the Mancuso clan a formidable presence both in the underworld and in Calabria's local economy.

Mancuso was widely regarded for his strategic intelligence and his ability to operate discreetly. Known for his low-profile demeanor, he maintained an image of calm authority while exerting significant influence behind the scenes. His efforts to mediate disputes within the 'Ndrangheta earned him a reputation as a stabilizing force during periods of internal strife. He was often called upon to broker peace between rival factions, preserving organizational unity and ensuring the continuity of business operations. This ability to maintain cohesion within a notoriously fractious criminal network further elevated his status.

One of the most significant chapters in Mancuso's criminal history came with his involvement in the massive anti-mafia investigation known as "Rinascita-Scott." Launched in 2019, the operation led to the arrest of over 300 individuals tied to the 'Ndrangheta, including Mancuso himself. The investigation exposed the vast scope of the organization's influence and laid bare the intricate web of connections between the mafia and various sectors of Italian society. The operation, which involved thousands of officers and years of surveillance, was a major blow to the 'Ndrangheta and a public humiliation for many of its leaders.

Mancuso's criminal empire brought with it tremendous wealth and power. As the head of one of the most powerful 'ndrine, he commanded significant financial resources, primarily derived from drug trafficking and the manipulation of local economies. His clan's control over public works and municipal contracts gave them de facto authority in many parts of Calabria, allowing them to dominate local institutions while maintaining a veneer of legitimacy. His influence also extended to other clans, many of which operated under his guidance or protection, cementing his role as the de facto leader of the 'Ndrangheta in the region.

Though direct political connections have never been conclusively proven, the clan's long-term operations and ability to secure lucrative public contracts suggest a level of integration with political and administrative structures. It is widely believed that the Mancuso clan benefited from corrupt relationships within local governance and possibly law enforcement. These connections likely facilitated their continued dominance and helped shield Mancuso from arrest for years.

Despite multiple arrests throughout his criminal career, Mancuso remained a central figure in the 'Ndrangheta until his 2019 capture during the Rinascita-Scott operation. His arrest marked a significant milestone in Italy's fight against organized crime and was celebrated by law enforcement as a major success. As of the latest available information, Mancuso remains incarcerated and is either awaiting trial or serving sentences related to his extensive criminal activities.

Mancuso's legacy is one of calculated dominance. His tenure as head of the Mancuso clan coincided with a period of significant expansion for the 'Ndrangheta, particularly in its international operations. His strategic leadership style helped stabilize the organization internally, even as law enforcement pressure increased. He is remembered not only for his power and wealth but for his ability to maintain order within one of the most dangerous and influential criminal networks in the world.

Known within criminal circles as "U Signurino"—a moniker that underscored his aristocratic demeanor and commanding presence—Mancuso inspired both fear and respect. His influence extended far beyond Calabria, with international connections that brought both opportunity and scrutiny. Despite his criminal background, his efforts to mediate internal disputes within the 'Ndrangheta reflect the paradox of a man who sought to preserve order within a world of violence and chaos.

Antonio "Gambazza" Pelle

Antonio Pelle, known within the underworld by the nickname "Gambazza," began his criminal career in the 1950s. His early years were marked by repeated arrests and multiple prison sentences, including significant time served for murder and attempted murder. In 1981, he was granted a pardon that would mark the beginning of his ascent within the 'Ndrangheta. Upon his release, Pelle rose to become the patriarch of the San Luca locale, one of the most influential territories within the Calabrian mafia. He was eventually recognized as the capo crimine, a title that, though largely symbolic, carried substantial weight within the hierarchy of the 'Ndrangheta and granted him a role in mediating and guiding the organization's broader direction.

Under Pelle's leadership, the Pelle clan expanded its reach across Europe through involvement in high-level criminal enterprises. These included drug trafficking, extortion, and manipulation of public contracts. The clan forged strategic alliances with international drug cartels, serving as a vital link in the importation and distribution of narcotics across the continent. Their operations were not limited to Calabria, and the scale of their trafficking network established the Pelle family as a significant power within the global narcotics trade.

Pelle was known for his strategic intelligence and for maintaining a low profile throughout his criminal career. He deliberately avoided public spectacle, preferring to work behind the scenes as a stabilizing force within the 'Ndrangheta. His ability to manage rivalries and prevent internal breakdowns earned him respect among other bosses, who viewed him as a voice of reason during times of upheaval. While feared by his enemies, he was regarded as a diplomatic figure among allies.

One of the most widely publicized events connected to Pelle was his attempt to mediate the San Luca feud—a brutal internal conflict between the Pelle-Vottari and Nirta-Strangio clans that began in 1991. Though he worked to broker peace, the feud escalated in violence and culminated in the 2007 Duisburg massacre in Germany, where six men were gunned down outside an Italian restaurant. Although Pelle's own faction was not directly responsible for the killings, the massacre drew international attention and exposed the 'Ndrangheta's vast operational reach and capacity for violence.

As the head of one of the most powerful 'ndrina, or 'Ndrangheta clans, Pelle amassed substantial wealth and influence. His control over narcotics networks and his clan's entrenchment in local economic structures allowed them to exert control not only over illicit markets but also over public resources and legitimate enterprises in Calabria. The clan's grip on public contracts further extended their influence into local governance, suggesting a degree of protection or complicity from officials within political and law enforcement circles.

Throughout his life, Pelle faced multiple arrests. His final capture occurred in 2009 after a period of hiding. By then, his influence had waned slightly, but he remained a respected elder within the organization. On November 4, 2009, at the age of 77, Antonio Pelle died of a heart attack at the hospital in Locri, Calabria. His death marked the close of a chapter in the 'Ndrangheta's leadership, as he had played a crucial role in preserving organizational unity during volatile periods.

Pelle's legacy remains intertwined with the 'Ndrangheta's continued resilience and expansion. His leadership style, which emphasized negotiation and restraint over unchecked violence, set a tone for future leaders seeking to balance tradition with the demands of modern criminal enterprise. Despite operating in a world of bloodshed and betrayal, Pelle was remembered for his efforts to hold the organization together and his attempts to prevent fratricidal wars that could destabilize the syndicate.

Behind the name "Gambazza," which referred to a leg injury he suffered in his youth, stood a man whose authority and cunning left a lasting mark on the Calabrian underworld. He remained the patriarch of the Pelle clan until his death, and many of his family members, sons and sons-in-law included, held high-ranking roles within the 'Ndrangheta. Despite his extensive criminal record, Pelle made repeated efforts to broker peace during one of the bloodiest chapters in the group's history, revealing the nuanced and often paradoxical role of leadership within organized crime.

Giovanni Tegano

Giovanni Tegano rose to prominence within the ranks of the 'Ndrangheta during the volatile 1980s, eventually becoming one of the principal leaders of the De Stefano-Tegano alliance. His influence crystallized during the Second 'Ndrangheta War, a brutal conflict that raged between 1985 and 1991 and claimed hundreds of lives. Tegano played a pivotal role in forging the strategic partnership between his clan and the De Stefano family, an alliance that was solidified not only through mutual interest but also by blood. In 1985, his niece, Antonietta Benestare, married Orazio De Stefano, a symbolic union that sealed the coalition between two of Reggio Calabria's most powerful criminal dynasties.

As the head of the De Stefano-Tegano faction, Tegano oversaw a sprawling network of illicit enterprises. The clan was heavily involved in murder, arms trafficking, and mafia association. These operations were not merely violent or opportunistic, they were systematically organized and ruthlessly enforced. Tegano's command over such criminal activities eventually led to multiple convictions, and he was sentenced to life in prison for his crimes. Despite the weight of these charges, his stature within the 'Ndrangheta remained significant, especially due to his role in transitioning the organization from a period of internal war to one of calculated peace.

Tegano distinguished himself through his reputation as a tactician rather than a brute. While he was no stranger to bloodshed, he became especially known for his ability to broker peace among rival clans. After years of carnage during the Second 'Ndrangheta War, it was Tegano who played a crucial role in negotiating a "pax mafiosa" in Reggio Calabria. This agreement carved the city into zones of influence, giving each clan territorial control in order to prevent further bloodshed. The ceasefire didn't signify the end of criminal activity, but it did allow the various factions to focus on business rather than internal destruction. In this sense, Tegano helped reshape the strategic outlook of the 'Ndrangheta during the 1990s.

His arrest on April 26, 2010, brought this chapter of his life to a close. After 17 years as a fugitive, he was captured in Reggio Calabria and led into custody under intense security. The scene outside the courthouse was striking: a crowd of supporters gathered to greet him, and one woman was heard shouting, "Giovanni is a man of peace!" The display reflected the complicated relationship between mafia figures and the communities they dominate, where fear, loyalty, and admiration can all coexist. At the time of his arrest, Tegano was considered one of Italy's most dangerous fugitives, a label that belied the local affection some still held for him.

While specific financial records remain hidden, Tegano's role as a top-tier boss in one of Italy's most powerful criminal organizations points to substantial wealth and influence. As with many 'Ndrangheta leaders, illicit proceeds were likely laundered through construction, drug trafficking, and local political arrangements, though the full scope of his financial empire remains speculative. Despite the lack of confirmed political ties, the clan's influence across Calabria suggests some level of cooperation or complicity within political and institutional spheres, a common feature in regions under mafia control.

Giovanni Tegano died on July 7, 2021, at the age of 81. He passed away while serving a life sentence under the strict 41-bis regime at the Opera prison in Lombardy, a form of incarceration specifically designed to isolate high-ranking mafia members from their criminal networks. His death marked the end of an era for the De Stefano-Tegano alliance, closing the book on one of the

'Ndrangheta's most influential peacemakers and power brokers.

Tegano's legacy is deeply tied to his ability to shift the strategic landscape of organized crime in Calabria. His contributions to the post-war order within the 'Ndrangheta laid the foundation for a more structured and financially driven criminal syndicate. While many mafia bosses are remembered for their brutality, Tegano is remembered just as much for his diplomacy. His behind-the-scenes role in shaping the balance of power among feuding clans earned him a unique position in the history of the 'Ndrangheta, one of both feared authority and reluctant admiration.

Despite his conviction for heinous crimes, Tegano's public arrest and the crowd's reaction illustrated the paradox often present in regions under mafia control. To many, he was not merely a criminal but a symbol of stability, even if that stability was built on violence and corruption. His influence as a peace negotiator and clan leader made him a central figure in the evolution of the modern 'Ndrangheta, whose reach now spans far beyond the hills of Calabria.

Michele "King of Cement" Zagaria

Michele Zagaria began his ascent in organized crime during the 1980s, aligning himself with powerful figures in the Casalesi clan such as Francesco Schiavone, known as "Sandokan," and Alberto Beneduce. His early involvement with the Camorra provided the foundation for a long and highly influential career. As he gained experience, Zagaria focused his efforts on infiltrating the construction and public works sectors, a strategy that earned him the nickname "King of Cement." Through control of these industries, he amassed both wealth and power, solidifying his position within the Camorra's leadership ranks.

Zagaria's influence was not confined to the Campania region. He expanded the clan's reach by forging strategic alliances with other major criminal organizations, including the 'Ndrangheta. These relationships enabled him to extend his operations into areas such as Emilia-Romagna and even Eastern Europe. His reputation as a power broker grew as he diversified his control and sought new opportunities for illicit expansion across borders.

He was involved in a wide range of criminal activities, including murder, extortion, drug trafficking, and corruption. His criminal enterprise spanned multiple regions and sectors, making him a central figure in modern Italian organized crime. Zagaria built his empire by infiltrating legitimate businesses, particularly in construction and public works, using these fronts to launder money and secure economic dominance. His ability to blend illicit and legitimate operations allowed him to accumulate vast resources while minimizing exposure to law enforcement.

Known for his reclusive nature, Zagaria carefully cultivated a public image as a reserved and strategic figure. He avoided the flamboyant displays of power favored by other mob leaders, choosing instead to operate in secrecy. Privately, he was meticulous and pragmatic, with a strong preference for long-term planning over impulsive violence. His leadership style emphasized discretion, economic penetration, and carefully selected alliances, which helped him evade capture for years.

Zagaria's criminal legacy was further cemented by his role in several major scandals. He was a central figure in the Spartacus Trial, a landmark legal case that resulted in multiple life sentences for members of the Casalesi clan, including Zagaria himself. The charges included murder and Mafia association. Additionally, he was implicated in the illegal disposal of toxic waste, a scandal that had devastating environmental and health effects in the Campania region. This operation highlighted the clan's deep infiltration into the waste management industry and its willingness to profit at the expense of public safety.

His wealth came largely from his domination of public works contracts and his extensive control over legitimate businesses across Italy and into Eastern Europe. His economic power enabled him to manipulate local governments and private enterprises alike. Through bribery and strategic influence, Zagaria ensured that public contracts were awarded to entities under his control, allowing the clan to maintain its financial dominance while avoiding direct confrontation with authorities.

Zagaria maintained strong connections with corrupt officials and politicians, relationships that proved instrumental in shielding his operations from law enforcement. These alliances allowed him to influence decisions and appointments in key regions, ensuring that the interests of the Casalesi clan were protected at all levels of government. His ability to manipulate public institutions made him one of the most politically connected figures in modern Italian organized crime.

After 16 years as a fugitive, Zagaria was finally captured in December 2011. He was found hiding in a secret bunker beneath a house in his hometown of Casapesenna. His arrest was the result of intensified law enforcement efforts and the deployment of advanced surveillance technologies that eventually led investigators to his hidden location. The capture of Zagaria marked a significant milestone in Italy's ongoing campaign against the Camorra.

Zagaria is currently serving multiple life sentences in an Italian prison for crimes including murder and Mafia association. His imprisonment was hailed as a major victory by Italian authorities, representing a decisive blow to one of the most entrenched and secretive criminal networks in the country. While he remains behind bars, his influence continues to be studied as a prime example of modern Camorra leadership.

His legacy endures as that of a master manipulator who demonstrated the power of economic infiltration and political corruption in sustaining criminal enterprises. Future crime groups have looked to his methods as a blueprint for expanding influence while minimizing attention. Zagaria is remembered today as one of the most elusive and powerful figures in the history of the Camorra.

Beyond his criminal empire, Zagaria had a taste for luxury and extravagance. Informants claimed that he kept exotic animals, including a tiger, at his residence to symbolize his wealth and dominance. He was also said to live by a strict personal code, though he often indulged in behaviors he forbade among his subordinates, revealing a "do as I say, not as I do" mentality that highlighted the contradictions of his leadership style.

Francesco "Sandokan" Schiavone

Francesco Schiavone, better known as "Sandokan," began his ascent through the Camorra ranks as a driver and bodyguard for the notorious Umberto Ammaturo. His first run-in with the law came in 1972, when he was arrested for illegal possession of firearms. Schiavone quickly became immersed in the violent power struggles that plagued the Naples underworld, aligning himself with Antonio Bardellino, the founder of the Casalesi clan. As rival factions were systematically eliminated during a series of bloody feuds, Schiavone's stature grew. By the 1990s, he had emerged as the undisputed boss of the Casalesi clan, recognized for his strategic acumen and authority within his generation of Camorra leaders.

Under Schiavone's leadership, the Casalesi clan expanded into a sprawling criminal empire that generated staggering profits. They skimmed millions from public contracts tied to major infrastructure projects, including the A1 highway between Rome and Naples and the construction of a prison in Santa Maria Capua Vetere. The clan also operated a vast and illicit waste management network, illegally dumping toxic materials and reaping financial rewards while jeopardizing public health. Their reach extended into the legitimate economy through their control of food distribution channels, notably involving well-known companies like Parmalat and Cirio. Much of the clan's dirty money was laundered through high-value real estate investments in cities such as Parma and Milan, solidifying their influence well beyond the Naples region.

Schiavone was as charismatic as he was calculating. Unlike some of his predecessors who relied on brute force, he prioritized a business-minded approach. Violence, while not entirely off the table, was reserved for strategic moments. He believed in keeping the organization discreet and maintaining profitability without attracting unnecessary attention from law enforcement. His leadership style emphasized long-term economic gain over dramatic displays of dominance, a philosophy that earned him respect and ensured the clan's enduring success during his reign.

The most high-profile event tied to Schiavone's rule was the "Spartacus Trial," a massive legal offensive targeting the Casalesi clan. Lasting over a decade, the trial culminated in life sentences for Schiavone and several top lieutenants. The proceedings were marred by violence and intimidation: five individuals linked to the trial, including an interpreter, were murdered, and a judge and two journalists received death threats. Despite these efforts to derail the process, the trial marked a historic moment in Italy's fight against organized crime.

By the mid-1990s, the Casalesi clan was estimated to be worth approximately $47 billion, a staggering figure that underscored their dominance within both the criminal underworld and the broader economy. During one wave of asset seizures in the 1990s, authorities confiscated over $788 million in properties and holdings tied to Schiavone and his family. These numbers reflected not only the scope of their illegal enterprises but also the effectiveness of Schiavone's methods in integrating criminal operations into seemingly legitimate business ventures.

Though detailed records of political connections remain elusive, the clan's control over public contracts and their entrenched role in waste management point to an extensive web of influence. Their ability to secure these contracts and profit from them without interruption for years suggests a degree of political accommodation or even active collusion with officials across multiple levels of government and industry.

Schiavone's reign came to an end on July 11, 1998, when police discovered him hiding in a concealed apartment behind a sliding granite wall in his luxurious Naples villa. He had been on the run for more than five years and was considered the most wanted Camorra figure in Italy at the time. In 2008, he was sentenced to life imprisonment following the conclusion of the Spartacus Trial, a sentence that marked the final chapter of his reign at the helm of one of Italy's most powerful criminal organizations.

As of the most recent information, Schiavone remains alive and incarcerated under the 41-bis prison regime, an austere form of confinement intended to sever Mafia leaders' ability to communicate with their networks. Though confined, his name remains synonymous with the rise of the Casalesi and the businesslike transformation of Camorra operations in the late 20th century.

Schiavone's legacy is one of strategic expansion, financial manipulation, and a deep integration of crime into legitimate institutions. His life and career were prominently featured in Roberto Saviano's investigative book *Gomorrah*, which exposed the Casalesi clan's inner workings to a global audience. The revelations helped elevate public awareness of the Camorra's reach and the systemic corruption that enabled it.

His nickname, "Sandokan," was inspired by a popular 1970s television series starring Kabir Bedi and was a nod to his dark, full beard and swashbuckling appearance. When police arrested him, they discovered a personal library devoted to Napoleon and several paintings he had created himself, clues to his interest in art and history. Schiavone's family was also deeply enmeshed in the clan's operations. His wife, Giuseppina Nappa, and several of his children faced legal consequences for their roles in the family's criminal activities, proving that in the Camorra, blood ties often ran as deep as business ones.

South and Central-American Organized Crime

Organized crime in Latin America took shape amid Colombia's explosive rise as the global cocaine hub during the 1970s and 1980s. Vast rural coca farms often employing thousands of local laborers became the foundation of powerful drug cartels. Among them, Pablo Escobar's Medellín Cartel grew into a sprawling criminal empire, at its peak supplying an estimated 60–80 percent of the world's cocaine and generating billions of dollars annually. Their terror tactics, bombings, assassinations, kidnappings, hindered extradition efforts and destabilized entire populations. Meanwhile, Colombia's rival Cali Cartel employed a subtler approach, relying on extensive bribery, money laundering, and global influence operations rather than overt violence. The downfall of these cartels between 1993 and 1995 left long-lasting effects on Colombia's institutions, economy, and rural communities, even as the structures of organized crime survived.

Pressure on Colombian networks forced traffickers to seek safer routes northward. Starting in the early 1980s, Mexican smuggling groups began by transporting cocaine on behalf of Colombian cartels but soon seized control of the supply chain by collaborating directly with Medellín and Cali distributors. What began as logistical support became a strategic shift: by the late 1980s, Mexican traffickers were operating their own distribution enterprises, ready to dominate the drug economy.

At the forefront of this shift was the Guadalajara Cartel, founded around 1978–1980 by Miguel Ángel Félix Gallardo alongside Rafael Caro Quintero, Ernesto Fonseca Carrillo "Don Neto," and Juan José Esparragoza

Moreno. This group pioneered the transformation of Mexican trafficking: it dominated heroin, marijuana, and later cocaine routes across the U.S.–Mexico border. They brokered deals with Colombian cartels, demanding as much as half of each cocaine shipment they transported, earning them tens of millions annually. Their political protection, allegedly tied to Mexico's Federal Security Directorate, enabled almost complete impunity.

A watershed moment occurred in 1985, when DEA agent Enrique "Kiki" Camarena was kidnapped, tortured, and murdered, retribution for the destruction of Rancho Búfalo, the cartel's massive marijuana plantation. This triggered Operation Leyenda, the DEA's largest homicide investigation ever. This violent retribution marked the beginning of the cartel's collapse and prompted the fragmentation of its empire into regional powerhouses like Sinaloa, Tijuana, and the Gulf cartel.

By the 1990s and 2000s, Mexican cartels had grown into sophisticated criminal corporations. Beyond cocaine, they controlled methamphetamine production, fentanyl labs, migrant smuggling networks, arms trafficking, cyber fraud, and illicit mining. Utilizing corruption, intimidation, and a global network, they extended their reach deep into North, Central, and South America.

The human toll has been staggering: Latin America now accounts for roughly 40 percent of the world's homicides despite representing just 9 percent of the world's population. Nations such as Mexico, Honduras, and El Salvador are plagued by cartel-fueled violence, migration crises, and institutional collapse. Armed groups like Colombia's ELN and post-FARC guerrillas are merging politics and crime, further complicating security efforts.

Modern cartels function like complex enterprises. The Sinaloa Cartel, led by Joaquín "El Chapo" Guzmán, Ismael "El Mayo" Zambada, and Juan José Esparragoza, employs a corporate hierarchy, tunnels, paramilitary enforcement units, money-laundering fronts, and transnational alliances. The Jalisco New Generation Cartel (CJNG), formed in 2009, surpasses them in aggression and militarization, using drones and heavy firepower. Meanwhile, paramilitary-style enforcers broke away from the Gulf Cartel in the late 1990s to form Los Zetas, whose extreme violence defined a new era in cartel warfare. The Gulf Cartel, longstanding since the 1930s, continues to operate out of Tamaulipas, frequently clashing with its former enforcers and other major syndicates.

Governments have adopted more comprehensive tactics in response. Mexico's 2016 judicial reform introduced oral trials, crime-scene professionalism, and plea agreements. In February 2025, the U.S. designated Sinaloa and CJNG as Foreign Terrorist Organizations, expanding its toolkit to include terror-related sanctions. Meanwhile, Colombia continues to contend with non-state criminal economies in post-FARC frontiers.

Yet even as cartels face pressure, they adapt. Their decentralized cells, shell companies, media manipulation, and institutional infiltration make them resilient. They launder profits through real estate, agriculture, mining, and the financial sector, concentrating power in border and remote regions where state presence is weak.

Latin American organized crime today is a globalized and adaptive phenomenon: born in Colombia's coca fields, matured in Mexico's cartel networks, and diversified across illicit and licit economies throughout the hemisphere.

Pablo Escobar

Pablo Escobar began his journey into crime as a teenager in Medellín, Colombia, engaging in petty offenses such as selling fake diplomas, smuggling stereo equipment, and stealing tombstones to resell. His first arrest occurred in 1974 for car theft. By the mid-1970s, Escobar had entered the cocaine trade, a move that would transform his criminal career and alter the global narcotics landscape. In 1976, he founded the Medellín Cartel, which quickly rose to dominate the cocaine supply chain into the United States. At its peak, the cartel controlled the vast majority of cocaine entering the U.S., making Escobar one of the most powerful drug lords in history.

He solidified his cartel's dominance by forming alliances with other traffickers, including Carlos Lehder and the Ochoa brothers. These partnerships enhanced the cartel's operational efficiency and reach. Escobar also developed connections with guerrilla groups and allegedly received foreign assistance to further expand his network. His ability to bridge criminal enterprises with armed factions and political actors helped the Medellín Cartel operate with impunity during its most violent years.

Escobar's criminal empire encompassed drug trafficking, murder, bombings, bribery, and racketeering. His organization was responsible for countless assassinations and acts of terrorism, including the bombing of Avianca Flight 203, which killed over 100 people. He monopolized the cocaine trade, reportedly shipping 70 to 80 tons of cocaine into the United States every month during the 1980s. The vast profits from this enterprise fueled a criminal infrastructure that extended across the Americas and into Europe.

In public, Escobar cultivated the image of a generous benefactor. He funded housing projects, built sports facilities, and offered financial assistance to the poor in Medellín. These efforts earned him the nickname "Paisa Robin Hood" and gained him genuine support from segments of Colombia's population. Privately, however, Escobar was known for his brutality and calculated use of violence and bribery. His infamous "plata o plomo" policy, offering targets the choice between silver (a bribe) or lead (a bullet,) became a defining tactic of his reign.

Escobar's name became synonymous with scandal and terror. In 1984, he ordered the assassination of Colombian Justice Minister Rodrigo Lara Bonilla, a bold move that escalated the government's offensive against the cartel. In 1989, he orchestrated the bombing of Avianca Flight 203, targeting a presidential candidate and killing innocent civilians. These acts marked some of the most violent chapters in Colombia's history and intensified international efforts to bring him to justice.

His wealth was staggering. Forbes estimated his net worth at $30 billion by the early 1990s, making him one of the richest men in the world at the time. Escobar used his fortune to influence Colombian politics, law enforcement, and the judiciary, often relying on bribes and intimidation to secure his interests. His power extended into local governments and police departments, where officials were often too afraid, or too well-paid, to oppose him.

Escobar also held political office. In 1982, he secured a seat as an alternate member of the Colombian Chamber of Representatives, a move that provided him with political immunity and an aura of legitimacy. His involvement in politics gave him access to powerful circles and further entrenched his ability to operate without interference.

Despite his immense power, Escobar's empire eventually began to unravel. Increased pressure from Colombian authorities, backed by international agencies, led to the gradual dismantling of the Medellín Cartel. On December 2, 1993, he was tracked down and killed by Colombian National Police on a rooftop in Medellín. A phone call to his family had led authorities to his location. While the official story states he died in a shootout, some believe Escobar may have taken his own life to avoid capture.

His death marked the end of the Medellín Cartel's dominance and ushered in a new era of drug trafficking led by rival organizations. The power vacuum left in his absence contributed to a reshaping of the global narcotics trade. Escobar's life became a symbol of both the excesses of narco-power and the challenges of combating organized crime at an international scale.

He left behind a complex legacy. On one hand, he demonstrated how drug trafficking could generate enormous wealth and global influence, setting a precedent for cartels that followed. On the other, he remains a deeply polarizing figure, reviled for his violence, yet admired by some for his philanthropic gestures. His story has been immortalized in numerous books, films, and television series, ensuring that his legend endures.

Among the many strange facts surrounding Escobar's life, it was reported that he spent over $2,500 a month just on rubber bands to bundle his cash. Rats were said to have consumed billions of dollars stored in his warehouses. In one of his boldest moves, Escobar once offered to pay off Colombia's entire national debt, estimated at $10 billion, in exchange for amnesty from extradition, a deal that was ultimately rejected but remains a striking example of his ambition and wealth.

Carlos "El Loco" Lehder

Carlos Lehder's rise to power began in the United States with minor criminal activities, including car theft and marijuana smuggling. His trajectory shifted dramatically during a stint in prison, where he met fellow inmate George Jung. Together, they crafted a plan to revolutionize the cocaine trade by using small aircraft to transport the drug into the U.S. Following his release, Lehder acquired Norman's Cay, a small island in the Bahamas, which he converted into a major transshipment hub. This strategic outpost allowed for unprecedented efficiency and volume in cocaine trafficking to Florida, setting a new standard for smuggling operations in the Western Hemisphere.

As a founding member of the Medellín Cartel, Lehder was instrumental in building a sophisticated transportation infrastructure that helped the cartel dominate the global cocaine trade. Norman's Cay became a critical node in the supply chain, enabling the rapid, covert movement of large quantities of cocaine into the United States. At its height, the Medellín Cartel was responsible for approximately 80% of the cocaine entering the U.S., with Lehder's logistical innovations playing a central role.

Lehder's eccentric and volatile personality earned him nicknames like "El Loco" and "Crazy Charlie." He openly embraced neo-Nazi ideology and founded the National Latin Civic Movement, a political party with a platform centered on anti-communism and nationalism. His radical beliefs, flamboyant behavior, and taste for extravagance made him a controversial figure even among fellow cartel members, who preferred a more discreet approach.

Among the most infamous chapters of his story was his attempt to enter Colombian politics through the National

Latin Civic Movement. One of its key platforms was opposition to extradition agreements with the United States, a cause that resonated with many in Colombia's criminal underworld. However, Lehder's increasing visibility, erratic conduct, and ideological extremism made him a liability, eventually alienating both allies and rivals within the cartel.

By the peak of his criminal career, Lehder had amassed a net worth estimated at $2.7 billion. His grip on Norman's Cay and his central role in the Medellín Cartel's logistics operations positioned him as one of the most powerful drug lords of his era. His influence extended internationally, as he expanded the cartel's reach into multiple continents while operating largely beyond the grasp of law enforcement.

Lehder's political ambitions brought him into direct conflict with both Colombian and American authorities. His overt attempts to manipulate Colombian policies through the National Latin Civic Movement and his neo-Nazi rhetoric invited intense scrutiny. While he enjoyed some initial support, his behavior increasingly drew the attention of law enforcement and hastened his fall from grace.

In 1987, Lehder was captured by Colombian authorities and swiftly extradited to the United States, where he faced multiple charges including drug trafficking and money laundering. He was sentenced to life imprisonment plus 135 years. However, his sentence was later reduced after he agreed to testify against Panamanian dictator Manuel Noriega, further complicating his legacy.

After spending more than three decades in U.S. prisons, Lehder was released in June 2020 and deported to Germany, where he held citizenship through his father.

In March 2025, he attempted to return to Colombia but was arrested upon arrival due to unresolved legal matters. A Colombian judge eventually ruled that his sentence had expired, and Lehder was released once again.

Carlos Lehder is remembered as one of the most innovative figures in the history of drug trafficking. His methods fundamentally changed how narcotics were transported, laying the groundwork for future operations across the Americas. His life story has been the subject of several books and documentaries, including his own memoir, *Vida y muerte del cartel de Medellín*, which offers an insider's look at the inner workings of the cartel.

Despite his violent and criminal past, Lehder had an unusual cultural side. He was a devoted fan of The Beatles and John Lennon, even installing a statue of Lennon at his hotel in Colombia. In a particularly audacious episode, Lehder once offered to pay off Colombia's national debt in exchange for amnesty and the freedom to continue his trafficking operations. His control over Norman's Cay was so absolute that the island functioned like an independent state, serving as a personal empire built on cocaine, ideology, and audacity.

Jose "El Mexicano" Gonzalo Rodriguez Gacha

José Gonzalo Rodríguez Gacha, born in Pacho, Cundinamarca, Colombia, emerged from a modest background to become one of the most powerful and feared figures in Colombia's drug trade. He began his criminal career in the emerald mining zones of Muzo, working under the influential emerald magnate Gilberto Molina Moreno. Known early on for his brutal efficiency as an enforcer, Rodríguez Gacha quickly made a name for himself. His ruthlessness and ambition paved the way for his transition into the burgeoning cocaine trade. He initially partnered with established trafficker Verónica Rivera de Vargas before rising further by joining forces with Pablo Escobar and other prominent traffickers to help found the Medellín Cartel.

As a top leader in the cartel, Rodríguez Gacha played a crucial role in developing cocaine trafficking routes through Mexico into the United States, focusing particularly on major cities like Los Angeles and Houston. He oversaw the construction of "Tranquilandia," one of the largest jungle-based cocaine laboratories ever built, employing more than 2,000 workers. This industrial-scale operation significantly enhanced the cartel's ability to produce and distribute cocaine, solidifying their dominance in the global drug market.

Rodríguez Gacha, nicknamed "El Mexicano" due to his love for Mexican culture, was instantly recognizable by his sombreros and the Mexican-themed names of his properties. He surrounded himself with mariachi bands, hosted elaborate fiestas, and lived an extravagant lifestyle. Despite his flamboyance, he was universally feared for his violence, authoritarian leadership, and willingness to use extreme force to maintain control.

One of his most controversial legacies was his role in founding and financing the paramilitary group "Muerte a Secuestradores" (MAS), which was created to combat guerrilla kidnappings. His violent reputation was further cemented by his involvement in the 1984 assassination of Colombian Justice Minister Rodrigo Lara Bonilla—an event that escalated the government's war against drug traffickers. Additionally, Rodríguez Gacha was implicated in the bombing of Avianca Flight 203 in 1989, a horrifying act that killed all 107 people on board and underscored the lengths the cartel would go to protect its interests.

At his peak, Rodríguez Gacha was named one of the world's billionaires by *Forbes* magazine in 1988. His immense fortune came from his cocaine empire, and he invested in a wide array of properties, including luxurious ranches and estates throughout Colombia. With his wealth, he was able to build and sustain private armies, which he used to wage war against both guerrilla groups and the Colombian state.

His confrontation with the government reached its zenith in the late 1980s. Known for hiring foreign mercenaries, including Israeli and British soldiers, to train his forces, Rodríguez Gacha turned parts of Colombia into militarized zones under his control. His open warfare against state institutions made him a high-priority target for Colombian and international law enforcement.

In December 1989, an informant revealed his whereabouts, leading to a military operation in Tolú. During a fierce shootout with police, Rodríguez Gacha, his son, and several of his bodyguards were killed. His death on December 15, 1989, marked a pivotal moment in the government's offensive against the Medellín Cartel and symbolized the intensifying violence of the Colombian drug wars.

Rodríguez Gacha's rise and fall have been portrayed in various forms of media, including the Netflix series *Narcos*, where actor Luis Guzmán played a character based on him. His story is often cited as a case study in the extreme brutality and unchecked ambition that characterized Colombia's narco era.

Known as "El Mexicano" due to his love for all things Mexican, Rodríguez Gacha infused his personal life with cultural homages, naming estates after Mexican towns and hosting festivals complete with mariachi bands. Surprisingly, despite his criminal reputation, some locals in his hometown viewed him as a community benefactor because of his financial contributions to local infrastructure and social projects.

Jorge Luis Ochoa Vasquez

Jorge Luis Ochoa Vásquez was born into a wealthy and respected family in Medellín, Colombia. His father, Fabio Ochoa Restrepo, was a prominent cattle breeder and a well-known figure in equestrian circles. Unlike many of his contemporaries in organized crime, Jorge Luis came from privilege and opportunity. In the mid-1970s, he and his brothers transitioned from the family's legitimate businesses into the world of narcotics trafficking, taking advantage of the explosive demand for cocaine in the United States. By 1978, the Ochoa brothers had established a robust distribution network in Miami, laying the foundation for what would soon evolve into the Medellín Cartel, one of the most powerful and infamous criminal organizations in history.

As one of the cartel's senior leaders, Ochoa played a pivotal role in coordinating the large-scale shipment of cocaine to the U.S. and Europe. At the peak of his operation, he claimed to be exporting an average of six metric tons of cocaine each month. Beyond managing logistics, Ochoa invested heavily in infrastructure to support the cartel's activities, including legitimate businesses such as livestock companies and even banks. These ventures helped launder proceeds and concealed the cartel's financial footprint. He was not only a trafficker but also a strategist, responsible for the smooth movement of product and money across continents.

Ochoa stood in contrast to his more flamboyant associate, Pablo Escobar. Known for his subdued demeanor, Ochoa kept a low public profile and avoided drawing unnecessary attention. He abstained from using cocaine and drank alcohol only on rare occasions. Passionate about traditional Colombian pastimes, he raised fighting bulls at his ranch, Los Lamos, and collected Harley-Davidson motorcycles. His businesslike approach to cartel operations and his reserved personality earned him a reputation as a pragmatic, level-headed leader within a world often dominated by violence and spectacle.

One of the defining episodes in Ochoa's career occurred in 1981, when his sister, Martha Nieves Ochoa Vásquez, was kidnapped by the leftist guerrilla group M-19. In response, the Medellín Cartel formed a paramilitary group called *Muerte a Secuestradores* ("Death to Kidnappers") and threatened to retaliate against any future kidnappers. The strategy worked: Martha was released unharmed and without a ransom payment. This event not only demonstrated the cartel's capacity for coordinated violence but also marked its first foray into political messaging. Ochoa was later implicated in the 1986 assassination of DEA informant Barry Seal, though he consistently denied any involvement.

At the height of his influence, Ochoa was listed among Forbes' twenty richest men in the world. In 1987, his estimated net worth was approximately $3 billion, a reflection of the cartel's global reach and dominance in the cocaine trade. He invested in numerous legitimate ventures that provided cover for his wealth, which extended well beyond Colombia and into the international financial system.

Ochoa's influence extended into Colombian politics, with unconfirmed reports suggesting he financed political campaigns, including those of future President Álvaro Uribe. Alongside other cartel leaders, he helped establish *Los Extraditables*, a group that sought to pressure the Colombian government to resist U.S. extradition efforts. Through violence, bribes, and public relations campaigns, they waged a high-profile battle against being tried in American courts.

In 1984, Ochoa was arrested in Spain on a U.S. warrant but was ultimately extradited to Colombia instead. There, he received a suspended sentence for unrelated charges. With the Colombian government seeking to reduce violence and regain control, it offered a plea deal in the early 1990s that promised reduced sentences and protection from extradition in exchange for surrender. Ochoa accepted the offer and turned himself in to authorities in January 1991. He was sentenced to eight years and four months in prison but served only five years and five months before being released in July 1996.

As of May 2025, Jorge Luis Ochoa Vásquez is alive and residing in Colombia. Since his release from prison, he has maintained a low profile and has not been linked to any further criminal activity. His retreat from the public eye has fueled speculation but left little concrete detail about his post-cartel life.

Ochoa's legacy is deeply embedded in the rise and fall of the Medellín Cartel. While overshadowed in popular culture by Pablo Escobar, Ochoa's strategic mind and organizational discipline were vital to the cartel's success. He has been portrayed in multiple television series, including *Narcos*, *Escobar, el patrón del mal*, and *Tres Caínes*, reflecting his central role in Colombia's narcotics history. He remains one of the most enduring and complex figures of the drug trafficking era, less notorious than Escobar but no less integral to the empire they built.

Fabio Ochoa Vasquez

Fabio Ochoa Vásquez was born into a wealthy and respected family in Medellín, Colombia. His father, Fabio Ochoa Restrepo, was a successful businessman and one of the country's most prominent horse breeders. The youngest of the Ochoa brothers, Fabio became involved in drug trafficking during the 1970s, alongside his older siblings Jorge Luis and Juan David. Together, they formed a close alliance with Pablo Escobar and other key players, becoming co-founders of the Medellín Cartel. Fabio's primary focus was on building and managing the cartel's distribution infrastructure, particularly its growing cocaine pipeline into Miami, which would become one of the most lucrative in the world.

As a major figure in the Medellín Cartel, Fabio oversaw the trafficking of massive quantities of cocaine, reportedly amounting to thousands of pounds each month. He was first indicted by U.S. authorities in 1984 and was later implicated in the 1986 assassination of DEA informant Barry Seal, although his direct involvement has never been definitively proven. Unlike the explosive public presence of Pablo Escobar, Fabio kept a low profile, preferring to remain behind the scenes and focus on the logistics and financial side of the business. His reserved demeanor and avoidance of headlines likely contributed to his ability to operate for as long as he did without capture.

In 1991, facing mounting pressure from Colombian and American authorities, Fabio and his brothers voluntarily surrendered to the Colombian government under a policy that promised reduced sentences and protection from extradition. The brothers served short prison terms and were released in 1996. However, shortly after his release, Fabio resumed his involvement in drug trafficking, violating the terms of the deal and reigniting international interest in his capture. In 1999, he was arrested again and extradited to the United States in 2001. Two years later, in 2003, he was convicted in a U.S. federal court on drug trafficking charges and sentenced to 30 years in prison.

At the peak of his criminal career, Fabio Ochoa Vásquez was listed by *Forbes* in 1987 among the world's billionaires, alongside his brothers. Their fortune was built on the Medellín Cartel's dominance over the global cocaine trade, and they invested in a range of businesses to launder and protect their wealth. As key members of *Los Extraditables*, a group formed by cartel leaders to oppose extradition to the United States,, the Ochoas used both violence and media campaigns to try to sway Colombian public opinion and government policy in their favor.

Despite his eventual arrest and long prison sentence, Fabio's fate changed in 2024. After serving nearly 25 years of his sentence, he was released from U.S. custody in December of that year and deported to Colombia. As of May 2025, he resides there, having largely faded from public view. Whether he remains involved in criminal activities is unknown, though no new charges have been reported since his release.

Fabio Ochoa Vásquez remains one of the most significant figures in the history of Colombian narcotrafficking. While overshadowed by the larger-than-life persona of Pablo Escobar, Fabio's role in the logistical and operational foundation of the Medellín Cartel was essential. His life has been depicted in numerous dramatizations, including the Netflix series *Narcos*, where he was portrayed by Roberto Urbina, and the Colombian series *Pablo Escobar: El Patrón del Mal*, where his character inspired the figure "Julio Motoa."

Beyond his criminal exploits, Fabio's story includes some unexpected turns. During his time in prison, he reportedly worked on several inventions related to renewable energy, showcasing a creative side not commonly associated with drug lords. And before the family ever entered the narcotics trade, they were known in Colombia for their achievements in horse breeding, with his father being a widely respected figure in equestrian circles. Fabio's transformation from heir to horseman to international trafficker captures the dramatic arc of one of the cartel era's most enduring dynasties.

Griselda "The Black Widow" Blanco

Griselda Blanco began her criminal career in her early teens, reportedly committing her first murder at the age of eleven. By the 1970s, she had established a significant cocaine trafficking operation in Queens, New York, alongside her second husband, Alberto Bravo. As the business grew, she relocated to Miami, Florida, where she quickly rose to prominence and became a central figure in the city's booming cocaine trade. Her early years in crime set the stage for her eventual dominance over one of the most violent and lucrative drug empires in American history.

Blanco solidified her power by pioneering inventive smuggling methods, most notably the use of specially designed lingerie to conceal and transport cocaine. Her approach combined tactical innovation with unmatched brutality. She forged key alliances with major Colombian cartels, especially the Medellín Cartel, which helped her expand her drug empire across the United States. Her influence even extended to mentorship roles for future trafficking titans, including a young Pablo Escobar, further embedding her legacy in the foundation of international narcotics trafficking.

She was deeply involved in a range of criminal activities, including drug trafficking, money laundering, and dozens of homicides. Blanco's organization was one of the most prolific of its time, smuggling vast quantities of cocaine into the United States and generating immense profits. Her cartel was directly linked to the Miami drug wars of the 1980s, with her enforcement teams carrying out executions that terrorized the streets. She established a vast distribution network across the country, using both violence and innovation to maintain control and eliminate competitors.

Publicly, Blanco maintained the appearance of a successful and sophisticated businesswoman, but privately, she was a ruthless and cunning crime boss. Her calculated use of fear and loyalty earned her several chilling nicknames, including "The Black Widow," owing to her alleged involvement in the deaths of her husbands. Her leadership style combined cold strategic thinking with extreme measures, ensuring obedience and dominance in a male-dominated criminal underworld.

Among her most infamous acts was the murder of her third husband, Darío Sepúlveda, following a custody dispute over their son, Michael Corleone Blanco. The killing was widely believed to have been ordered by Blanco herself. Another major scandal arose during her trial for multiple homicides, when her chief hitman, Jorge Ayala, was found to have had inappropriate relationships with secretaries in the prosecutor's office. The scandal compromised the integrity of the case and forced prosecutors to offer her a plea deal, avoiding the death penalty and drastically reducing her sentence.

At the peak of her power, Blanco amassed a fortune estimated at up to $2 billion, placing her among the wealthiest drug lords in history. She wielded considerable influence across law enforcement and political spheres, often securing protection and compliance through a potent mix of bribery and intimidation. Her ability to operate with such impunity for so many years was largely a result of these connections.

Blanco's alleged ties to corrupt officials and politicians allowed her to expand her operations virtually unchecked for much of her criminal career. She supposedly maintained influence over both local and federal law enforcement agencies through well-placed bribes and credible threats, which hampered attempts to dismantle her cartel and shielded her from arrest for years.

Her eventual downfall came on February 17, 1985, when DEA agents apprehended her in her home. She was charged with drug trafficking and multiple murders. Her arrest marked the collapse of her criminal empire, which had already begun to erode due to increased law enforcement scrutiny and betrayals from within her inner circle. Her imprisonment signaled the end of a bloody and profitable chapter in the Miami drug wars.

Blanco remained incarcerated for nearly two decades before quietly returning to Colombia. On September 3, 2012, at the age of 69, she was gunned down in Medellín by a motorcyclist who shot her twice in the head outside a butcher shop. Ironically, the technique used in her assassination was one she was credited with inventing: the motorcycle drive-by shooting. Her death closed the book on one of the most violent and controversial careers in the history of drug trafficking.

Her legacy continues to influence organized crime, especially among female traffickers. Blanco proved that a woman could rise to the highest ranks of the drug trade through a potent mix of ingenuity and ferocity. She is remembered as one of the most powerful and notorious women in the history of organized crime, her story dramatized in numerous documentaries and films, most recently in Netflix's *Griselda*, starring Sofía Vergara.

Among the more unusual facts about her life is her choice to name her youngest son Michael Corleone Blanco, in homage to *The Godfather* film series, an indication of her deep fascination with mafia culture. Another lasting mark on history was her creation of the motorcycle drive-by shooting, a method of assassination that would later be used to end her own life.

Maria Teresa Osorio de Serna

Maria Teresa Osorio de Serna, believed to have been born between 1945 and 1950 in Colombia, emerged as a key figure allegedly tied to one of the most powerful criminal enterprises in history, the Medellín Cartel. Her rise is attributed not to acts of overt violence or cartel leadership, but to her reported role in laundering vast sums of money during the height of the cartel's influence in the 1980s and 1990s. This financial management position placed her at the operational heart of the cocaine trade without drawing the same attention as the cartel's more public figures.

Osorio de Serna has been charged by the U.S. Drug Enforcement Administration (DEA) with conspiracy to distribute cocaine and money laundering. Since 2005, she has been listed among the DEA's most wanted international fugitives. Interestingly, despite these serious accusations, Colombian law enforcement holds no active charges or investigations against her. This absence of domestic legal action underscores the opaque and clandestine nature of her alleged involvement, suggesting a highly sophisticated ability to operate behind the scenes and shield her activities from local scrutiny.

Due to her near-total elusiveness, little is definitively known about Osorio de Serna's personal characteristics or leadership style. However, her ability to evade capture for decades suggests a preference for discretion and a calculated, strategic mindset. Unlike other high-profile cartel affiliates, she has never been publicly photographed in the company of major figures or caught up in public scandals, reinforcing the perception of her as a ghost within the criminal underworld.

Her profile gained renewed attention following the 2016 recapture of Joaquín "El Chapo" Guzmán. With his removal from the DEA's most wanted list, Osorio de Serna's name moved higher in prominence, though some analysts argue that this placement may reflect bureaucratic inertia rather than current threat level. Nonetheless, her enduring presence on the list indicates the U.S. government still considers her a significant target in the fight against transnational narcotics crime.

While direct evidence of her financial holdings remains scarce, Osorio de Serna's alleged involvement in laundering money for the Medellín Cartel suggests access to immense sums. Her apparent capacity to remain at large for decades without leaks, betrayals, or major blunders implies not only financial stability but potentially a support network capable of shielding her from global law enforcement.

No confirmed political or law enforcement alliances have been documented. Yet the lack of criminal proceedings in Colombia, despite her high-profile status with the DEA, has raised questions about whether she benefited from systemic oversights, corruption, or protective arrangements.

To date, Osorio de Serna has not been captured. She has effectively disappeared from public record, eluding detection and avoiding any definitive confirmation of her whereabouts. Her continued freedom highlights the enduring challenges that law enforcement agencies face in dismantling the financial infrastructure behind international drug cartels.

Her status remains unresolved, there are no verified reports of her death, and law enforcement has failed to locate her despite nearly two decades on the DEA's list. Her legend has grown in part because of this void of information, creating an aura of mystique unmatched by more infamous, but less elusive, figures.

Osorio de Serna's legacy serves as a stark reminder of the behind-the-scenes operators who enable drug empires to thrive. Her case illustrates the structural challenges of international law enforcement when facing actors who work in shadows rather than on the frontlines. Her profile also spotlights how financial operatives can wield massive influence without brandishing weapons or commanding armies.

Among the more surprising facts is her use of multiple aliases, including María Teresa Correa, Gloria Bedoya, Iris Conde, and Teyer Washington. These names, found across various databases, reflect her capacity to shift identities and avoid consistent tracking. Additionally, DEA records about her remain inconsistent, featuring contradictory data on her birth year and last known residence, further complicating efforts to apprehend her. Notably, despite being a top U.S. target, she remains legally uncharged in Colombia, underscoring the deep disconnect between international and domestic enforcement in such cases.

Gilberto "The Chess Player" Rodriguez Orejuela

Gilberto Rodríguez Orejuela was born on January 30, 1939, in Mariquita, Tolima, Colombia, and later moved with his family to Cali. He began his professional life as a drugstore clerk and eventually opened his own pharmacy. In the 1970s, he co-founded the Cali Cartel with his brother Miguel, along with associates José Santacruz Londoño and Hélmer Herrera. Unlike the notoriously violent Medellín Cartel, the Cali Cartel took a more discreet and calculated approach, emphasizing bribery and infiltration of political and law enforcement institutions to consolidate power and influence.

Under Rodríguez Orejuela's leadership, the Cali Cartel rose to dominate the global cocaine trade. The organization employed highly sophisticated smuggling techniques, such as concealing cocaine in concrete posts and frozen vegetables, to transport massive quantities of the drug internationally. At the same time, the cartel invested heavily in legitimate enterprises, including pharmacies and banks, to launder its immense profits, allowing it to operate behind a veneer of respectability.

Nicknamed "The Chess Player," Rodríguez Orejuela was renowned for his strategic brilliance and meticulous planning. He preferred manipulation and systemic control to brute violence, often relying on intelligence and psychological pressure to accomplish objectives. His methodical and low-profile leadership style set him apart from other cartel figures, contributing significantly to the Cali Cartel's prolonged success.

One of the most notable chapters in Rodríguez Orejuela's life was his alleged covert role in aiding the downfall of Pablo Escobar by supplying intelligence to authorities. Following Escobar's death, the Cali Cartel became law enforcement's primary target. In 1995, Rodríguez Orejuela was captured by Colombian authorities while hiding in a secret compartment behind a wardrobe, an arrest that signaled a turning point in the war on drugs.

At the height of its power, the Cali Cartel generated billions of dollars annually, making it one of the wealthiest criminal organizations in history. Rodríguez Orejuela invested his fortune in various sectors, including pharmaceuticals, banking, and professional sports. He and his brother were owners of the América de Cali football team, further extending their influence into mainstream Colombian society.

A key element of the Cali Cartel's strategy was its deep entanglement with political and judicial structures. Rodríguez Orejuela orchestrated an extensive network of bribery, reaching politicians, judges, and law enforcement officials. These connections allowed the cartel to function with relative impunity for years, shielding its leadership from serious prosecution.

After his 1995 arrest, Rodríguez Orejuela was sentenced to 15 years in a Colombian prison but was released in 2002 under controversial circumstances. He was re-arrested in 2003 and extradited to the United States in 2004. Two years later, he pleaded guilty to drug trafficking and money laundering charges, receiving a 30-year federal prison sentence and forfeiting $2.1 billion in assets.

Rodríguez Orejuela died on May 31, 2022, at the age of 83, in a U.S. federal prison in Butner, North Carolina. He had been suffering from numerous health conditions, including cancer and heart complications, at the time of his death.

His legacy is one of criminal brilliance and systemic corruption. As a founder of the Cali Cartel, Rodríguez

Orejuela helped create one of the most powerful drug trafficking networks the world has ever seen. His preference for strategy over bloodshed allowed the cartel to operate in the shadows for far longer than its rivals. His story has been featured prominently in popular culture, including in the Netflix series *Narcos*, where actor Damián Alcázar portrayed him.

Despite his infamy, Rodríguez Orejuela had surprising personal traits. He was an avid reader of classic literature while orchestrating his global drug shipments. In his memoirs, he reflected that if given the chance, he would take the same path again, an unapologetic epitaph to a life defined by criminal empire-building and strategic dominance.

Miguel Rodriguez Orejuela

Miguel Rodríguez Orejuela was born in Mariquita, Tolima, Colombia, and moved with his family to Cali during his youth. In the 1970s, he co-founded the Cali Cartel alongside his brother Gilberto and associates José Santacruz Londoño and Hélmer Herrera. In stark contrast to the brutal violence of their rival, the Medellín Cartel, the Cali Cartel operated through more covert means, preferring to expand their reach by infiltrating political systems and bribing law enforcement rather than engaging in open warfare.

Under Miguel's leadership, the Cali Cartel became a dominant player in the global cocaine trade. The organization employed highly sophisticated smuggling techniques and funneled its vast profits into legitimate business ventures to facilitate large-scale money laundering. Their influence extended into nearly every sector of Colombian society, including politics, law enforcement, and even professional sports.

Known for his strategic mindset and methodical demeanor, Miguel emphasized intelligence and manipulation over brute force. His leadership style was instrumental in establishing the Cali Cartel's reputation as a calculated, business-oriented criminal empire, markedly different from the volatile reputation of the Medellín network. His calm, systematic approach allowed the cartel to grow into one of the most powerful and profitable drug trafficking organizations in the world.

A pivotal moment in the history of Colombian drug cartels was the fall of Pablo Escobar, and Miguel Rodríguez Orejuela reportedly played a key role. The Cali Cartel is said to have discreetly supplied intelligence to authorities, which contributed to Escobar's eventual death. In the power vacuum that followed, law enforcement turned its full attention to the Cali syndicate. In 1995, Miguel was arrested by Colombian authorities, delivering a critical blow to the cartel's operations and signaling a shift in the country's war on drugs.

At the height of its power, the Cali Cartel generated billions of dollars annually. Miguel used his immense wealth to invest in a range of sectors, including pharmaceuticals, banks, and the sports industry. He and his brother were owners of the América de Cali football team, one of Colombia's most successful and celebrated teams during their tenure, further solidifying their influence over national institutions and popular culture.

The strength of the Cali Cartel lay in its deep entanglement with Colombia's political and legal structures. Miguel was known to maintain extensive networks of bribery, which reached politicians, judges, and law enforcement officials. These connections shielded the cartel for years, enabling it to flourish even under increasing scrutiny from international authorities.

After his initial arrest in 1995, Miguel Rodríguez Orejuela was sentenced to 15 years in Colombia but was released in 2002 under controversial circumstances. In 2003, he was re-arrested and extradited to the United States in 2005. A year later, he pleaded guilty to charges of drug trafficking and money laundering, receiving a 30-year federal prison sentence. He remains incarcerated in the U.S. as of May 2025, with a projected release date of 2028.

Miguel Rodríguez Orejuela's legacy is tightly woven into the history of transnational crime. His role in developing a discreet, corruption-based model for cartel success helped distinguish the Cali Cartel from its bloodier rivals. His life and actions have been dramatized in popular media, including the Netflix series *Narcos*, in which actor Francisco Denis portrayed him.

Though known primarily for his criminal empire, Miguel also had a surprising cultural and personal side. He was married to Martha Lucía Echeverry, who held the title of Miss Colombia in 1974. He and his brother's ownership of América de Cali not only reflected their financial clout but also their desire to embed themselves in the cultural fabric of Colombia.

Daniel "El Loco" Barrera

Daniel Barrera Barrera, widely known by the nickname "El Loco," began his ascent in Colombia's criminal underworld during the 1980s. Operating initially alongside his brother Omar in San José del Guaviare, Barrera supplied chemicals essential for cocaine processing. After Omar's murder, Barrera vowed revenge, a turning point that earned him his infamous moniker. In 1990, he was arrested but managed to escape prison later that year. His escape marked the start of his rise as a formidable trafficker. Over time, he evolved into a critical intermediary between coca-producing guerrilla groups like the FARC and major cartels. As his power grew, Barrera transitioned from a middleman to an empire builder, orchestrating one of Colombia's most significant drug trafficking networks.

Barrera's criminal enterprise revolved around purchasing coca paste from FARC units and selling the processed cocaine to multiple cartels and paramilitary groups, including the Norte del Valle Cartel and the AUC. His operations were massive, processing around 30,000 kilograms of cocaine every month, which added up to roughly 360,000 kilograms a year. His network extended well beyond Colombia, linking with the Sinaloa Cartel in Mexico and distributing cocaine to the United States, Europe, and Brazil. Barrera used his alliances across ideological divides, forming strategic ties with both leftist guerrillas and right-wing paramilitaries to maintain control over production zones and trafficking corridors.

Known for his ruthless ambition and cold calculation, Barrera orchestrated numerous assassinations to eliminate rivals and expand his influence. He played a pivotal role in the 2004 killing of Miguel Arroyave, commander of the AUC's Bloque Centauros, alongside Pedro Oliveiro Guerrero ("Cuchillo"). He was also implicated in the 2008 murder of Wilber Varela, alias "Jabón," a powerful figure in the Norte del Valle Cartel. These assassinations removed major competitors and strengthened his grip on the Colombian drug trade.

Despite his violent reputation, Barrera was careful to keep a low public profile. He used multiple aliases and underwent extensive plastic surgery to disguise his appearance. He even went as far as burning his fingertips to avoid biometric identification. These evasive tactics, combined with his extensive bribery of local law enforcement, allowed him to operate with impunity for decades. His ability to co-opt both guerrilla and paramilitary actors, often paying protection money to both, highlights the murky alliances that characterize Colombia's criminal ecosystem.

Barrera's wealth was staggering. He earned tens of millions of dollars annually, laundering money through front businesses and investing in real estate, ranches, and other ventures across Colombia. In 2013, authorities seized nearly 300 of his properties. His financial success was matched by his influence over corrupt police and political contacts, enabling him to sustain his empire and evade capture for years.

His eventual downfall came on September 18, 2012, in San Cristóbal, Venezuela. The arrest was the result of a highly coordinated international operation involving Colombian and Venezuelan authorities, the U.S. DEA, CIA, U.K. MI6, and other agencies. At the time of his capture, Barrera had dramatically altered his appearance through surgery and was using fake identification. His arrest marked the culmination of one of the most intensive manhunts in recent Colombian history.

Following his extradition to the United States in 2013, Barrera pleaded guilty to multiple charges, including large-scale drug trafficking and money laundering. In July 2016, he was sentenced to 35 years in a U.S. federal prison and ordered to forfeit $10 million. As of now, he remains incarcerated in the United States.

Barrera's legacy is significant in the context of Colombian organized crime. His reign represented one of the last major Colombian traffickers to operate independently of Mexican cartels. His fall signaled a shift in the balance of power, with Mexican groups like the Sinaloa Cartel ascending to dominate hemispheric drug trafficking. His ability to build cross-ideological alliances and his role in violent restructuring of cartel hierarchies exemplify the complex political and criminal entanglements that have shaped Colombia's narco landscape.

A number of surprising facts surround Barrera's story. His obsessive measures to avoid capture, including plastic surgeries and fingertip mutilation, underscore the lengths to which he went to maintain anonymity. Equally remarkable was his ability to pay off both FARC guerrillas and AUC paramilitaries, who were bitter enemies, reflecting his pragmatic, profit-driven approach to criminal enterprise. His arrest marked a rare moment of collaboration between international intelligence agencies, involving the CIA, MI6, DEA, and Venezuelan law enforcement in a multinational effort to bring down one of Colombia's most elusive and violent drug lords.

Dairo Antonio "Otoniel" Usuga

Dairo Antonio Úsuga David, better known by his alias "Otoniel," was born on September 15, 1971, in Necoclí, Antioquia, Colombia. His entry into armed conflict began at the age of 18 when he joined the leftist guerrilla group Popular Liberation Army (EPL). Following the EPL's demobilization in 1991, he shifted allegiances to the right-wing paramilitary group United Self-Defense Forces of Colombia (AUC). After the AUC disbanded, Otoniel and his brother Juan de Dios Úsuga David, alias "Giovanny," took over leadership of the criminal group Los Urabeños, later renamed the Clan del Golfo. After Giovanny's death in 2012, Otoniel assumed full control, transforming the organization into Colombia's most formidable drug trafficking network.

Under Otoniel's command, the Clan del Golfo expanded its criminal portfolio beyond drug trafficking to include extortion, illegal mining, and a wide range of violent enforcement tactics. The group seized control of key cocaine trafficking routes and became notorious for human rights violations, such as forced displacement and the recruitment of child soldiers. Its operations spanned not only Colombia but also extended into international markets, making Otoniel one of the most powerful drug lords of his era.

Known for his cunning and operational discipline, Otoniel was able to evade capture for over a decade. He frequently relocated through remote jungle hideouts and relied on an extensive network of informants and corrupt officials to shield his movements. Despite his brutal leadership and violent methods, he attempted to recast his image during his trial as a remorseful figure, publicly urging others not to follow in his footsteps.

One of the most dramatic episodes in Colombia's recent history was Otoniel's capture on October 23, 2021. The operation that led to his arrest was one of the largest since the takedown of Pablo Escobar. It involved more than 500 soldiers, 22 helicopters, and intelligence coordination with both the United States and the United Kingdom. His extradition to the U.S. followed in May 2022, and in August 2023, he pleaded guilty to drug trafficking charges and was sentenced to 45 years in prison.

At the peak of his criminal empire, Otoniel oversaw the export of hundreds of tons of cocaine each year, earning billions of dollars in illicit revenue. His power extended not only through criminal networks but also through significant influence over local governance and law enforcement in Colombia. These connections were often secured through intimidation and bribery, allowing his organization to operate with relative impunity for years.

The eventual downfall of Otoniel was driven by the Colombian government's intensified campaign to dismantle the Clan del Golfo. His capture in 2021 and subsequent extradition marked the end of his criminal reign. He was sentenced to 45 years in prison and ordered to pay a $216 million fine, a landmark conviction in the international war on drugs.

As of May 2025, Otoniel is serving his sentence at the ADX Florence supermax prison in Colorado. His incarceration represents one of the most significant victories against organized crime in Colombia's modern history, though the Clan del Golfo continues to operate under new leadership.

Otoniel's legacy is defined by his central role in Colombia's drug conflict and the violence that accompanied it. His strategic use of paramilitary structures and criminal alliances helped reshape the landscape of organized crime in the country. While his capture was hailed as a major win by Colombian and U.S. officials, his former organization remains active, highlighting the enduring challenge of dismantling entrenched criminal empires.

Despite his criminal past, Otoniel managed to evade authorities for more than a decade by utilizing an intricate web of safehouses, informants, and loyal subordinates. His arrest was considered so momentous that Colombian President Iván Duque likened it to the fall of Pablo Escobar. Following his capture, Otoniel publicly expressed regret, declaring, "Do not take the same path that I took. The armed conflict must pass into history. Weapons must pass into history."

Miguel "El Padrino" Angel Felix Gallardo

Miguel Ángel Félix Gallardo began his criminal career as a member of the Mexican Federal Judicial Police and later served as a bodyguard for Sinaloa Governor Leopoldo Sánchez Celis. These early roles gave him access to high-level political circles and provided the critical connections he would later use to enter and dominate the drug trade in Mexico.

In the late 1970s, Félix Gallardo made a defining move by co-founding the Guadalajara Cartel alongside Rafael Caro Quintero and Ernesto Fonseca Carrillo. Under his leadership, the cartel quickly became a dominant force in the global narcotics trade throughout the 1980s. His operational expertise and ability to centralize various trafficking factions under one powerful organization marked the beginning of Mexico's ascent in the international drug market.

A major factor in the cartel's success was Félix Gallardo's ability to forge strategic partnerships with Colombian cartels, especially the Cali Cartel. These relationships were often mediated by traffickers such as Juan Matta-Ballesteros and enabled the Guadalajara Cartel to move vast quantities of cocaine from Colombia through Mexico and into the United States. These deals allowed the cartel to take a large share of the profits while consolidating control over the most lucrative smuggling routes.

His criminal activities were vast and brutal. Félix Gallardo was involved in large-scale drug trafficking, money laundering, and murder. The Guadalajara Cartel was responsible for smuggling enormous quantities of cocaine, marijuana, and heroin into the United States. His empire rested on a complex, well-coordinated network that dominated trafficking routes across Mexico. During its peak, the cartel essentially monopolized the illegal drug trade in the region, maintaining supremacy through violence, fear, and bribery.

Publicly, he portrayed himself as a respectable businessman and philanthropist, but behind the scenes, he was orchestrating one of the most powerful and violent drug trafficking empires in history. He was known for being calculating, strategic, and utterly ruthless, traits that made him both feared and admired within the criminal underworld. Corruption and brutality were central to his rule, and he didn't hesitate to eliminate rivals or silence dissenters to maintain his grip on power.

One of the most infamous scandals involving Félix Gallardo was his role in the 1985 kidnapping, torture, and murder of DEA agent Enrique "Kiki" Camarena. The event caused an international firestorm and resulted in unprecedented pressure from the United States on Mexican authorities. Camarena's death ultimately set in motion the events that would lead to Félix Gallardo's downfall and the collapse of the Guadalajara Cartel.

Beyond that tragedy, Félix Gallardo was also implicated in a major scandal that exposed his extensive connections with high-ranking Mexican politicians and law enforcement officials. These revelations underscored the deep-rooted corruption within Mexican institutions and painted a clear picture of how intertwined organized crime and politics had become under his reign.

At the height of his power, Félix Gallardo's wealth was estimated in the billions, making him one of the richest drug lords in history. His influence extended across numerous sectors, including law enforcement, the judiciary, and political offices. Through an intricate system of bribery and intimidation, he ensured that the cartel's operations ran smoothly and with minimal interference from authorities.

His connections to powerful figures like Governor Leopoldo Sánchez Celis granted him a level of protection that few other criminals enjoyed. He had significant sway over both local and federal law enforcement agencies, allowing him to operate with virtual impunity for many years. By manipulating the system through corruption and fear, Félix Gallardo kept authorities at bay while his empire flourished.

However, his dominance would not last forever. On April 8, 1989, he was finally arrested by Mexican authorities on charges related to drug trafficking and the murder of DEA agent Camarena. The combined pressure from U.S. and Mexican law enforcement, along with growing international scrutiny, led to his capture and signaled the beginning of the end for the Guadalajara Cartel.

Today, Félix Gallardo is serving a 37-year sentence, now under house arrest due to deteriorating health after being transferred from a maximum-security facility in 2022. His imprisonment was hailed as a major victory by both Mexican and American officials in the fight against organized crime and narcotics trafficking.

His legacy is deeply entrenched in the history of the Mexican drug trade. He demonstrated the effectiveness of uniting rival traffickers under a single umbrella and leveraging political alliances to dominate international trafficking routes. This centralized leadership model became a blueprint for future cartels that would emerge in his wake.

Félix Gallardo is remembered not only as one of the most powerful drug traffickers in history but also as a figure who fundamentally reshaped the structure of organized crime in Mexico. His life and operations have been chronicled in books, documentaries, and television series, most notably in *Narcos: Mexico*, where his story reached a new generation of viewers.

Among the more surprising facts about his life is that he reportedly continued to direct cartel operations from prison using a mobile phone, until he was moved to a higher-security facility. He even authored a memoir while incarcerated, offering rare insights into his personal experiences and the inner workings of the Guadalajara Cartel.

Rafael Caro Quintero

Rafael Caro Quintero, born on October 24, 1952, in La Noria, Badiraguato, Sinaloa, emerged from humble beginnings to become one of Mexico's most notorious drug lords. The death of his father forced him to leave school early to help support his large family. His path soon led him into the world of drug cultivation and trafficking, where he quickly rose through the ranks. By the late 1970s, Caro Quintero co-founded the Guadalajara Cartel alongside Miguel Ángel Félix Gallardo and Ernesto Fonseca Carrillo. Together, they built one of the most powerful and influential drug trafficking organizations in Mexico's history.

Caro Quintero's criminal empire was founded on innovation and scale. He pioneered large-scale marijuana cultivation operations, most famously the vast "Rancho El Búfalo," which covered over 1,000 hectares and employed thousands of workers. The Guadalajara Cartel didn't stop at marijuana. Under Caro Quintero's leadership, it expanded into heroin and cocaine trafficking, forging key alliances with Colombian cartels and establishing efficient smuggling routes into the United States. His logistical acumen and agricultural strategies elevated him into the upper echelons of the drug world.

Known for his sharp mind and strategic foresight, Caro Quintero was seen as both ruthless and pragmatic. While he operated a violent criminal enterprise, he also cultivated a Robin Hood-like image in his hometown, funding infrastructure projects and contributing to local development. These gestures earned him a degree of local admiration, even as his cartel fueled addiction and violence across the hemisphere.

One of the most infamous chapters in Caro Quintero's life came in 1985, when he was implicated in the abduction, torture, and murder of DEA agent Enrique "Kiki" Camarena. The killing, which was in retaliation for Camarena's undercover work exposing cartel operations, sparked a major diplomatic crisis between the United States and Mexico. Caro Quintero fled to Costa Rica but was quickly captured and extradited to Mexico, where he was sentenced to 40 years in prison.

At the height of his influence, Caro Quintero amassed a fortune estimated in the hundreds of millions of dollars. His power stretched across Mexico and into the United States, bolstered by systemic corruption that shielded him from law enforcement. The Guadalajara Cartel's ties to political and law enforcement officials were extensive, allowing its leaders to operate with near impunity for years.

After serving 28 years of his sentence, Caro Quintero was unexpectedly released in 2013 due to a legal technicality, a decision that was later overturned. He immediately went into hiding, becoming a high-profile fugitive and the subject of intense manhunts by both U.S. and Mexican authorities. In July 2022, he was finally recaptured in Sinaloa. Following protracted legal battles, he was extradited to the United States in February 2025 and now faces trial for his decades-long involvement in drug trafficking and the murder of Camarena.

As of May 2025, Caro Quintero remains alive and in U.S. custody, awaiting trial. His arrest and extradition mark the closing chapters of one of the most consequential lives in the history of organized crime.

Caro Quintero's legacy has been immortalized in popular culture, most notably in the Netflix series *Narcos: Mexico*, where his story serves as both a gripping narrative and a stark warning about the scope and cost of the drug war. His name remains synonymous with the rise of modern Mexican cartels and the violence that accompanied their ascent.

Despite his bloody career, he continued to be remembered in his hometown as a benefactor, a contradiction that underscores the complexity of his legacy. His 2013 release, based on a legal technicality, remains one of the most controversial moments in recent Mexican judicial history and a reminder of how far-reaching the influence of cartel power can be.

Juan Jose Esparragoza "El Azul" Moreno

Juan José Esparragoza Moreno, better known as "El Azul," began his professional career in law enforcement, joining Mexico's now-defunct Dirección Federal de Seguridad (DFS) in the 1970s. It was during his tenure with the DFS that he established key connections with individuals involved in organized crime, which would later serve as the foundation for his rise within the narco underworld. Transitioning fully into criminal activity, he became one of the founding members of the Guadalajara Cartel, alongside notorious figures such as Miguel Ángel Félix Gallardo, Ernesto Fonseca Carrillo, and Rafael Caro Quintero.

Over the course of his career, Esparragoza Moreno played a significant role in the operations of three major cartels: the Guadalajara Cartel, the Juárez Cartel, and the Sinaloa Cartel. He was deeply involved in drug trafficking, money laundering, and coordinating complex criminal enterprises. His key responsibilities often involved forming and managing alliances with other criminal organizations and overseeing massive drug trafficking operations, making him a linchpin in the logistics and diplomacy of the Mexican drug trade.

El Azul was known for his discreet, diplomatic style. Unlike many of his counterparts who craved the spotlight or ruled with open brutality, he operated quietly, building networks and brokering peace between rival factions. This understated, calculated approach earned him a reputation as a stabilizing force within the cartel ecosystem. His nickname, "El Azul" (The Blue), reflected not only his dark complexion but also his calm, composed demeanor.

One of the most controversial chapters of Esparragoza Moreno's history was his alleged involvement in the aftermath of the 1985 kidnapping and murder of DEA agent Enrique "Kiki" Camarena. Although his direct role in the killing remains unclear, he was arrested in 1986 on drug trafficking charges and served a seven-year prison sentence. Upon his release, he resumed his criminal activities and eventually rose to prominence within the Juárez and Sinaloa cartels.

As a high-ranking member of these powerful drug organizations, Esparragoza Moreno accumulated substantial wealth and wielded considerable influence. His strategic mind and diplomatic skills enabled him to help expand the reach of the cartels, making him one of Mexico's most influential and enduring crime figures.

His early career in the DFS gave him access to valuable connections within the Mexican government and law enforcement, which were critical to his ability to protect and expand his criminal operations. These relationships allowed him to avoid detection and arrest for extended periods, illustrating the depth of corruption that shielded high-level drug traffickers.

On June 7, 2014, Esparragoza Moreno reportedly died of a heart attack while recovering from injuries sustained in a car accident. However, this report has never been officially confirmed. Allegedly, his body was cremated before proper identification could take place, leading to widespread skepticism. To this day, Mexican authorities have not verified his death, and he remains listed as a fugitive by agencies such as the FBI, which continues to offer a reward for information leading to his capture.

Esparragoza Moreno's legacy is defined by his quiet but powerful presence in the drug world. He helped shape the operational structure of major Mexican cartels, favoring negotiation and alliance-building over overt warfare. His rumored death, paired with his enduring status as a fugitive, has only added to the mystique surrounding his life and career.

Known for his dark skin, El Azul's nickname reflected a physical trait as much as his unique temperament. He consistently preferred diplomacy and backroom deals over the bloody rivalries that defined other cartel eras. Despite his high-level involvement, he managed to remain largely out of the public eye, with very few photographs or personal details ever made public, cementing his status as one of the most enigmatic figures in organized crime history.

Joaquin "El Chapo" Guzman

Joaquín "El Chapo" Guzmán began his criminal career during his teenage years in the 1970s, selling marijuana in his hometown of La Tuna, Badiraguato, Sinaloa. He later rose through the ranks under the leadership of Miguel Ángel Félix Gallardo, the head of the Guadalajara Cartel, where he was responsible for managing drug shipments and logistics. Following Félix Gallardo's arrest in 1989, Guzmán seized the opportunity created by the power vacuum and co-founded the Sinaloa Cartel. He quickly expanded his influence through innovative smuggling techniques and the establishment of a vast and efficient distribution network.

He consolidated his power by forming strategic alliances with other traffickers, including Ismael "El Mayo" Zambada and the Beltrán Leyva brothers. These relationships allowed the cartel to dominate drug trafficking across the Americas and strengthened its operational capabilities. Guzmán's leadership and ability to coordinate massive-scale logistics made the Sinaloa Cartel one of the most formidable criminal organizations in the world.

Guzmán engaged in a wide range of criminal activities, including drug trafficking, money laundering, murder, and racketeering. His organization was responsible for smuggling enormous quantities of cocaine, heroin, methamphetamine, and marijuana into the United States and other countries. The cartel employed a range of sophisticated smuggling methods, including underground tunnels, submarines, and vehicles with hidden compartments. These operations generated billions in revenue, fueling the cartel's expansion and cementing its global dominance.

Publicly, Guzmán cultivated the image of a benefactor, funding infrastructure projects and assisting the poor in his hometown, which earned him a Robin Hood-like reputation among locals. Privately, he was known for his ruthlessness and for employing calculated violence to eliminate rivals. Despite his brutality, he was also recognized for his sharp understanding of global drug markets and logistics, allowing him to manage one of the largest narcotics empires in history.

His criminal career was marked by a series of high-profile scandals. In 2015, he escaped from Mexico's Altiplano prison through a mile-long tunnel dug directly into his cell, an event that humiliated Mexican authorities and demonstrated the extent of his resources and influence. During his trial in the United States, explosive testimony revealed that he allegedly paid a $100 million bribe to former Mexican President Enrique Peña Nieto to halt efforts to capture him.

At the height of his power, Forbes estimated Guzmán's net worth at $1 billion, making him one of the richest individuals in Mexico. He used his wealth and influence to bribe or intimidate law enforcement and political figures, ensuring that the cartel's operations continued largely unimpeded. His power extended deep into multiple sectors of society, where officials were often too corrupt or too fearful to challenge his authority.

He maintained extensive political and law enforcement connections, leveraging these relationships to protect and grow his criminal enterprises. During his trial, testimonies revealed that his organization paid millions in bribes to a wide range of government officials. His control over local and federal law enforcement agencies in Mexico, achieved through both financial incentives and threats, allowed him to operate with impunity for many years.

His eventual capture came on January 8, 2016, following a six-month manhunt after his escape. Authorities located him at a safe house in Los Mochis, Sinaloa, where he was apprehended after a shootout. His downfall was driven by intensified law enforcement efforts, international cooperation, and betrayals from within his own organization. In 2017, he was extradited to the United States to face trial.

He is currently serving a life sentence plus 30 years at the United States Penitentiary Administrative Maximum Facility (ADX) in Florence, Colorado. He was convicted on numerous charges, including drug trafficking and murder conspiracy. His incarceration marked a significant win for international law enforcement and represented the fall of one of the most powerful drug traffickers in modern history.

Guzmán's legacy is one of scale, brutality, and strategy. He demonstrated how a cartel could become a global power through a combination of violence, corruption, and logistical innovation. His methods set a precedent for future crime groups looking to emulate his model of global drug trafficking.

He remains one of the most infamous drug lords in history, and his story continues to be studied by law enforcement, researchers, and the media. His life has become the subject of books, television series, and documentaries.

Among the many strange details of his life, Guzmán reportedly owned a private zoo, several beach houses, and four private jets, reflecting the lavish lifestyle his cartel profits afforded him. He even began planning a biographical film about himself before his final arrest, further illustrating his larger-than-life persona and desire to control his narrative.

Ismael "El Mayo" Zambada

Ismael Zambada García, born on January 1, 1948, in El Álamo, Culiacán, Sinaloa, Mexico, began his criminal career in the 1970s. Starting as an enforcer, he gradually rose through the ranks of the Guadalajara Cartel. After the 1989 arrest of Miguel Ángel Félix Gallardo, Zambada co-founded the Sinaloa Cartel alongside Joaquín "El Chapo" Guzmán. While many of his contemporaries were captured or killed, Zambada managed to maintain a low profile and avoid arrest for decades, operating from the shadows and earning a reputation as one of the most elusive figures in organized crime.

As a leader of the Sinaloa Cartel, Zambada was responsible for orchestrating large-scale drug trafficking operations. The cartel smuggled massive quantities of cocaine, heroin, methamphetamine, and marijuana into the United States. Zambada also oversaw money laundering, arms trafficking, and brutal acts of violence to secure control over key territories and smuggling routes. His leadership played a central role in establishing the Sinaloa Cartel as one of the most powerful and far-reaching criminal organizations in the world.

Zambada was known for his sharp intellect and preference for operating discreetly. He shunned media attention, rarely appearing in public or allowing photographs to be taken. This strategic invisibility helped him avoid capture and allowed him to build and sustain a criminal empire that spanned continents. Unlike other cartel leaders who sought notoriety or operated flamboyantly, Zambada focused on pragmatism, loyalty, and stability within the organization.

In 2009, Zambada surprised the public by granting a rare interview to Mexican journalist Julio Scherer García. The conversation offered a unique glimpse into his mind and operations, marking a moment of vulnerability and candor from a man otherwise known for secrecy. The interview became a significant moment in Mexican media and criminal history, revealing his awareness of the life he led and the toll it took.

Zambada's wealth, built over decades, was staggering. He invested heavily in agriculture, livestock, and other legitimate enterprises as a means of laundering drug money and maintaining a facade of legality. Within the underworld, he was often referred to as the *capo de capos*, the boss of bosses, due to his enduring authority and influence within the Sinaloa Cartel. He maintained a vast network of operatives and oversaw billions in drug revenues.

Although little is officially confirmed, Zambada's extraordinary ability to avoid arrest for over 50 years has led many to suspect he enjoyed protection from political or law enforcement contacts. His long run of freedom, in a field where most kingpins fall swiftly, remains a testament to either his strategic genius or deeply rooted connections, or both.

On July 25, 2024, U.S. authorities arrested Ismael "El Mayo" Zambada at a private airfield near El Paso, Texas, capturing him alongside Joaquín Guzmán López, one of "El Chapo" Guzmán's sons. According to U.S. officials, Guzmán López convinced Zambada to board a private plane under the pretense of inspecting real estate, then flew him into U.S. custody. However, Zambada later claimed he was forced onto the aircraft against his will. The arrests were part of a coordinated effort targeting the remaining leadership of the Sinaloa Cartel The arrest marked a turning point in the U.S.-Mexico war on drugs and shocked many who believed Zambada might never be caught.

Zambada is currently in U.S. custody, facing multiple federal charges ranging from drug trafficking and money laundering to conspiracy and violence-related offenses. He has pleaded not guilty, and his trial is pending.

Zambada's legacy is defined by his ability to lead from the shadows. For more than five decades, he managed to command one of the most powerful drug syndicates in the world while staying out of the spotlight and beyond the reach of authorities. His story continues to fascinate law enforcement, journalists, and scholars attempting to understand the inner workings of transnational organized crime.

In his 2009 interview, Zambada expressed a surprising moment of introspection, stating that he feared the consequences of his choices and wished for a peaceful life, if only it were possible. Despite being one of the most dangerous men in the world, he managed to remain a free man for over half a century, one of the longest stretches of impunity in cartel history.

Hector Luis Palma Salazar

Héctor Luis Palma Salazar, known as "El Güero," was born on April 29, 1960, in Noria de Abajo, Mocorito, Sinaloa. He began his criminal career as a car thief before rising to prominence as a hitman for Miguel Ángel Félix Gallardo, the notorious leader of the Guadalajara Cartel. Palma's efficiency and brutality in carrying out assignments earned him the trust of Gallardo and a steady promotion through the cartel's ranks. Following the eventual fragmentation of the Guadalajara Cartel, Palma allied with Joaquín "El Chapo" Guzmán. Together, they co-founded the Sinaloa Cartel, which would go on to become one of the most powerful and enduring criminal organizations in the world.

As a senior leader within the Sinaloa Cartel, Palma played a critical role in coordinating large-scale drug trafficking operations. He oversaw the logistics of transporting cocaine from Colombia into the United States, focusing on route efficiency and border infiltration. His expertise in managing distribution networks helped secure the Sinaloa Cartel's dominance in the international narcotics trade during the late 1980s and early 1990s, a period marked by increasing violence and escalating competition among rival cartels.

Palma's personality was a blend of strategic acumen and ruthless pragmatism. Despite the brutality of his actions, he was known to operate according to a personal code, particularly emphasizing loyalty. His nickname, "El Güero," which means "the fair-skinned," referred to his noticeably light complexion, a feature that made him stand out in his region of Mexico. Palma's reputation as both a cunning tactician and a vengeful adversary solidified his standing among allies and enemies alike.

Perhaps the most infamous chapter of Palma's life involved a deeply personal and horrifying betrayal. His wife and two young children were murdered by Rafael Clavel Moreno, allegedly under orders from rival cartel figures. Clavel seduced Palma's wife, convinced her to withdraw $7 million in cartel funds, and then killed her. He later murdered Palma's children by throwing them off a bridge in Venezuela. Clavel mailed Palma a videotape of the acts along with his wife's severed head. This gruesome event prompted Palma to unleash a wave of retaliatory killings, targeting those responsible and reasserting his control through sheer terror.

During his peak, Palma accumulated immense wealth from his role in the Sinaloa Cartel. His influence stretched across Mexico and into the United States, enabling him to establish and maintain power through a mix of fear, bribery, and strategic alliances. His operations were made possible, in part, by widespread corruption in Mexican law enforcement. Palma often eluded capture by posing as a Federal Judicial Police officer, complete with forged credentials and an armed escort, which allowed him to move freely and continue his operations with relative impunity.

Palma's downfall came in dramatic fashion. On June 23, 1995, he survived a plane crash in Nayarit, Mexico. When authorities arrived, they discovered him wearing a police uniform and carrying a gold-plated pistol engraved with a palm tree, a personal symbol. He was arrested and later extradited to the United States in 2007, where he was sentenced for drug trafficking. After serving time, Palma was released in 2016 and returned to Mexico, where he was promptly re-arrested and remains incarcerated as of May 2025. His legal battles continue, with various charges and proceedings influencing his status in the Mexican prison system.

Palma's life has been dramatized in popular media, most notably in the Netflix series *Narcos: Mexico*, where actor Gorka Lasaosa portrays him. His violent trajectory, from low-level criminal to high-ranking cartel co-founder, serves as a chilling example of the human cost and personal devastation intertwined with the drug trade.

"El Güero" Palma's nickname, highlighting his pale complexion, has become synonymous with his legacy. Despite his criminality, he was known to adhere to a strict personal code, placing high value on loyalty and family, traits that clashed tragically with the fate of his own. His capture following a plane crash added a surreal twist to his already notorious story, further cementing his place in the lore of Mexico's criminal underworld.

Amado "The Lord of the Skies" Carrillo Fuentes

Amado Carrillo Fuentes began his criminal career under the guidance of his uncle, Ernesto "Don Neto" Fonseca Carrillo, a prominent figure in the Guadalajara Cartel. Early on, he managed cocaine shipments in Ojinaga, Chihuahua, learning the intricacies of border operations from seasoned traffickers like Pablo Acosta Villarreal and Rafael Aguilar Guajardo. These experiences laid the groundwork for his eventual rise to power within Mexico's drug trade. After the fall of Guadalajara, Carrillo shifted his focus to Juárez, a strategic move that allowed him to consolidate power and eventually assume control of the Juárez Cartel.

Carrillo made his defining move in 1993 by orchestrating the assassination of his former boss, Rafael Aguilar Guajardo. With Aguilar eliminated, Carrillo took control of the Juárez Cartel and expanded its operations rapidly, establishing a formidable trafficking network that reached deep into Colombia and the United States. His network's scale and sophistication earned him the nickname "El Señor de los Cielos," the Lord of the Skies, due to his extensive use of aircraft in drug transportation.

He strategically aligned himself with other major traffickers, including Pablo Escobar, the Cali Cartel, Joaquín "El Chapo" Guzmán, the Arellano Félix family, and the Beltrán Leyva organization. These alliances fortified his position as one of the most dominant drug lords of the 1990s, enabling him to move vast quantities of cocaine through Mexico into the United States while avoiding the infighting and turf wars that plagued other groups.

Carrillo's criminal portfolio included drug trafficking, money laundering, and murder. His cartel was notorious for smuggling enormous volumes of cocaine using an innovative logistics approach. At its peak, his fleet reportedly included more than 30 aircraft, including large commercial jets like Boeing 727s. These planes were used to move drugs across international borders with precision and efficiency, while Carrillo also laundered money through Colombian financial systems to sustain and grow his empire.

Publicly, he crafted the image of a powerful and wealthy businessman. Privately, he ran one of the most violent and expansive narcotics operations in the world. His strategic mind and ability to evade law enforcement made him both feared and admired within the criminal underworld. He was known for blending ruthlessness with innovation, ensuring the cartel's dominance by eliminating threats and adopting the latest technologies to stay ahead of authorities.

One of the most defining events of his career was the assassination of Aguilar Guajardo, which catapulted Carrillo into power. But perhaps the most scandalous chapter came when it was discovered that General José de Jesús Gutiérrez Rebollo, Mexico's top anti-drug official, was on Carrillo's payroll. This revelation not only exposed the deep corruption within the Mexican government but also sparked a national political crisis that embarrassed high-ranking officials and eroded public trust.

At the height of his power, Carrillo's wealth was estimated at $25 billion, placing him among the richest drug lords in history. His fortune bought him access to government insiders and law enforcement protection, allowing the Juárez Cartel to operate virtually unchallenged. Through a mix of bribes and threats, Carrillo exercised influence over various sectors of society, shielding his empire from interference.

His relationships with politicians and officials were not limited to bribes. The exposure of his connection to General Gutiérrez Rebollo underscored just how far his reach extended. Carrillo had successfully embedded himself within the very structures designed to stop him, making it difficult for authorities to pursue him without internal resistance. His dominance was further protected by loyal lieutenants and a fearsome reputation.

Eventually, however, the pressure mounted. Facing increased surveillance and law enforcement coordination, Carrillo took a drastic step in an attempt to escape justice, he sought plastic surgery to change his appearance and avoid recognition. On July 5, 1997, he died from complications during the procedure, either from a malfunctioning respirator or a reaction to medication. His death stunned both the underworld and the public, revealing the extraordinary lengths he was willing to go to preserve his freedom.

Carrillo's demise caused immediate chaos within the Juárez Cartel. Power struggles ensued, and his brother Vicente Carrillo Fuentes stepped in to take control. The organization never quite regained the same level of dominance under his successor, and Carrillo's absence marked the end of a highly effective, if brutal, era in the Mexican drug trade.

His legacy lives on through the logistics and infrastructure model he perfected. Carrillo proved that with the right combination of aviation, alliances, and money laundering, a cartel could scale into a multinational criminal corporation. His story continues to be told in documentaries and television, including the Telemundo series *El Señor de los Cielos*, inspired by his life.

Among the more surprising facts about Carrillo was his massive investment in aviation. His fleet of aircraft was not only impressive in scale but revolutionary in how it redefined cross-border drug trafficking. Despite his death, his influence persists, a blueprint for how drug empires could be run with corporate-level precision.

Vicente Carrillo Fuentes

Vicente Carrillo Fuentes rose to power in the wake of personal tragedy. Following the death of his brother, Amado Carrillo Fuentes, infamously known as "The Lord of the Skies," in 1997, Vicente assumed control of the Juárez Cartel. Inheriting a vast and powerful drug trafficking empire, he led the organization through one of its most turbulent and violent eras. Under his leadership, the cartel maintained its grip on key narcotics smuggling routes into the United States, solidifying its status as one of the most formidable criminal syndicates in Mexico.

Carrillo Fuentes orchestrated wide-ranging criminal operations during his tenure. The Juárez Cartel was primarily engaged in the large-scale smuggling of cocaine across the U.S.-Mexico border, but its activities also extended to money laundering, arms trafficking, and brutal enforcement tactics. To safeguard the cartel's interests, he employed violence as a strategic tool, ruthlessly eliminating rivals and maintaining territorial control through intimidation and bloodshed. His leadership coincided with some of the deadliest years of cartel warfare, particularly in conflict zones like Ciudad Juárez.

In stark contrast to some of his flashier contemporaries, Carrillo Fuentes was known for his discreet and calculated approach. He eschewed media attention and flamboyant displays of wealth, preferring to operate from the shadows. His management of the cartel was defined by pragmatism and an emphasis on maintaining strategic alliances, which helped the organization persist even amid mounting pressure from law enforcement and rival cartels.

One of the most defining aspects of Carrillo Fuentes' reign was the cartel's prolonged turf war with the powerful Sinaloa Cartel. The battle for dominance over smuggling corridors in northern Mexico led to years of violence that claimed thousands of lives. His name became synonymous with the brutality of Mexico's drug war, and he was widely believed to have ordered numerous assassinations to consolidate power and quash dissent within and outside his organization.

At the peak of its influence, the Juárez Cartel under Carrillo Fuentes trafficked narcotics valued in the billions, with profits reinforcing his status as one of the country's top drug lords. While details about his political or law enforcement connections remain murky, the cartel's long-standing ability to operate with relative impunity suggests some level of institutional protection or corruption. Allegations of collusion and bribery surrounded many high-profile Mexican criminal figures of the era, and Carrillo Fuentes was no exception.

His downfall came on October 9, 2014, when he was captured by Mexican authorities in Torreón, Coahuila. The arrest dealt a heavy blow to the Juárez Cartel, accelerating its decline and splintering its once-cohesive network. The collapse of centralized leadership opened the door to rival groups and internal factions, further destabilizing the region.

Following his arrest, Carrillo Fuentes was sentenced in Mexico to 28 years in prison on charges of organized crime, weapons violations, and money laundering. In February 2025, he was extradited to the United States, where he now faces additional charges, including leading a continuing criminal enterprise and participating in major drug trafficking operations. His extradition marked the latest chapter in a long-standing legal pursuit that spanned decades and two nations.

Carrillo Fuentes' legacy is one of violence, territorial dominance, and the complex realities of Mexico's modern drug trade. His tenure is often studied for its insights into cartel structure, inter-organizational warfare, and the systemic challenges of combating transnational criminal empires. Despite his relatively subdued public persona, his influence reshaped the trajectory of organized crime in the region.

One surprising fact about Carrillo Fuentes is his inclusion under the U.S. Foreign Narcotics Kingpin Designation Act in 2000, which froze his assets and prohibited American individuals and businesses from engaging with him. For years, he managed to evade capture, underscoring the immense difficulty authorities faced in apprehending top-tier cartel leaders who operated with deep resources and protective networks.

Benjamin Arellano Felix

Benjamín Arellano Félix was born in Culiacán, Sinaloa, Mexico, and rose to prominence during a pivotal shift in Mexico's drug trafficking landscape. In the late 1980s, after the arrest of his uncle Miguel Ángel Félix Gallardo, Benjamín and his brothers assumed control over the Tijuana corridor, one of the most lucrative and strategically important smuggling routes into Southern California. Under Benjamín's leadership, the Arellano Félix Organization (AFO) evolved into one of the most feared and powerful drug cartels in Mexico, known both for its vast drug empire and its unrelenting brutality.

During its peak, the AFO was responsible for the trafficking of massive quantities of cocaine, marijuana, methamphetamine, and heroin into the United States. Benjamín, as the cartel's principal strategist, oversaw its operations as it carved out a dominant position along the border. The cartel's rule was marked by widespread use of extreme violence, including targeted assassinations, torture, and public displays of intimidation. The AFO also systematically infiltrated Mexican institutions through corruption, ensuring a steady flow of bribes and coerced cooperation from law enforcement, politicians, and members of the judiciary.

Benjamín distinguished himself from his brother Ramón, who was infamous for his violent tendencies and street-level enforcement, by focusing on the larger strategic and financial operations of the cartel. Known for his organizational discipline and cool demeanor, Benjamín preferred to stay behind the scenes, running the AFO like a well-oiled criminal enterprise. His reserved nature and business-focused mindset helped the cartel expand across northern Mexico and into the U.S. market with ruthless efficiency.

One of the most notorious scandals involving the AFO occurred in 1993, when the organization was implicated in the assassination of Cardinal Juan Jesús Posadas Ocampo at the Guadalajara airport. The killing of a senior religious figure shocked the country and sparked international outrage. Although the cartel claimed the cardinal was killed in a case of mistaken identity, the incident triggered a major escalation in the Mexican government's war against drug trafficking organizations and brought unprecedented scrutiny upon the AFO.

At the height of its power, the AFO was believed to generate hundreds of millions of dollars annually. While the full extent of Benjamín's wealth remains obscured by layers of laundering and hidden assets, it is widely accepted that his financial empire was vast. Like many cartel leaders, he used front businesses and real estate investments to conceal illicit profits. His influence extended well beyond street-level operations, bolstered by deep ties to corrupt officials who allowed the AFO to operate with near impunity for years.

Benjamín's downfall came on March 9, 2002, when he was arrested by the Mexican Army in the city of Puebla. After years of eluding capture, the arrest marked a major victory for law enforcement. He remained in Mexican custody until his extradition to the United States in April 2011, where he faced serious charges including racketeering and money laundering. In April 2012, he was sentenced to 25 years in U.S. federal prison and ordered to forfeit $100 million. He is currently serving his sentence at a high-security federal facility in Virginia, with a projected release date in 2032.

Despite his incarceration, the legacy of Benjamín Arellano Félix continues to reverberate throughout the criminal underworld. His tenure as the AFO's leader helped cement the organization's reputation for extreme violence, strategic corruption, and its key role in fueling the drug war between rival factions. His story has been dramatized in television and documentaries, including a portrayal by actor Alfonso Dosal in the Netflix series *Narcos: Mexico*, helping to cement his role in the broader narrative of the Mexican drug trade.

Benjamín was one of several siblings who formed the backbone of the AFO's leadership. His brothers Ramón, Eduardo, and Francisco Javier, along with his sister Enedina, were all involved in the cartel's operations. Enedina, in particular, is believed to have assumed greater leadership responsibilities following the arrests and deaths of her brothers. Few know that Benjamín was arrested as early as 1982 in California for drug trafficking but managed to escape custody and return to Mexico, a harbinger of the impunity the family would enjoy for decades. The story of the AFO has since become a central chapter in the violent and complex history of drug trafficking between Mexico and the United States.

Ramon Eduardo Arellano Felix

Ramón Arellano Félix was born in Culiacán, Sinaloa, and rose to infamy as one of the most feared enforcers in Mexico's drug war. He was one of several siblings who co-founded the Tijuana Cartel in the wake of the Guadalajara Cartel's collapse in the late 1980s. While his brother Benjamín oversaw strategy and finances, Ramón took command of enforcement and security, building a reputation for unmatched brutality. His rise within the cartel was rapid and vicious, and he soon became the face of the organization's violent arm.

As the Tijuana Cartel's chief enforcer, Ramón commanded a paramilitary-style force composed of former police officers, cartel loyalists, and local gang members. He orchestrated assassinations, kidnappings, and acts of torture across the region, eliminating rivals and intimidating anyone who dared oppose the AFO. Under his oversight, the cartel continued its large-scale smuggling operations, transporting cocaine, marijuana, and methamphetamine into the United States. His ability to project violence was not only functional, it was psychological. The cartel's enemies knew that crossing Ramón often meant certain death.

Unlike Benjamín's calculated and quiet leadership, Ramón thrived on flamboyance and theatrics. He traveled in convoys with heavily armed bodyguards and was known to participate personally in executions. His public persona was one of dominance and fear, and he cultivated an image that blurred the line between myth and reality. His methods ensured discipline within the cartel and instilled terror in rivals and law enforcement alike.

One of the most infamous episodes associated with Ramón was the 1993 killing of Cardinal Juan Jesús

Posadas Ocampo at the Guadalajara airport. Though the official story claimed the cardinal was mistakenly caught in a crossfire, many believe he was deliberately targeted, either due to mistaken identity or as a warning to enemies. The murder shocked Mexico and galvanized the government's efforts to rein in cartel activity, putting the Arellano Félix brothers in the national and international spotlight.

Despite the chaos he unleashed, Ramón's power brought wealth. The Tijuana Cartel's grip on the U.S.-Mexico border allowed for massive drug revenues, though exact figures tied to his personal fortune remain unclear. The AFO's control of the Tijuana corridor gave it dominance over a key trafficking route into Southern California, enriching the organization and its leaders. As with most major cartels, this wealth was maintained through systematic bribery and manipulation of local and federal law enforcement.

For years, Ramón operated with near impunity thanks to an extensive network of corrupt police and officials. The cartel's ability to buy protection allowed Ramón to move freely and strike without fear of arrest. But that impunity didn't last forever. On February 10, 2002, Ramón's violent run came to an abrupt end. While in Mazatlán, Sinaloa, allegedly preparing to assassinate Sinaloa Cartel boss Ismael "El Mayo" Zambada, he was pulled over during a routine traffic stop. Reports indicate he opened fire on the officers, killing one before being gunned down. Others have suggested his death was the result of betrayal and a coordinated hit by rival factions.

His identity was confirmed through DNA testing, and his body was cremated shortly after the shootout. Ramón's death dealt a significant blow to the Tijuana Cartel, and within a month, his brother Benjamín was also arrested. The twin losses effectively crippled the organization, initiating a slow but steady decline in its dominance and ushering in years of internal conflict.

Despite his death, Ramón's legacy as one of Mexico's most violent and iconic cartel figures endures. His life has been portrayed in multiple documentaries and dramatized series, most notably in *Narcos: Mexico*, where actor Manuel Masalva depicted his menacing persona. His story is often cited as a turning point in Mexico's war on drugs, marking the beginning of a more aggressive federal crackdown on organized crime.

In 1997, the FBI placed Ramón on its Ten Most Wanted Fugitives list, a testament to his status as a major international criminal. At the time of his death, he was traveling under a false identity, "Jorge Pérez López." His notoriety and flamboyance have made him a lasting figure in both criminal history and pop culture, embodying the raw violence that defined the height of cartel warfare in Mexico.

Enedina "La Jefa" Arellano Felix

Enedina Arellano Félix emerged as one of the most influential female figures in the history of organized crime through her role in the Tijuana Cartel. A member of the infamous Arellano Félix family, she initially remained behind the scenes, using her accounting degree from a private university in Guadalajara to manage the cartel's finances and launder its illicit profits. The Tijuana Cartel was founded by her brothers in the late 1980s and quickly became one of the most violent and dominant drug trafficking organizations in Mexico. As the cartel's male leadership fell, either through arrests or killings, Enedina gradually assumed a more prominent role, eventually becoming the cartel's de facto leader following the 2008 arrest of her brother Eduardo.

Under her leadership, the Tijuana Cartel continued trafficking cocaine, marijuana, and methamphetamine into the United States. However, Enedina's style marked a clear departure from the brutal tactics employed by her brothers. She adopted a more business-like, financially driven model, focusing on laundering money through legitimate fronts and forging strategic alliances rather than resorting to violence. Her operational approach was calculated and discreet, helping to preserve the cartel's strength while avoiding the high-profile bloodshed that had previously drawn intense law enforcement scrutiny.

Unlike many of her male counterparts in the drug trade, Enedina maintained a remarkably low profile. She was not known for flamboyance or public displays of wealth. Instead, she wielded influence through economic savvy and quiet authority. Her strategic leadership helped stabilize the Tijuana Cartel during a period when many Mexican criminal organizations were fragmenting or being absorbed by rivals. She steered the cartel through turbulent transitions with a focus on sustainability over territorial warfare.

Enedina's ability to lead and transform the cartel has been the subject of media interest and cultural portrayal. Most notably, she was depicted by actress Mayra Hermosillo in the Netflix series *Narcos: Mexico*, bringing her story to international attention. Her leadership is often cited as a turning point for the cartel, signaling a shift from violence-based control to a more corporate, clandestine model of drug trafficking.

Though precise details about the cartel's earnings under her command remain elusive, it is widely acknowledged that the Tijuana Cartel continued to generate immense profits. Enedina's financial expertise played a central role in managing and expanding those earnings through complex laundering schemes. Her nicknames, "La Jefa" (The Boss) and "La Narcomami" (The Narcomom,) reflect her dual reputation as a commanding presence and a stabilizing force within the organization.

Despite being sanctioned under the U.S. Foreign Narcotics Kingpin Designation Act in 2000, Enedina has never been captured. She remains a fugitive, with her current location unknown. Her elusiveness is a testament to her disciplined, low-visibility approach, an unusual trait in an industry dominated by high-profile male figures.

Enedina Arellano Félix's legacy challenges long-standing assumptions about gender roles in organized crime. She demonstrated that criminal empires could be run not just through violence, but through shrewd financial management and discretion. Her rise from accountant to cartel matriarch underscores a unique brand of power, one built not on fear alone, but on strategic control and business acumen.

Ismael Higuera Guerrero

Ismael Higuera Guerrero emerged as a powerful figure within the Tijuana Cartel, also known as the Arellano Félix Organization (AFO), during the late 1980s and early 1990s. Born into a family deeply involved in the cartel's operations, he climbed the ranks to become the AFO's chief of operations, responsible for overseeing drug shipments, managing smuggling routes, and enforcing cartel control over key corridors like Tijuana and Mexicali. His operational role made him one of the most feared and influential men within the organization.

Higuera Guerrero played a central role in importing multi-ton quantities of cocaine and marijuana from Colombia into Mexico, which were then smuggled across the U.S. border. He supervised millions of dollars in drug proceeds, arranged bribes to corrupt officials, and led enforcement teams that relied on kidnapping, torture, and murder to maintain cartel dominance. His leadership solidified the AFO's grip on one of the most strategic trafficking regions in North America.

Feared for his ruthlessness, Higuera Guerrero kept a low public profile while commanding a brutal reputation within the drug underworld. Unlike some cartel figures who sought media attention or political notoriety, he focused strictly on operations and enforcement, earning a reputation for methodical and uncompromising violence.

In May 2000, Higuera Guerrero's criminal career came to a halt when Mexican soldiers and federal police raided his beachfront home in Ensenada. The arrest was a significant blow to the AFO, which was already under intense pressure from law enforcement. After spending several years in Mexican custody, he was extradited to the United States in 2007. He later pleaded guilty to federal racketeering charges, admitting to leading a violent criminal enterprise and coordinating widespread corruption.

Although his exact fortune remains unclear, his high-ranking position allowed him to accumulate considerable wealth through drug trafficking and extortion. His role also involved organizing systematic bribe payments to law enforcement and government officials, a key element in maintaining the AFO's power in the border region.

Higuera Guerrero was sentenced to 40 years in U.S. federal prison and ordered to forfeit $5 million in criminal proceeds. However, the Bureau of Prisons does not list anyone by his name, suggesting he may be living under an alias. Additionally, records show that he entered into a plea agreement with a cooperation addendum, though the specific records are sealed.

His time in leadership left a lasting mark on the AFO's legacy. He helped define the cartel's reputation for extreme violence, institutional corruption, and relentless territorial control. His cooperation with U.S. authorities represented a significant turning point in the broader effort to dismantle the Tijuana Cartel's leadership.

In addition to his own actions, Higuera Guerrero's family was also deeply involved in cartel operations, his son, Ismael Higuera Flores, was arrested in 1998 for drug and weapons possession. Higuera Guerrero's story reflects the evolution of Mexican cartel leadership during the height of the drug war: disciplined, violent, and deeply embedded in both organized crime and institutional corruption.

Nazario Moreno Gonzalez

Nazario Moreno González, born on March 8, 1970, in Apatzingán, Michoacán, came from a poor, rural background. In his youth, he migrated to the United States, where he became involved in drug trafficking and encountered various legal troubles. After returning to Mexico, Moreno's rise within the criminal underworld culminated in 2004, when he assumed leadership of La Familia Michoacana following the arrest of its previous boss, Carlos Rosales Mendoza. Under Moreno's guidance, the organization evolved from a regional gang into a powerful and fearsome cartel, distinguished not only by its violent operations but also by a quasi-religious ideology that Moreno personally cultivated.

La Familia Michoacana, under Moreno's control, expanded its reach across Michoacán and beyond, engaging in a wide array of criminal activities. The cartel was particularly dominant in methamphetamine production and trafficking, but it also profited from extortion, kidnapping, and contract killings. Its reign was marked by extreme violence, exemplified by a chilling 2006 incident in which five severed heads were rolled onto a nightclub dance floor as a macabre message of "divine justice." Such acts underscored the cartel's willingness to use shock and fear to enforce control and intimidate rivals.

Moreno's leadership style set him apart from other drug lords. Charismatic and enigmatic, he carefully crafted a spiritual persona that blended criminality with moral posturing. Often portraying himself as a religious guide, he wrote a book titled *Pensamientos del Más Loco* ("Thoughts of the Craziest One"), a collection of moral aphorisms and behavioral codes distributed among his followers. Within La Familia, Moreno enforced strict rules, including prohibitions on drug use and mandates for family values. His strange fusion of brutal violence and professed spirituality gained him a loyal and almost cult-like following, further solidifying his power.

One of the most dramatic episodes in Moreno's life came in December 2010, when Mexican federal authorities claimed he had been killed in a shootout. Despite government reports, Moreno's body was never recovered, prompting rumors and speculation that he had survived. These suspicions were confirmed in 2014 when he was revealed to be alive and leading the Knights Templar Cartel, a splinter group that had risen from the remnants of La Familia Michoacana. Later that year, on March 9, 2014, Moreno was killed during a shootout with Mexican security forces in Tumbiscatío, Michoacán, exactly one day after his 44th birthday. Forensic analysis confirmed his identity, finally putting to rest years of uncertainty surrounding his fate.

During his tenure, Moreno wielded significant wealth and influence, even though exact figures are difficult to determine. His control of drug trafficking routes and the widespread presence of his cartels in Michoacán allowed him to amass power both financially and territorially. He extended this influence through systematic infiltration of local governments and law enforcement agencies, taking full advantage of corruption to shield his operations. These connections, however, also made dismantling his networks exceedingly difficult for Mexican authorities.

His death in 2014 marked a turning point in Mexico's war against drug cartels, significantly weakening the Knights Templar Cartel. Though the group lingered on, it never regained the dominance it enjoyed under Moreno's leadership. His demise was seen as a major victory for law enforcement, though it also left a power vacuum that contributed to further instability in the region.

Moreno's legacy remains one of the most perplexing in the history of organized crime. While he is reviled for the extreme violence and criminal enterprises he led, in some communities he is venerated. Shrines and altars dedicated to "San Nazario" have been discovered, revealing a level of devotion more typical of folk saints than drug lords. His unique blend of spirituality and savagery has drawn attention from journalists and scholars alike, as they seek to understand how such contradictory personas can coexist and command loyalty.

Among the more surprising facts about Moreno was his fascination with comic book heroes, particularly the Mexican character Kalimán. This influence shaped his self-image as a kind of protector of the people, despite his cartel's ruthless methods. His peculiar double life as both preacher and predator has inspired portrayals in popular media, including the television series *El Chapo*, which explored the blurred lines between criminality, faith, and myth in the Mexican underworld.

Servando "La Tuta" Gomez Martinez

Servando Gómez Martínez, born on February 6, 1966, in Arteaga, Michoacán, began his professional life far from the world of organized crime. A former primary school teacher, he earned the nickname "El Profe," the Professor, a moniker that would stay with him long after he traded chalkboards for criminal enterprise. His descent into the drug world began in the early 2000s, when he became involved with La Familia Michoacana, a cartel that uniquely combined drug trafficking with a pseudo-religious ideology. As internal conflicts fractured the organization, Gómez Martínez co-founded the Knights Templar Cartel around 2011, stepping into the role of leader following the death of its former head, Nazario Moreno González.

Under Gómez Martínez's command, the Knights Templar Cartel expanded its portfolio of criminal enterprises far beyond traditional drug trafficking. While methamphetamine production and distribution remained central, the cartel also delved into extortion, kidnapping, illegal mining, and arms trafficking. One of its more chilling tactics was the imposition of "taxes" on local businesses and farmers in Michoacán, a form of extortion masked as communal order. The cartel's brutality became infamous, as did its far-reaching control over the local economy and society.

Gómez Martínez stood out among his peers for his media savvy and flair for public relations. He routinely appeared in videos and interviews, positioning himself as a moral crusader rather than a drug lord. In these public messages, he portrayed himself as a protector of the people, claiming that the Knights Templar acted to preserve order and justice in regions abandoned by the state. The cartel adopted medieval imagery and rituals, modeling itself after the ancient Christian military order from which it took its name. Members wore tunics with red crosses and conducted initiation ceremonies steeped in symbolism, lending a strange sense of ideological legitimacy to their criminal activities.

This peculiar blend of crime and theatrics drew both fascination and controversy. In 2014, Gómez Martínez became the center of a political scandal when videos surfaced showing him in meetings with local politicians and businessmen. These revelations laid bare the depth of the cartel's infiltration into political and economic structures in Michoacán. The fallout was significant, triggering public outrage and leading to the resignation of the state's governor. The scandal confirmed long-held suspicions that corruption was not just incidental but integral to the cartel's survival.

Although hard financial figures are elusive, Gómez Martínez's influence over critical drug routes and regional industries indicates considerable wealth and power. His organization had tentacles in both local communities and international markets, facilitating a complex web of operations that extended far beyond Michoacán. Through a combination of fear, corruption, and social manipulation, Gómez Martínez managed to sustain a criminal empire under the guise of moral righteousness.

This charade finally collapsed on February 27, 2015, when federal police captured Gómez Martínez in Morelia, Michoacán. In a surprising turn, the arrest occurred without a single shot being fired. Authorities had been monitoring his network and movements for months, ultimately leading to his apprehension in a quiet, clinical operation that belied the drama of his criminal career.

As of May 2025, Servando Gómez Martínez remains behind bars in Mexico. In December 2022, he was sentenced to 47 years and six months in prison for charges related to organized crime and drug trafficking. His incarceration marked a symbolic end to a period defined by the Knights Templar's bizarre fusion of violence and virtue, though the effects of his leadership are still felt in Michoacán.

Gómez Martínez's legacy is complex and deeply contradictory. He sought to redefine cartel leadership through religious rhetoric, symbolic theatrics, and direct communication with the public. In doing so, he left a distinctive mark on the history of organized crime in Mexico. Scholars and journalists have analyzed his media tactics and ideological branding as a sign of the evolving sophistication and manipulation within modern criminal enterprises.

Among the more surprising facts about Gómez Martínez is that he continued to receive a government salary as a teacher until at least 2010, years after his transition into cartel leadership. He was also known for his belief in tarot readings and reportedly used them to guide key decisions. Perhaps most memorably, the cartel's adoption of medieval symbolism, from ceremonial garb to moral codes, reflected Gómez Martínez's unique vision of organized crime as something righteous, even ordained. That contradiction remains central to how history will remember "El Profe."

Nemesio "El Mencho" Ruben Oseguera Cervantes

Nemesio Oseguera Cervantes, widely known as "El Mencho," began his criminal journey in the 1980s after moving to the United States. There, he became involved in drug trafficking, a path that led to multiple arrests and deportations. Upon returning to Mexico, he joined the Milenio Cartel, quickly ascending through the ranks due to his strategic thinking and ruthless methods. Following the cartel's fragmentation, he co-founded the Jalisco New Generation Cartel (CJNG) in 2010, transforming it into one of the most dominant and feared criminal organizations in Mexico.

Under El Mencho's leadership, the CJNG expanded its reach across the globe, engaging in a wide array of illicit activities including drug trafficking, extortion, kidnapping, and fuel theft. The group has earned a reputation for its extreme brutality, often resorting to torture and public executions to instill fear. The cartel has also demonstrated operational sophistication by employing drones in attacks and luring recruits with deceptive job offers, showcasing a modernized approach to organized crime.

El Mencho is known for maintaining a low public profile, a stark contrast to the flamboyant personas adopted by other drug lords. He is regarded as highly strategic and disciplined, placing a strong emphasis on operational security. His leadership style rewards loyalty and efficiency, helping him build a resilient and effective criminal network while successfully avoiding capture for years.

In 2015, the CJNG carried out one of the most audacious acts of cartel violence when it shot down a Mexican military helicopter, killing several soldiers in an effort to thwart El Mencho's apprehension. This attack marked one of the most direct and violent confrontations between a drug cartel and the Mexican government. His notoriety has been further fueled by the arrests of close family members, including his wife and children, drawing sustained attention from international media.

Although El Mencho's personal wealth is difficult to quantify, the scale and scope of CJNG's operations point to his control over a vast fortune. His status as a high-value target is underscored by the $15 million reward offered by the U.S. government for information leading to his capture, one of the highest bounties for any fugitive in the world.

The CJNG's ability to operate with relative impunity has been facilitated by widespread corruption. The cartel has successfully infiltrated various levels of government and law enforcement, often using bribery and intimidation to secure its interests. Reports of local officials aiding the cartel highlight the systemic challenges authorities face in dismantling such a deeply embedded organization.

Despite extensive efforts by both Mexican and U.S. authorities, El Mencho remains a fugitive. His ability to evade capture is attributed to a combination of rural hideouts, loyal operatives, and high-level corruption. However, increased international pressure and sanctions have intensified efforts to locate and apprehend him, making his eventual capture a top priority for both nations.

As of May 2025, El Mencho has not been captured, and persistent rumors of his death remain unconfirmed. Law enforcement agencies continue to pursue leads amid growing speculation, but no concrete evidence has surfaced to verify these claims.

El Mencho's legacy is defined by the meteoric rise of the CJNG and its unprecedented use of militarized tactics. He has reshaped the landscape of Mexican organized crime, focusing on rapid global expansion and modernized operational strategies. His leadership has had a profound and lasting impact on the dynamics of cartel warfare and criminal enterprise in Mexico and beyond.

Before embarking on a criminal career, El Mencho briefly served as a police officer in Tomatlán, Jalisco, an irony that underscores the deep entanglement between law enforcement and organized crime in Mexico. He is known to have a passion for cockfighting and reportedly owns several ranches dedicated to the sport. His infamy has also been immortalized in narcocorridos, a genre of Mexican music that glorifies drug lords, reflecting his larger-than-life presence in popular culture.

Oscar Malherbe de Leon

Óscar Malherbe de León began his ascent in the criminal world in the 1970s in Matamoros, Tamaulipas. His early years were humble, working as a shoeshiner and car washer, before he turned to car theft, which marked his entry into the underworld. In 1976, his trajectory shifted significantly when he was recruited by Casimiro Espinosa Campos, known as "El Cacho," a prominent figure within the Gulf Cartel. After Espinosa's death in 1984, Malherbe aligned himself with the rising cartel leader Juan García Ábrego, quickly becoming one of his most trusted and powerful lieutenants.

Malherbe played a critical role in the Gulf Cartel's operations, particularly in managing the transportation of large-scale cocaine shipments from Colombia. Working closely with the Cali Cartel, he coordinated the logistics of smuggling operations and oversaw clandestine airstrip networks in Tamaulipas, which were key to facilitating the flow of narcotics into the United States. His operational expertise and strong relationships with Colombian suppliers made him indispensable to the cartel's expansion and profitability.

Known for his intelligence and strategic mind, Malherbe stood out within the organization. He was valued not just for his ruthlessness, but also for his ability to handle complex operations and cultivate crucial alliances. His composed and calculated demeanor earned him respect within the cartel and made him a central figure in its hierarchy.

Following García Ábrego's arrest in 1996, Malherbe briefly assumed leadership of the Gulf Cartel. However, his time at the top was short-lived. On February 26, 1997, he was captured by authorities in Mexico City. In a failed attempt to avoid imprisonment, he reportedly offered a

$2 million bribe to officials, which was rejected. His arrest delivered a significant blow to the Gulf Cartel's leadership structure and marked the beginning of a turbulent era for the organization.

At the height of its power, the Gulf Cartel controlled a major share of the cocaine trade into the United States, generating billions of dollars in revenue. As one of the principal intermediaries between the cartel and Colombian suppliers, Malherbe was deeply embedded in the financial engine that powered the organization's growth and influence.

Like other Gulf Cartel leaders, Malherbe operated within a network of corrupt law enforcement and political officials. These connections enabled the cartel to evade capture and operate with relative impunity for years. The seamless integration of the cartel's activities into legal and governmental structures was a hallmark of its long-standing success.

Malherbe's downfall came with his arrest in 1997. He was imprisoned at the Federal Social Readaptation Center No. 1 in Almoloya de Juárez, one of Mexico's highest-security facilities. Though U.S. authorities requested his extradition, a Mexican judge denied the petition, citing insufficient evidence presented by the United States, and ruled that Malherbe would be tried in Mexico.

As of May 2025, Óscar Malherbe de León remains incarcerated in Mexico, serving a sentence for multiple charges, including drug trafficking and homicide. His continued imprisonment underscores the lasting legal consequences of his time at the helm of one of Mexico's most powerful cartels.

Malherbe's legacy is closely tied to the Gulf Cartel's rise as a dominant force in international drug trafficking during the late 20th century. His arrest not only weakened the cartel's leadership but also triggered internal conflicts and power struggles, paving the way for the emergence of new factions and leaders.

Nicknamed "El Licenciado," which translates to "The Graduate," Malherbe carried a title often associated with legal professionals in Mexico, though it remains unclear whether he actually held a law degree. Despite his criminal role, he was known for maintaining a refined appearance, often dressing in business attire and presenting himself with the polished demeanor of a corporate executive rather than a drug trafficker.

Antonio "Tony Tormenta" Ezequiel Cardenas Guillen

Antonio Cárdenas Guillén was born in Matamoros, Tamaulipas, a city that would later become a key hub in Mexico's drug war. He entered the criminal world in the late 1980s alongside his brother, Osiel Cárdenas Guillén, who would eventually rise to lead the powerful Gulf Cartel. Antonio remained in the background during Osiel's rule, but following his brother's arrest in 2003, Antonio and Jorge Eduardo Costilla Sánchez assumed joint leadership of the cartel. Antonio took charge of operations in Matamoros, a strategic smuggling corridor into the United States, and played a central role in maintaining control over this lucrative region.

As a top figure in the Gulf Cartel, Antonio oversaw the trafficking of massive quantities of cocaine and marijuana from South America into the U.S. He also managed large-scale extortion networks, kidnappings, and money laundering operations that funneled illicit profits back into the organization. His leadership style differed from his brother's; while Osiel had been flamboyant and confrontational, Antonio kept a low public profile. He preferred to work from the shadows, focusing on the logistical and operational mechanics of the cartel's vast enterprise. His discretion and discipline made him a more elusive target for law enforcement, even as his influence quietly grew.

Despite his understated approach, Antonio's leadership helped strengthen the Gulf Cartel's grip on northern Mexico. He was responsible for maintaining control over Matamoros and expanding the cartel's reach throughout Tamaulipas and across the border. Known as "Tony Tormenta," or "Tony the Storm," his nickname reflected his reputation for orchestrating violent operations and reacting decisively to threats. While not publicly theatrical, his methods were ruthless, and he was feared by both rivals and subordinates.

Antonio's most notorious moment came on November 5, 2010, when Mexican marines launched a full-scale operation to capture him in Matamoros. What followed was one of the most intense urban battles of Mexico's drug war. Over 660 marines, supported by 17 vehicles and 3 helicopters, engaged in an eight-hour firefight with Antonio's forces. The chaos brought the city to a standstill. International bridges linking Matamoros to the United States were temporarily closed, and terrified residents sheltered in place as gunfire echoed through the streets. Antonio was killed during the operation, along with several of his bodyguards and associates. His identity was confirmed shortly thereafter, ending a months-long manhunt.

Although the precise scale of Antonio's wealth remains unknown, his control over one of the most valuable smuggling corridors in the hemisphere and his senior position within the Gulf Cartel suggest that he accumulated considerable power and resources. At the time of his death, the U.S. government had placed a $5 million bounty on his capture, a testament to his status as a high-priority target. His ability to operate for years with minimal public exposure also speaks to the layers of protection surrounding him, including deep corruption within regional law enforcement.

The Gulf Cartel's operations under Antonio were reportedly supported by systemic corruption in Tamaulipas. Local police and political figures turned a blind eye, or actively participated, in cartel activities, enabling the group to operate with a degree of impunity. While concrete details about specific political connections remain scarce, Antonio's reach and longevity suggest he had access to sensitive information and institutional cover.

Antonio's death marked a turning point for the Gulf Cartel. Without his leadership, the organization quickly splintered. Factions within the cartel began vying for control, sparking internal conflicts that weakened the group's structure. This fragmentation created an opening for rival organizations, most notably Los Zetas, who had already broken away from the Gulf Cartel, to seize more territory and escalate the violence across the region.

Antonio also left behind a small but deadly private army known as Los Escorpiones, or The Scorpions. Composed of former police officers, this elite enforcement group served as his personal security detail and played a key role in maintaining order within the cartel. Their loyalty and tactical training made them one of the most formidable units in the Gulf Cartel's arsenal.

In the years following his death, Antonio's legacy has lived on in both crime history and pop culture. A character loosely based on him appeared in the 2017 TV series *El Chapo*, portraying a version of the enigmatic and brutal drug lord. While not as publicly infamous as his brother Osiel, Antonio's calculated leadership and violent end made him one of the most significant figures in the history of the Gulf Cartel and Mexico's ongoing struggle with organized crime.

Heriberto Lazcano

Heriberto Lazcano was born in Apan, Hidalgo, Mexico, and joined the Mexican Army at the age of 17. His military career led him into the elite Grupo Aeromóvil de Fuerzas Especiales (GAFE), where he received advanced training in counterinsurgency, special operations, and battlefield tactics. This elite background would later define his role in the criminal underworld. In 1998, Lazcano deserted the military and was quickly recruited by Osiel Cárdenas Guillén to join a cadre of ex-commandos forming a new enforcement wing for the Gulf Cartel. This group became known as Los Zetas, originally tasked with protecting cartel leadership and executing high-risk operations. Over time, as leaders were killed or captured, Lazcano rose through the ranks. By 2004, he had taken control and led the transformation of Los Zetas from an enforcement arm into a fully autonomous criminal cartel.

Under Lazcano's leadership, Los Zetas evolved into one of the most violent and diversified criminal organizations in the Western Hemisphere. While drug trafficking remained a core operation, the group expanded aggressively into extortion, kidnapping, oil theft, human smuggling, and arms dealing. Los Zetas quickly earned a reputation for their brutality, often employing military-style tactics, beheadings, and public mass killings to intimidate rivals and secure control over territory. Their influence extended from Mexico's northern border with the United States all the way to Central America, and they left a trail of violence in their wake that redefined the level of savagery associated with organized crime in the region.

Despite heading one of the most feared cartels in the country, Lazcano maintained an unusually low public profile. Rarely photographed and seldom seen in public, he operated from the shadows, preferring anonymity to notoriety. Yet, those who knew him described a man of stark contradictions. Known for his military discipline and strategic intelligence, Lazcano was also deeply religious. He reportedly funded the construction of a chapel in his hometown and frequently carried Catholic religious artifacts. It was said that he attended mass regularly, a detail that contrasted sharply with the violent nature of his criminal enterprise.

One of the most bizarre and controversial moments in Lazcano's life ironically came after his death. On October 7, 2012, acting on a citizen's tip, Mexican marines engaged Lazcano and an associate in a firefight in Progreso, Coahuila. Both men were killed in the exchange, and Lazcano's identity was later confirmed through fingerprint analysis and photographs. However, within hours of his death, his body was stolen from the funeral home by a heavily armed group. The theft fueled widespread speculation and conspiracy theories, with some questioning whether he had actually died at all. Despite the disappearance of the corpse, Mexican authorities stood by their confirmation of his death.

Though exact numbers are unknown, Lazcano's command over vast criminal territories and diversified revenue streams likely brought him substantial wealth. The U.S. government offered a $5 million reward for information leading to his capture, while Mexico's government offered 30 million pesos, approximately $2 million. Los Zetas' reach, brutality, and efficiency made them one of the most profitable and feared criminal syndicates in the region.

While there is no confirmed evidence that Lazcano maintained direct alliances with political officials, the operations of Los Zetas benefited enormously from corruption and the infiltration of law enforcement agencies. His military background gave him an edge in structuring the organization like a paramilitary unit, and local governments often proved too weak, or too intimidated, to resist the cartel's presence. Los Zetas' operational freedom in many regions was attributed to both fear and the systemic corruption of municipal and state institutions.

Lazcano's death was seen as a critical moment in Mexico's drug war, but it did not dismantle Los Zetas. The organization continued under new leadership, though internal fractures and external pressure have since weakened its structure. Nonetheless, Lazcano's legacy persists. He is remembered as one of the most ruthless and militarized figures in Mexican organized crime history. His tenure marked a shift toward the cartel-as-corporation model, expansive, diversified, and ruthlessly efficient.

Despite commanding a reign of terror, Lazcano remained devout in his Catholic faith, a paradox that baffled many observers. He funded religious projects and was said to carry rosaries and icons even into battle. His military training gave him a tactical edge that set Los Zetas apart from their rivals, bringing battlefield efficiency to the drug war. The posthumous theft of his body remains one of the most surreal episodes in the history of Mexico's narco conflict, prompting lingering questions about his final moments and the true nature of his legacy.

Arturo Beltran Leyva

Arturo Beltrán Leyva began his criminal career as a key figure within the Sinaloa Cartel, working closely with Joaquín "El Chapo" Guzmán. Alongside his brothers Carlos, Alfredo, and Héctor he served as both underboss and security chief, playing a pivotal role in cartel operations. However, in 2008, following the arrest of his brother Alfredo, which Arturo blamed on a betrayal by El Chapo, the Beltrán Leyva brothers broke away from the Sinaloa Cartel and formed their own organization: the Beltrán Leyva Cartel.

The newly formed cartel quickly became a major player in the drug trade. It was deeply involved in the production, transportation, and wholesale distribution of multiple narcotics, including cocaine, marijuana, heroin, and methamphetamine. The organization established control over vital drug trafficking corridors into the United States and diversified its criminal portfolio to include money laundering, arms trafficking, and orchestrated violence against civilians and law enforcement across Mexico.

Beltrán Leyva was widely feared for his ruthlessness and respected for his strategic mind. He was known for his ability to build powerful alliances and infiltrate high-ranking institutions within the Mexican government. Through a combination of bribery and intimidation, he secured influence over political, judicial, and law enforcement figures, allowing his organization to operate with relative impunity.

In December 2009, Arturo Beltrán Leyva became the target of a high-profile operation by the Mexican Marines. Acting on intelligence, authorities located him in a luxury apartment complex in Cuernavaca. What followed was a 90-minute shootout involving nearly 200 marines. Beltrán Leyva and several of his bodyguards were killed in the confrontation. The successful operation was hailed as one of the most important victories in Mexico's ongoing war against drug cartels.

At the height of his influence, Beltrán Leyva was regarded as one of the most powerful drug lords in Mexico. His cartel's activities spanned the country and extended into the United States, generating vast sums of illicit income. In 2008, the U.S. Department of the Treasury placed him under sanction via the Foreign Narcotics Kingpin Designation Act, freezing his assets and prohibiting U.S. businesses and individuals from engaging with him financially.

Beltrán Leyva's cartel was particularly notorious for its ability to corrupt officials at every level. One of the most egregious examples was the infiltration of Mexico's Attorney General's office, where key officials were found to be receiving large bribes in exchange for intelligence on anti-drug efforts. This institutional penetration shielded the cartel from law enforcement for years.

The operation that ended Arturo Beltrán Leyva's life took place on December 16, 2009. The assault on his Cuernavaca hideout marked a devastating blow to the cartel's leadership. His death created an immediate power vacuum within the organization, sparking infighting and a rapid decline in cohesion and control.

Beltrán Leyva's death resulted in the disintegration of his once-formidable criminal empire. As the cartel splintered, rival factions emerged, leading to a spike in violence as groups competed for dominance over lucrative trafficking routes and territories. The internal fragmentation weakened the cartel's national and international operations.

Despite the brutal nature of his business, Beltrán Leyva was known for his extravagant personal life. He reportedly hosted lavish parties featuring prominent musicians and entertainers. His death was heavily publicized, with graphic images of his bullet-ridden body widely circulated by the media. These photos became a symbolic representation of the Mexican government's hardline stance against organized crime.

Edgar Valdez "La Barbie" Villarreal

Edgar Valdez Villarreal, better known by his nickname "La Barbie," began his journey into the criminal underworld during his teenage years in Laredo, Texas. While still in high school, he was already dealing marijuana, which eventually drew legal scrutiny and forced him to flee to Mexico. There, his fluency in English and deep familiarity with American culture made him a valuable asset to the Beltrán-Leyva Cartel. Valdez quickly rose through the ranks, becoming a top lieutenant and later the leader of the cartel's feared enforcement arm, "Los Negros." His unique cross-border ties and strategic acumen helped solidify his position within the Mexican drug trafficking hierarchy.

Valdez played a central role in the cartel's operations, overseeing the movement of massive quantities of cocaine from South America into the United States. As the head of Los Negros, he orchestrated a reign of terror, using extreme violence to enforce cartel control and eliminate rivals. His crew was known for kidnappings, torture, executions, and high-profile assassinations. His methods earned him a reputation for both brutality and effectiveness, helping to preserve the cartel's influence during a particularly volatile period of Mexico's drug war.

Despite his ruthless enforcement tactics, Valdez cultivated a flamboyant and ostentatious public image. He reportedly spent $200,000 on a biographical film about his life, though it was never released, and lived lavishly in Mexico City, owning multiple high-end properties. His style mixed calculated violence with showmanship, setting him apart from other cartel leaders who preferred to operate in the shadows.

One of the most infamous episodes involving Valdez was his alleged harboring of José Jorge Balderas Garza, the man responsible for shooting Paraguayan soccer star Salvador Cabañas in 2010. The incident brought increased scrutiny to Valdez, who was also believed to have ties to international criminal networks, including the Israeli mafia. His ability to build alliances across continents and cartels underscored the transnational nature of modern organized crime.

Valdez's empire made him enormously wealthy, with operations generating millions in drug profits. He flaunted his wealth openly, adopting the extravagant lifestyle typical of Mexico's narco-elite. Yet, despite his high-profile presence, he managed to avoid capture for several years, thanks in part to alleged cooperation with U.S. agencies such as the DEA and FBI. Some reports suggest that Valdez provided intelligence on rival cartels, using this information to disrupt competitors and rise further within the underworld.

His downfall came on August 30, 2010, when Mexican Federal Police captured him near Mexico City after a year-long manhunt. The arrest was heralded as a major victory in the government's war against the cartels. In 2015, Valdez was extradited to the United States, where he faced multiple charges including drug trafficking and money laundering. In June 2018, he was sentenced to 49 years and one month in federal prison and ordered to forfeit $192 million in criminal proceeds. As of April 2025, he remains incarcerated at USP Coleman II, a high-security federal prison in Florida.

Valdez's legacy is a complex blend of violence, strategy, and betrayal. His arrest and cooperation with U.S. authorities significantly weakened the Beltrán-Leyva Cartel and provided valuable intelligence that fueled further operations against organized crime. Despite his fall from power, the effects of his tenure continue to ripple through the landscape of Mexico's criminal underworld.

Among the more surprising elements of his story is the origin of his nickname, "La Barbie," bestowed upon him by a high school football coach because of his striking resemblance to a Ken doll. That image of a clean-cut American youth stood in stark contrast to the brutal cartel enforcer he would become. His international connections, media aspirations, and ultimate betrayal of cartel allies made him one of the most notorious and enigmatic figures of the drug war era.

Eastern European Organized Crime

The collapse of communism across Eastern Europe unleashed a surge in organized crime. Fragile institutions, weak rule of law, porous borders, and widespread corruption created fertile ground for criminal networks to flourish. From human trafficking and drug smuggling to arms trade and cybercrime, these groups exploited the region's newfound openness and economic instability.

Among the most influential are the Albanian mafia, which emerged in the 1990s as a major force in pan-European cocaine trafficking. Known for its rigid code rooted in "besa" (honor) and clan-based discipline, it shifted operations into Italy, the UK, Canada, and South America. The term "narco-state" has even been used to describe Albania due to deep political penetration by these networks.

In the post-Soviet space, Russian, Ukrainian, Georgian, Serbian, and Romanian mafias rapidly institutionalized as notorious "thieves-in-law" emerged. They capitalized on the chaos of privatization, engaging in racketeering, arms trafficking, cyber fraud, and protection rackets. Eurasian syndicates have also forged alliances with Western European mafias and Latin American cartels, reflecting their growing global integration.

In the Balkans, crime organizations thrived via smuggling routes, refugee flows, and ethnic tensions. Criminal enterprises in countries like Croatia, Bosnia, Montenegro, and Slovenia often collaborate with Albanian or Serbian groups. Meanwhile, the Slovak mafia, though smaller, plays roles in extortion, money-laundering, and cross-border trafficking.

Eastern European syndicates are also deeply engaged in cybercrime, with Russian and Ukrainian groups leveraging hacker networks, ransomware, and encrypted communications to extort global victims. Their modern playbook merges traditional rackets with digital innovation, while using money laundering through real estate, casinos, and cryptocurrencies.

Governments and law enforcement across Europe are under mounting pressure. The UNODC warns of human trafficking and illegal commodities trade, while Europol notes the complex ties between mafia-style organizations and mainstream economics. Notably, the surge in stimulant trafficking through gateways like Antwerp has fueled violent clashes involving Eastern European gangs.

Today, Eastern European crime syndicates stand as sophisticated global players, extending networks from Vancouver and London to Singapore and Buenos Aires. Their operations blend brutal street-level tactics with financial camouflage and political cover.

Simeon "Brainy Don" Mogilevich

Semion Yudkovich Mogilevich was born on June 30, 1946, in Kyiv, Ukraine. He earned a degree in economics from the University of Lviv in 1968, an academic background that would later earn him the nickname "Brainy Don" due to the sophistication of his criminal operations. During the 1970s and 1980s, Mogilevich began engaging in fraudulent schemes, notably targeting fellow Soviet Jews who were emigrating from the USSR. He would offer to sell their possessions and forward them the money abroad but instead kept the proceeds for himself. These early scams marked the beginning of his criminal career and demonstrated a talent for exploiting financial systems.

By the early 1990s, Mogilevich had expanded his influence internationally, establishing a stronghold in Hungary where he acquired legitimate businesses and formed a sprawling criminal organization. His operations grew to encompass a wide range of illegal activities, supported by an intricate network of companies that masked his true intentions. One of his most notorious schemes involved YBM Magnex International Inc., a company listed on the Toronto Stock Exchange. Mogilevich is accused of orchestrating massive fraud through YBM, defrauding investors of over $150 million. The scheme attracted the attention of international authorities and led to widespread investigations.

Beyond the YBM fraud, Mogilevich's criminal empire is believed to be involved in arms trafficking, drug smuggling, prostitution, extortion, and international money laundering. His ability to use legitimate businesses as fronts, supported by a network of shell corporations and financial instruments, allowed him to maintain a global presence while staying largely out of reach of law enforcement. His style of operation, intelligent, calculated, and cloaked in legitimacy, helped him build what many call the "Red Mafia," a sophisticated syndicate operating across multiple continents.

In 2009, Mogilevich was placed on the FBI's Ten Most Wanted Fugitives list for his role in the YBM Magnex fraud. However, despite the international attention, Russian authorities arrested him only briefly in 2008 on tax evasion charges. He was released the following year, with officials stating that the charges were not severe enough to justify continued detention. This incident fueled speculation about his protection from within powerful circles in Russia.

Mogilevich is believed to have amassed billions through his criminal enterprises. His wealth is managed through an expansive and opaque network of businesses and financial institutions, making it difficult to trace or confiscate. His organization remains one of the most powerful and well-structured criminal groups in the world. Reports also suggest that Mogilevich has long-standing ties to political and law enforcement figures, which have enabled him to operate with near impunity. These connections are believed to have shielded him from serious prosecution and contributed to his ability to remain a free man despite being wanted internationally.

Despite being indicted in multiple countries and remaining a fugitive in the eyes of U.S. authorities, Mogilevich has largely evaded prosecution. His continued residence in Moscow, where he is believed to live freely, complicates any efforts to bring him to justice, especially given the lack of an extradition treaty between Russia and the United States. Law enforcement agencies worldwide continue to monitor his activities, but his legal situation remains unchanged.

As of the latest available information, Semion Mogilevich continues to reside in Moscow and is still wanted by the FBI for charges including racketeering and fraud. His ability to stay out of prison despite intense international scrutiny underscores the reach and protection he enjoys. His criminal legacy has left a profound mark on transnational organized crime, particularly in the use of complex financial structures and legitimate businesses to facilitate and disguise illicit activity.

Despite his role as one of the world's most elusive crime figures, Mogilevich is a surprisingly academic individual. He holds a formal degree in economics and has employed that education to orchestrate elaborate financial crimes. He is also known to have used numerous aliases throughout his career, including Seva Mogilevich, Semen Yukovich Telesh, and Sergei Yurevich Schnaider, further complicating efforts to track and apprehend him.

Sergei Mikhailov

Sergei Mikhailov began his journey into organized crime from humble beginnings. Originally working as a waiter in Moscow, he entered the criminal world after being convicted of fraud in 1984. Following his release from prison, Mikhailov shifted his focus toward more ambitious ventures. In the late 1980s, as the Soviet Union teetered on the brink of collapse, he co-founded the Solntsevskaya Bratva alongside Viktor Averin in the Solntsevo District of Moscow. The gang thrived in the chaos of the era, recruiting disaffected local youths and forging alliances with established criminals. With the political and economic structures of the Soviet regime unraveling, Mikhailov capitalized on the opportunity to build one of the most powerful and far-reaching criminal organizations in Russia.

Under Mikhailov's leadership, the Solntsevskaya Bratva developed into a sophisticated and diversified criminal enterprise. Its operations included racketeering, extortion, drug trafficking, arms smuggling, money laundering, and contract killings. Mikhailov was instrumental in establishing international partnerships with other criminal groups, including Colombian drug cartels and Italian mafia families. These connections facilitated a global network of operations and allowed the Bratva to expand well beyond the borders of Russia, engaging in transnational crime with a level of organization that rivaled any Western syndicate.

Mikhailov was known for his strategic mindset and ability to blend into both the underworld and the legitimate business sphere. He invested heavily in businesses used to launder illicit profits, helping the organization maintain a facade of legality. His leadership style fused traditional mafia tactics with corporate strategies, creating an organizational structure that was both ruthless and efficient. This approach not only ensured operational success but also allowed the Solntsevskaya Bratva to present itself as a legitimate economic force during a time when many Russian industries were undergoing chaotic privatization.

One of the most high-profile incidents in Mikhailov's career occurred in 1996 when he was arrested in Switzerland on charges related to the use of false documents and violations of property ownership laws. He spent two years in custody awaiting trial, during which time public interest in his case surged. However, he was ultimately acquitted due to a lack of sufficient evidence. The case was marred by the murder of key witness Vadim Rosenbaum in Amsterdam before he could testify, a development that cast a dark shadow over the proceedings and fueled speculation about the Bratva's reach and capacity for silencing threats.

Although the exact value of Mikhailov's wealth remains unknown, it is widely accepted that his criminal operations generated substantial revenue. The gang's dominance in illicit markets, combined with investments in legitimate real estate and business ventures both in Russia and abroad, contributed to his fortune. The financial power of the Solntsevskaya Bratva allowed them to wield influence across multiple sectors, creating a blend of underworld dominance and surface-level legitimacy that was difficult for authorities to penetrate.

The Bratva's long-term success was also bolstered by reported connections with political figures and law enforcement officials. These relationships provided the organization with a measure of protection, allowing them to operate with relative impunity during key periods. Bribes, favors, and mutual interests created a buffer that shielded Mikhailov and his associates from sustained prosecution and allowed them to maintain their grip on power.

Despite the Swiss arrest and ongoing scrutiny from international law enforcement, Mikhailov managed to avoid long-term incarceration. The Solntsevskaya Bratva continued to evolve, adapting to new political landscapes and shifting criminal markets. As of the latest public records, Mikhailov remains alive, though his current activities and whereabouts are largely unknown. He has taken a low-profile approach in recent years, retreating from public view and allowing speculation to swirl about the extent of his ongoing influence.

Mikhailov's role in founding and shaping the Solntsevskaya Bratva left a permanent mark on the world of organized crime. The structure, tactics, and global operations he helped design have served as a blueprint for other criminal organizations, and his strategies are still studied by law enforcement and criminologists trying to understand and combat Russian organized crime. His life and operations have been chronicled in various media, including documentaries and books like *McMafia* by Misha Glenny.

The reach of the Solntsevskaya Bratva under Mikhailov's leadership extended far beyond Russia. The organization established footholds in the United States, Israel, and numerous European countries, partnering with other criminal syndicates to amplify their impact. The gang's global alliances enhanced its capacity for drug trafficking and money laundering, cementing its place among the most powerful and feared criminal organizations in the world. Mikhailov's rise from a waiter to a criminal kingpin stands as a defining example of the opportunities that emerged in the lawless aftermath of the Soviet collapse.

Leonid Bilunov

Leonid Bilunov was born in 1949, without much being publicly documented about his early years. During the Soviet era, he became involved in criminal activities and eventually aligned himself with the Solntsevskaya Bratva, one of Russia's most powerful and feared criminal organizations. His rise through the ranks was driven by a keen strategic mind and an exceptional talent for building influential relationships that expanded his reach both inside and outside the criminal underworld.

Bilunov's criminal operations included racketeering, extortion, and large-scale money laundering. He leveraged his role within the Solntsevskaya Bratva to build a diversified portfolio of illicit enterprises, which eventually gave way to legitimate ventures. His activities crossed borders and made him a known figure not only in Russia but also in international business and criminal networks.

Despite his underworld affiliations, Bilunov developed a reputation for sophistication and charisma. He carefully crafted a public persona that merged the worlds of high society and organized crime. Frequently appearing in media and social functions, he portrayed himself as a legitimate businessman and philanthropist, seeking to distance himself from his criminal background. This calculated image management contributed significantly to his survival in both legal and public arenas.

In the 1990s, Bilunov's past caught up with him in the form of legal troubles, including extradition requests and criminal investigations. Yet he consistently avoided major convictions. He often cited his charitable work and business contributions as proof of his reformation, which helped him maintain a favorable public image even under scrutiny.

Through a combination of criminal profits and strategic investments, Bilunov amassed substantial wealth. His holdings in real estate and finance allowed him to embed himself in international business circles. His continued financial success was underpinned by shrewd partnerships and a reputation for navigating high-stakes environments with tactical precision.

Bilunov's ability to avoid significant legal repercussions raised suspicions about his ties to political and law enforcement figures. Various reports suggest that these connections played a key role in shielding him from prosecution and supporting his business activities across multiple countries.

Though frequently investigated, Bilunov never suffered a major downfall. His skillful rebranding and philanthropic work helped to deflect public and legal pressure. His story stands as a striking example of how image manipulation and strategic alliances can insulate a figure with a criminal past from the consequences typically associated with such a life.

As of May 2025, Leonid Bilunov is believed to be alive and residing in France. He remains active in both business and philanthropy, continuing to operate in Russian and international circles while maintaining a public presence.

Bilunov's legacy is layered and controversial. He is remembered not only for his rise in the Solntsevskaya Bratva but also for his transformation into a prominent businessman and public figure. His life represents the blurred line between criminality and legitimacy that characterizes much of post-Soviet Russia's elite.

Among the more surprising aspects of his life is the publication of his memoir, *Three Lives*, in which he chronicles his journey from poverty to prominence, offering insights into his internal transformation. He also appeared in the 2010 documentary *Thieves by Law*, where he discussed the world of Russian organized crime and shared firsthand accounts of his involvement. Despite his criminal origins, Bilunov has been recognized for his charitable efforts, including significant donations to the restoration of churches in France, reinforcing the contradictions that define his complex public image.

Zakhary "Shakro Molodoy" Kalashov

Zakhary Kalashov, better known as "Shakro Molodoy," began his rise within the criminal underworld in 1971 when he was reportedly "crowned" as a thief-in-law in Tbilisi, Georgia. His early years were marked by a series of prison sentences between 1971 and 1985, shaping his resilience and strengthening his reputation among other criminals. After serving his time, Kalashov relocated to Moscow in 1989, where he cultivated alliances with some of the most powerful figures in the Russian underworld, including Aslan Usoyan, known as "Ded Khasan," and Vyacheslav Ivankov, famously called "Yaponchik." Over the ensuing decades, Kalashov's influence grew steadily, and he came to be regarded as one of the most authoritative and respected leaders within both the Russian and Georgian criminal communities.

Kalashov's criminal portfolio was broad and lucrative. He was involved in money laundering on an international scale, orchestrated sophisticated extortion and racketeering schemes, and was connected to operations involving kidnapping and drug trafficking. His name was also linked to the "Brothers' Circle," a powerful transnational criminal organization that united elite mob figures from across the former Soviet Union. This syndicate facilitated cooperation across borders and enabled its members to expand their reach into various European markets. Kalashov's strategic mind and low-profile demeanor allowed him to thrive behind the scenes, where he exercised control without drawing unnecessary attention. His ability to mediate internal conflicts further cemented his role as a stabilizing force among rival factions.

One of the most significant chapters in Kalashov's career came in 2005 when Spanish authorities launched "Operation Wasp," targeting high-ranking members of the Brothers' Circle. Kalashov fled to the United Arab Emirates to avoid arrest but was apprehended in 2006 and extradited to Spain. In 2010, he was convicted and sentenced to seven and a half years in prison, along with a €20 million fine for money laundering and racketeering. His sentence was later increased to nine years and the fine raised to €22.5 million, reflecting the severity and scale of his crimes. Years later, in 2016, Kalashov again made headlines when he was arrested in Moscow for his role in an extortion case connected to a deadly shootout at the upscale Elements restaurant. The investigation exposed deep-rooted corruption, leading to the arrest of several high-ranking officials from Russia's Investigative Committee who were accused of accepting bribes to release Kalashov's associates.

Throughout his criminal reign, Kalashov accumulated vast wealth through his control over international criminal operations, particularly in money laundering and extortion. His reach extended well beyond Russia, influencing illicit activities across Europe and the broader post-Soviet region. His ability to operate for decades without significant interference raised questions about possible protection from political or law enforcement contacts. Although specific relationships were never fully confirmed, the involvement of senior officials in his later legal troubles suggests at least some degree of integration with official sectors.

After completing his sentence in Spain, Kalashov was extradited to Russia in 2014. Just two years later, he was rearrested in Moscow in connection with the extortion case tied to the Elements shootout. In 2018, he was sentenced to nine years and ten months in a maximum-security penal colony. While in prison, reports surfaced of severe health issues, including near-total blindness. Citing medical grounds, Russian authorities granted

Kalashov early release in March 2024, ending one of the longest and most complex criminal careers in modern Russian history.

Kalashov's legacy is that of a master strategist whose leadership solidified the post-Soviet criminal order. His influence on organized crime spanned generations and borders, marked by a balance of force, diplomacy, and deeply rooted networks. He is remembered not just for his wealth and power, but for his role in uniting disparate factions under a more centralized and cooperative criminal framework.

Despite his hardened reputation, Kalashov's life included some notable and surprising elements. His nickname, "Shakro Molodoy," or "Young Shakro," was a nod to his early prominence within the criminal world. Like Aslan Usoyan, Kalashov was of Yazidi Kurdish descent, a minority community known for its unique cultural and religious identity. His arrest and conviction in Spain were seen as one of the most impactful blows against Russian organized crime in Western Europe, underscoring the transnational nature of his operations and the wide reach of the network he helped to build.

Tariel Oniani

Tariel Oniani was born in 1952 in Tkibuli, Georgia, and experienced hardship early on when his father died in a mining accident. At the age of 17, he was convicted of armed robbery. While serving time in prison, he was initiated as a *vor v zakone*, a prestigious rank within the criminal underworld signifying elite status. By the 1980s, Oniani had risen to become one of the most powerful and influential crime figures in Moscow.

His criminal empire eventually extended beyond Russia, reaching into Western Europe. In the 1990s, Oniani operated in Paris before relocating to Spain, where he became deeply involved in a range of illicit enterprises including money laundering, human trafficking, and organized crime. He diversified his operations by acquiring stakes in multiple businesses, notably a construction company that employed illegal Georgian immigrants. In 2005, Spanish authorities launched a major operation against his organization, resulting in numerous arrests. Although he initially escaped capture, the operation marked a turning point in his criminal trajectory.

Oniani was known for his strategic thinking and assertive expansion tactics. He was unafraid to push into rival territories, which sparked intense conflicts within the criminal underworld. His approach defied conventional boundaries, making him both a respected and feared figure among other gang leaders.

One of the most infamous chapters in Oniani's life was his long-standing feud with fellow crime boss Aslan Usoyan, also known as "Grandpa Hassan." The rivalry escalated into a brutal gang war that led to the assassination of Vyacheslav Ivankov, a revered mediator in the criminal community, in 2009. Ivankov's murder was widely seen as a consequence of the ongoing conflict between Oniani and Usoyan.

Through his extensive operations in extortion, illegal gambling, and laundering illicit funds, Oniani amassed significant wealth and controlled a vast criminal network. His dominance within the Georgian mafia, particularly the Kutaisi clan, further solidified his status in both European and Russian criminal circles.

Oniani's cross-border operations were made possible by his connections with various political and law enforcement officials. These relationships helped him avoid prosecution for years, but as these protections eroded, he became increasingly vulnerable to arrest and extradition.

In 2009, Russian authorities arrested Oniani for the kidnapping of a businessman. He was convicted and sentenced to 10 years in prison. Upon completing his sentence in April 2019, he was immediately re-arrested due to an outstanding extradition request from Spain, where he faced charges related to money laundering and organized crime. He was extradited to Spain in October 2019.

As of May 2025, Tariel Oniani remains alive and is currently incarcerated in Spain, serving time for a range of criminal convictions. His life continues to attract attention from international law enforcement and scholars of organized crime.

Oniani's legacy is defined by his rise to power, transnational influence, and involvement in some of the most notorious underworld conflicts of the modern era. His name is frequently cited in analyses of Eurasian criminal syndicates and their global reach.

Among the more surprising aspects of his career is a 2008 meeting aboard his private yacht, where he attempted to negotiate peace between rival factions. The gathering was raided by Russian authorities, resulting in several arrests. Despite his criminal history, Oniani invested in legitimate ventures, including an airline and construction companies, which he used to launder illegal profits. His daughter, Gvantsa, was briefly detained during the 2005 Spanish crackdown on his organization, a testament to how deeply his criminal activities affected his personal life.

Aslan "Grandpa Hasan" Usoyan

Aslan Usoyan, born in Tbilisi, Georgia, began his criminal career in the 1950s, engaging in petty crimes like pickpocketing and currency speculation during the Soviet era. Sometime in the 1960s, he was officially "crowned" as a thief-in-law, a prestigious title within the Russian criminal hierarchy that signified both respect and seniority. Over the following decades, Usoyan gradually expanded his reach, building a formidable criminal empire that extended from Moscow to the Urals, Siberia, and into Central Asia. His rise was marked not by flamboyant violence, but by careful alliances and strategic influence, eventually making him one of the most powerful crime figures in post-Soviet Russia.

Usoyan's empire spanned an extensive range of illicit enterprises. He controlled drug trafficking networks, illegal gambling rings, and arms smuggling operations. Extortion and racketeering were standard tools in his playbook, and he also exercised control over large swaths of the construction and real estate industries. Beyond traditional criminal ventures, he was even accused of supplying funds and weapons to the Kurdistan Workers' Party (PKK), a Kurdish militant group, a move that further hinted at his wide geopolitical footprint and controversial dealings.

Known for his discretion and strategic mindset, Usoyan operated largely behind the scenes. He avoided public attention and preferred to act as a mediator within the criminal community, helping to settle disputes between rival factions. His reputation for diplomacy, combined with his seniority, earned him widespread respect and positioned him as a unifying figure during times of tension between powerful criminal groups.

Usoyan's life was marked by multiple assassination attempts. In 2010, he survived a high-profile shooting in Moscow, which only reinforced his image as a hardened survivor and symbol of stability. However, his luck ran out in 2013, when a sniper fatally shot him outside his favorite restaurant in Moscow. The assassination was widely believed to be the result of escalating tensions with rival factions, particularly those aligned with Georgian mob boss Tariel Oniani. His death stirred fears of renewed turf wars in the Russian underworld.

While exact financial figures are difficult to confirm, Usoyan was believed to have accumulated substantial wealth through both illegal and legitimate business activities. His holdings in the construction and real estate sectors alone were reportedly extensive, and his influence reached well beyond Russia's borders. His name surfaced in connection with several major developments, most notably projects related to the 2014 Sochi Winter Olympics, hinting at his quiet integration into official circles.

Usoyan's ability to operate so freely for decades raised questions about his connections within political and law enforcement bodies. While no concrete affiliations were ever made public, his role in major construction initiatives and his long-standing freedom from serious prosecution suggest at least a degree of protection or strategic alignment with corrupt elements in official institutions.

His downfall came on January 16, 2013, when he was assassinated by a sniper in central Moscow. The killing, attributed to factional conflict within the Russian and Georgian criminal networks, abruptly ended the reign of a man long seen as a stabilizing presence in a volatile world. The hit was widely seen as a turning point, ushering in uncertainty and potential fragmentation among the once-unified criminal factions.

Usoyan's funeral drew hundreds of mourners, including numerous underworld figures, demonstrating the scope of his influence and the void his death left behind. It was a final show of reverence for a man whose quiet but firm leadership helped define an entire era of organized crime in the post-Soviet landscape.

Usoyan's legacy is one of both consolidation and complexity. Known as "Grandpa Hasan," he was considered a father figure among criminals, guiding a fractured underworld toward relative unity and discipline. His reputation for balance and arbitration left an enduring impact on how organized crime operated in Russia and its neighboring regions. Even in death, he remains a symbol of mafia order in a world increasingly defined by chaos and competition.

Despite his criminal empire, Usoyan was known for some surprising aspects of his identity. Of Yazidi Kurdish descent, he belonged to a small and distinct ethnic minority. His cultural background added another layer to his complex public persona. He also held deep ties to Sochi, a city he reportedly considered his "second homeland," and was heavily involved in its development in the lead-up to the Winter Olympics, a symbol of how seamlessly criminal power could blend with legitimate enterprise under the right leadership.

Marat Balagula

Marat Balagula was born on September 8, 1943, in Chkalov (now Orenburg), USSR, to Soviet Jewish parents. After World War II, his family relocated to Odesa, Ukraine. There, Balagula earned degrees in mathematics and economics and later secured a job aboard the Soviet cruise ship *MS Ivan Franko*. The position gave him the opportunity to engage in black-market trading, exchanging Western goods for profit. In 1977, seeking a better life, he immigrated to the United States with his family and settled in Brighton Beach, Brooklyn, a growing hub for Russian-speaking immigrants.

Initially working as a textile cutter, Balagula soon ventured into business, opening the Odesa restaurant and nightclub, which became a popular gathering spot within the local community. He later expanded into the gasoline industry, acquiring a chain of gas stations and establishing an elaborate bootlegging operation that evaded both state and federal fuel taxes. After the 1985 murder of his associate and then-leader of the Russian mob, Evsei Agron, Balagula emerged as the new de facto boss of Russian organized crime in New York, cementing his influence over the expanding empire.

Balagula's criminal operations were vast and complex. He masterminded a gasoline bootlegging scheme that defrauded the U.S. government of roughly $85 million in taxes by using shell companies and manipulating fuel sales. In 1986, he was implicated in a $750,000 credit card scam that resulted in his conviction and a prison sentence. His ventures also extended into international drug trafficking, coordinating heroin shipments from Thailand to the U.S. via Poland, as well as arms trafficking, where he purchased weapons in Florida and smuggled them into the USSR for sale on the black market.

Known for his intellect and strategic thinking, Balagula operated with a calculated and corporate approach, in stark contrast to his more street-level predecessor Agron. His operations mimicked legitimate businesses in structure, and his diplomatic demeanor allowed him to build strong relationships with influential crime families, including the Lucchese and Colombo organizations. These alliances were vital to maintaining his position at the top of the Russian mob in New York.

One of the most infamous moments in Balagula's rise came in 1986, when he was confronted by rival gangster Vladimir Reznikov. Reznikov demanded $600,000 and a stake in Balagula's lucrative operations, threatening his life if he refused. Not long afterward, Reznikov was gunned down outside a nightclub in a hit believed to have been carried out with the help of the Lucchese family. This assassination not only eliminated a threat but also reinforced Balagula's dominance over his criminal territory.

At the peak of his empire, Balagula's gasoline bootlegging scheme alone generated an estimated $150 million per month in revenue, with monthly profits reaching $30–40 million. His wealth enabled him to purchase luxury properties, including a $1.2 million home on Long Island, and invest in international ventures such as a diamond mine in Sierra Leone. Despite his immense wealth, Balagula managed to maintain a relatively low profile in both the media and public view.

There is no direct evidence that Balagula had significant political connections, but his ability to run high-level operations while avoiding detection for years speaks volumes about his sophistication. His knack for setting up front companies and laundering money through legitimate ventures displayed a deep understanding of the regulatory systems he manipulated to his advantage.

Eventually, Balagula's expansive criminal activities caught up with him. In 1986, he was convicted of credit card fraud and sentenced to eight years in prison. In 1989, he was arrested in Frankfurt, West Germany, after fleeing the United States. He was later extradited and, in 1992, convicted of gasoline bootlegging, receiving an additional ten-year sentence. He served his time and was released from prison in 2004.

On December 19, 2019, Marat Balagula died of cancer in New York City at the age of 76. His death marked the end of a significant chapter in the history of Russian organized crime in the United States.

Balagula is credited with laying the groundwork for Russian mob operations in America. His ability to forge alliances with Italian crime families, establish profitable rackets, and run a criminal empire like a multinational corporation made him a pivotal figure in the evolution of modern organized crime. His life and exploits have been portrayed in books and inspired fictional characters, including Marat Buzhayev in the film *We Own the Night*.

Despite the scale of his empire, Balagula maintained a modest public image and was commonly referred to in his community as simply being "in the gasoline business." He once declined a film director's request to shoot a scene at his restaurant, fearing the publicity. His bootlegging operation was so lucrative that the Five Families imposed a two-cent-per-gallon "family tax" on his sales, making it one of their most profitable ventures after narcotics trafficking.

Alimzhan "Taiwanchik" Tokhtakhunov

Alimzhan Tokhtakhunov was born on January 1, 1949, in Tashkent, Uzbekistan, then part of the Soviet Union. He earned the nickname "Taiwanchik" due to his Asiatic facial features. Originally aspiring to a sports career, he played for the youth team of Pakhtakor Tashkent and later worked as an administrator for CSKA Moscow. However, his passion for card games and growing ties to criminal elements gradually pulled him into the underworld. In the 1980s, he was twice imprisoned under the Soviet charge of "parasitism," typically used against those without official employment. Following the collapse of the USSR, Tokhtakhunov relocated to Western Europe, first to Germany and then France, where he expanded his business dealings and, allegedly, his criminal network.

Tokhtakhunov has been linked to a wide range of criminal activities. In 2002, a U.S. federal grand jury indicted him for attempting to rig the pairs figure skating event at the Salt Lake City Winter Olympics by bribing judges, a case that garnered global attention. He was also a key figure in the Taiwanchik-Trincher Organization, a high-stakes illegal gambling and money laundering ring based in part out of Trump Tower in New York City, which laundered more than $100 million. Interpol has connected him to several additional criminal ventures, including drug trafficking, arms dealing, and trafficking in stolen vehicles, painting a picture of a figure deeply embedded in international organized crime.

Despite his criminal associations, Tokhtakhunov cultivated a surprisingly public persona. He is regarded as a "vor v zakone," a high-ranking figure within the Russian criminal hierarchy, and has attended elite social events, often seen mingling with celebrities and athletes. While denying all criminal allegations against him, he has portrayed himself in the media as a legitimate businessman and philanthropist. His highly visible lifestyle set him apart from many underworld figures who preferred to remain in the shadows.

One of the most infamous episodes in Tokhtakhunov's history was his alleged role in fixing the figure skating competition at the 2002 Winter Olympics in Salt Lake City. The U.S. accused him of bribing judges to influence the outcome, leading to his arrest in Italy. However, an Italian court denied the U.S. extradition request, and he was released. Another scandal erupted in 2013 when U.S. authorities charged him with orchestrating an illegal gambling and money laundering ring operating out of Trump Tower. Despite the seriousness of the charges, Tokhtakhunov remained in Russia, beyond the reach of American law enforcement.

Tokhtakhunov's operations have generated significant wealth, with the gambling and laundering scheme alone moving over $100 million. He wielded influence in areas ranging from sports to high society and was known to maintain connections with prominent figures both within and outside of Russia. Although there is no public documentation of direct political ties, his ability to evade extradition and remain untouched by prosecution suggests a degree of protection or influence within powerful circles.

Multiple indictments and an Interpol red notice have not led to his arrest. Residing in Russia, which has no extradition treaty with the United States, Tokhtakhunov has remained a free man, highlighting the challenges of international law enforcement in cases involving powerful transnational criminals.

As of the most recent reports, Alimzhan Tokhtakhunov is still alive and continues to reside in Russia. He remains a fugitive, wanted by the United States for a host of criminal charges.

Tokhtakhunov's story stands as a symbol of the global nature of organized crime and the difficulties in holding powerful figures accountable across national borders. His involvement in internationally publicized scandals and his ability to remain outside the reach of justice have earned him notoriety and made him a prominent case study in the intersection of crime, politics, and diplomacy.

Known as "Taiwanchik," or "Little Taiwanese," due to his appearance, Tokhtakhunov was once deeply involved in the world of sports, both as a football player and an administrator. In recent years, he has appeared in documentaries and interviews, often dismissing allegations against him and suggesting he is the target of politically motivated persecution.

Darko Saric

Darko Šarić was born on October 21, 1970, in Pljevlja, Montenegro. He began his criminal activities in the 1990s with petty offenses but quickly rose through the ranks of the underworld. By the early 2000s, he had built an expansive smuggling operation, capitalizing on Montenegro's strategic coastal access to move cocaine from South America to Europe. His criminal organization, commonly referred to as the "Šarić clan," soon became one of the most dominant drug trafficking networks in the Balkans.

Šarić's empire specialized in the transatlantic transport of cocaine. One of the most significant busts occurred in 2009, when authorities seized roughly 2.8 tons of cocaine off the coast of Uruguay directly linked to his network. In addition to narcotics, his organization laundered drug money through a variety of businesses spread across the region, including hotels and media outlets. The clan was also known for its involvement in violent crimes, including attempted murders and direct threats aimed at government officials, further establishing its fearsome reputation.

Despite his illicit dealings, Šarić cultivated an image of legitimacy. He maintained a low public profile and operated largely behind the scenes, investing heavily in legal ventures to conceal his true income. His public persona was that of a successful businessman, which allowed him to blend into elite social circles and delay law enforcement scrutiny for years.

One of the most dramatic episodes in his career came with Operation Balkan Warrior in 2009, a coordinated effort by international law enforcement targeting Šarić's organization. The crackdown led to numerous arrests and large-scale drug seizures. In a shocking revelation in

2010, Serbian officials disclosed that Šarić had allegedly plotted the assassination of several high-ranking politicians, including the president and justice minister, in retaliation for the operation.

At the peak of his criminal career, Šarić's organization reportedly generated billions of euros annually. This immense wealth gave him leverage across both the criminal underworld and legitimate economic sectors throughout the Balkans. His vast financial resources also enabled him to fund political relationships and shield his network from prosecution, though the full extent of his influence remains speculative.

International pressure eventually forced Šarić to surrender in 2014, ending his years as a fugitive. He was extradited to Serbia, where he faced a series of legal battles. In 2018, he was sentenced to 15 years in prison for drug trafficking, followed by an additional nine-year sentence in 2020 for money laundering. These convictions marked a major victory for law enforcement in the region.

As of May 2025, Darko Šarić remains incarcerated in Serbia. His legal team continues to file appeals, but he remains behind bars, serving his combined sentences. His downfall significantly disrupted the Balkan drug trade and altered the criminal landscape.

Šarić's impact continues to resonate across the Balkans. The collapse of his empire led to the rise of rival factions, most notably the Kavač and Škaljari clans. These splinter groups have since been embroiled in violent turf wars, further destabilizing organized crime networks in the region.

Despite the weight of the evidence against him, Šarić once claimed that his fortune came from the sale of a newsstand chain for €30 million, a claim met with widespread skepticism. His organization's use of advanced communication tactics, including encrypted messages and coded newspaper ads, demonstrated a level of operational sophistication that kept law enforcement at bay for years.

Zoran "Skolet" Uskokovic

Zoran Uskoković's rise to notoriety began in 1992, when he was arrested on suspicion of involvement in the murder of Branislav Perović, an inspector with Belgrade's homicide division. Though he was eventually acquitted, the arrest thrust him into the public spotlight and established him as a prominent figure in Serbia's criminal underworld. Over time, he expanded his reach, reportedly engaging in a variety of illicit enterprises while building a presence that spanned both the criminal and business communities.

While the specifics of Uskoković's activities remain somewhat opaque, he was widely regarded as a major player in organized crime. His name emerged in connection with drug trafficking, extortion, and violent crimes, with law enforcement and media consistently tying him to key criminal networks. Perhaps most infamously, he was implicated in the high-profile assassination of Željko Ražnatović, better known as Arkan, who had been both a feared paramilitary leader and a powerful underworld figure in his own right. Though Uskoković publicly denied involvement, the accusations persisted, casting a long shadow over his reputation.

Known for his assertiveness and, at times, ruthless behavior, Uskoković was said to exert control through a mixture of charm, intimidation, and calculated aggression. His relationships with criminal associates were complex, marked by moments of loyalty and volatility alike. Unlike many in his position, he also made forays into legitimate business, owning restaurants and investing in construction projects. These ventures not only bolstered his wealth but also helped mask the extent of his criminal reach.

The most infamous chapter of his life was undeniably his alleged connection to the murder of Arkan in January 2000. The two had once shared a close personal and professional relationship, with joint interests in various business dealings, including the transfer of football players. However, tensions reportedly escalated between them over financial disputes and unpaid debts. Following Arkan's assassination, Uskoković took the unusual step of publicly denying any role, citing their former friendship as evidence. Despite his statements, the theory that he orchestrated the killing gained traction among rivals and investigators alike.

Through both his criminal activities and business investments, Uskoković accumulated significant wealth and wielded considerable influence. In Belgrade, he was viewed as one of the city's most powerful underworld figures. His operations spanned across multiple industries, giving him a level of financial leverage that extended beyond street-level crime and into legitimate sectors of the economy.

Though no direct political or law enforcement ties have been publicly confirmed, Uskoković's ability to operate for years without major legal consequences suggests some form of protection or alliance. It is widely believed that he cultivated relationships with influential individuals on both sides of the law, which allowed him to move freely and expand his empire with minimal interference.

His downfall came suddenly and violently. On April 27, 2000, Uskoković was ambushed and killed in the Vidikovac neighborhood of Belgrade, along with his bodyguard, a police officer named Miloš Stevanović. The hit was widely attributed to the Zemun Clan, a rival criminal group that had been gaining traction in Serbia's underworld. Many saw the assassination as retaliation for

Uskoković's suspected involvement in Arkan's murder and a signal of a new era in organized crime.

The assassination of Zoran Uskoković represented a major shift in the balance of power within Belgrade's criminal landscape. With his death, the Zemun Clan was able to consolidate its influence and rise to dominance. The power vacuum he left behind triggered a reorganization of criminal alliances and territorial control throughout the region.

Uskoković's legacy is one steeped in the chaos and violence that defined Serbia's criminal environment in the 1990s. His life and death remain symbolic of an era when the lines between politics, business, and crime were often indistinguishable. To this day, his story remains a point of fascination in Serbian media and among those who study the evolution of organized crime in the Balkans.

Despite his notoriety, Uskoković actively invested in legitimate ventures across Europe. He maintained a complicated relationship with Arkan, marked by business, friendship, and eventual hostility, which played a pivotal role in his rise and demise. His legacy was tragically echoed in 2021 when his son, also named Zoran Uskoković, was murdered in Belgrade, an act many believe to be rooted in the same criminal conflicts that defined his father's life.

Vyacheslav "Yaponchik" Ivanko

Vyacheslav Ivankov was born on January 2, 1940, in Tbilisi, Georgian SSR, but he grew up in Moscow, where he spent his youth as an amateur wrestler. His first encounter with the law came after a bar fight, and following his release, he transitioned into black-market dealings. These early activities led him deeper into the Soviet underworld, where he steadily built his reputation. In 1974, while serving time in Moscow's Butyrka prison, Ivankov was formally initiated as a *vor v zakone*, a "thief-in-law," marking his official rise within the Russian criminal hierarchy. By the 1980s, he was a major figure in Moscow's underworld, respected for his experience and feared for his brutality.

Throughout the Soviet era, Ivankov engaged in a wide array of criminal activities, including racketeering, armed robbery, drug trafficking, and arms smuggling. He served multiple prison sentences for various offenses. In 1992, Ivankov relocated to the United States and settled in Brighton Beach, Brooklyn, where he established a powerful criminal network. His organization quickly expanded its reach into cities like Miami, Los Angeles, and Boston, engaging in extortion, drug trafficking, and money laundering. His transnational operations cemented his reputation as one of the most formidable Russian mobsters of his time.

Ivankov was known for his direct, hands-on leadership style. Unlike some bosses who delegated their criminal operations, he often participated personally, particularly in extortion schemes. He was both strategic and ruthless, traits that earned him considerable authority within criminal circles. Despite his background, Ivankov projected a charismatic public persona and was articulate in interviews, often downplaying or outright denying the existence of the Russian mafia. His ability to balance intimidation with diplomacy made him an especially dangerous figure.

One of the most famous incidents in his criminal career occurred in 1995, when he was arrested by the FBI for attempting to extort $3.5 million from two Russian businessmen. The case led to a conviction in 1996, and he was sentenced to ten years in a U.S. federal prison. After serving his time, Ivankov was deported back to Russia in 2004, where he faced charges related to a 1992 triple homicide. However, in 2005, a Russian court acquitted him due to lack of evidence, allowing him to regain his freedom despite public scrutiny.

Ivankov's criminal empire was vast, with operations spanning Russia, the United States, and parts of Europe. His networks were involved in a variety of illicit activities, generating significant revenue and reinforcing his standing as a major international crime boss. His influence extended beyond the criminal world, Ivankov was believed to have ties to Russian intelligence and possibly collaborated with state actors to protect and advance his interests. These alleged connections likely helped shield him from law enforcement throughout much of his career.

However, his life came to a violent end. On July 28, 2009, Ivankov was shot by a sniper outside a Moscow restaurant. He succumbed to his injuries on October 9, 2009, at the age of 69. The assassination was widely believed to be part of a broader power struggle within the Russian underworld. Following his death, authorities charged three men with his murder, alleging they acted on behalf of a rival mobster seeking to eliminate Ivankov from the criminal landscape.

Ivankov's legacy is defined by his role in expanding Russian organized crime beyond the borders of the former Soviet Union. He was instrumental in setting up criminal operations in the United States and symbolized the globalization of post-Soviet criminal networks. His life has since become the subject of numerous books, documentaries, and academic research into transnational crime, reinforcing his status as a pivotal figure in modern underworld history.

Known by the nickname "Yaponchik," or "Little Japanese," due to his slightly Asian facial features, Ivankov stood out even among other criminals. His son, Eduard Ivankov, remained active in criminal circles and often represented his father's interests in both Russia and abroad, maintaining links with other prominent underworld figures.

Asian Organized Crime

Asia's organized crime networks are a mosaic of centuries-old traditions and modern, highly adaptive structures. From the prison-born triads of southern China to the ritualistic yakuza in Japan and the violent drug cartels of Southeast Asia, these syndicates reach across national boundaries, morphing fluidly into today's sprawling criminal enterprises.

Originating in the early 19th century as secret societies, Chinese triads like Sun Yee On, 14K, Wo Shing Wo, and the Big Circle Boys have maintained influence far beyond mainland China, in Hong Kong, Macau, Taiwan, and international diasporas. These groups are deeply embedded in gambling rackets, prostitution, loan sharking, and drug smuggling. The 14K triad, for example, channels heroin and opium trafficked across Southeast Asia and global routes, utilizing a decentralized, franchise-like structure. Recent European law enforcement efforts have cracked down on Chinese mafia activities across Italy, France, and Germany□.

Japan's yakuza, formally recognized through groups like Yamaguchi-gumi, Sumiyoshi-kai, and Inagawa-kai, operate openly under quasi-legal structures, comprising around 20,000 active members. Steeped in ritual such as yubitsume finger-cutting and hierarchical oaths, they balance illicit ventures like drug trafficking, extortion, prostitution, and construction kickbacks with legitimate investments in entertainment and finance. Although legal reforms since the early 2000s have chipped away at their power, the emergence of fragmented tokuryū gangs indicates the yakuza's decline has opened room for more agile and anonymous criminal groups.

The Golden Triangle, bordering Myanmar, Laos, and Thailand has endured centuries as a drug hub, first for opium and later for heroin. Today, it's the nucleus of synthetic drug production, especially methamphetamine. The Sam Gor syndicate, combining triad, Burmese militia, and other Asian criminal forte, controls an estimated 40–70 percent of the Asia-Pacific meth market, generating up to $8 billion annually. These groups have built vertically integrated operations, linking manufacture to global distribution via maritime and land corridors reaching Australia, South Korea, New Zealand, and beyond.

These syndicates don't operate in isolation. The yakuza, triads, and Southeast Asian drug lords often align with Pacific rackets, Middle Eastern smugglers, and Mexican cartels. Their alliances facilitate not only drug routes but also human trafficking, cyber fraud, and arms flows. Wan Kuok-koi ("Broken Tooth,") former head of Macau's 14K, became notorious for high-tech scams and cyber-enabled crimes, even as legitimate front organizations yielded international scrutiny and U.S. sanctions.

Governments from Japan to Southeast Asia and across Western democracies are grappling with highly sophisticated syndicates. Their challenges include cyber-enabled financial exploitation, smuggling of people and wildlife, and regional cartel alliances. Record meth and ketamine seizures in 2023, 190 tons, valued at nearly $80 billion, highlight both production scale and evolving enforcement needs. These intertwined networks demand cross-border cooperation and nuanced strategies to unravel financial and logistical webs that span multiple continents.

Kazuo "The Bear" Taoka

Kazuo Taoka was born on March 28, 1913, in Sanshōmura, Japan. Orphaned at a young age, he grew up in a harsh environment that ultimately led him to join local street gangs in Kobe during the 1930s. These early affiliations marked the beginning of his rise in the Japanese criminal underworld. In the aftermath of World War II, Taoka became the third kumicho (boss) of the Yamaguchi-gumi in 1946. At the time, it was a small yakuza group based in Kobe, but under his leadership, the organization rapidly expanded by absorbing smaller gangs and extending its reach across Japan.

Taoka made pivotal moves to strengthen the Yamaguchi-gumi, including forging alliances with other yakuza groups and introducing a formal hierarchical structure that streamlined operations. He implemented roles such as wakagashira (underboss), enhancing efficiency and command within the organization. These changes helped unify the group and laid the foundation for it to become the most powerful yakuza syndicate in the country.

Under Taoka's command, the Yamaguchi-gumi engaged in a wide array of criminal enterprises, including illegal gambling, extortion, and drug trafficking. To further bolster their operations, the organization also infiltrated legitimate industries like construction, real estate, and entertainment. This dual strategy allowed the Yamaguchi-gumi to launder illicit profits and maintain a facade of legitimacy. By integrating legal businesses into the cartel's operations, Taoka ensured a steady stream of income and minimized the scrutiny often associated with overt criminal activity.

Known as the "Godfather of Godfathers," Taoka was renowned for his strategic mind and commanding presence. His leadership was marked by strict discipline, and he was revered for his ability to maneuver through Japan's post-war power dynamics. His charisma and authority earned unwavering loyalty from his subordinates, which proved crucial as the organization grew in size and complexity.

In 1978, Taoka survived an assassination attempt by a member of the rival Matsuda-gumi. He was shot in the neck at a nightclub in Kyoto but recovered from his injuries. The failed attempt on his life sparked a violent conflict between the Yamaguchi-gumi and Matsuda-gumi. His survival only enhanced his legendary reputation within the yakuza world and demonstrated his resilience in the face of internal and external threats.

During his tenure, the Yamaguchi-gumi grew into Japan's largest yakuza syndicate, boasting more than 10,000 members spread across over 500 affiliate groups. The organization's ventures into both legal and illegal enterprises turned it into a formidable economic force. The revenue generated from these activities cemented its dominance in the criminal world and extended its influence well beyond the underworld.

Taoka also cultivated connections with politicians and law enforcement, which allowed the Yamaguchi-gumi to operate with relative impunity for years. These relationships were instrumental in facilitating the group's expansion and shielding it from serious legal challenges. However, the exposure of these ties eventually attracted public scrutiny, leading to increased pressure on authorities to clamp down on organized crime during the later years of his leadership.

His health began to deteriorate in the late 1970s due to heart disease, and he ultimately died from a heart attack on July 23, 1981, at the age of 68. His passing created a power vacuum within the Yamaguchi-gumi, igniting internal struggles that would significantly impact the group's future.

Following his death, Taoka's widow, Fumiko Taoka, temporarily assumed leadership of the Yamaguchi-gumi, guiding the organization until a successor could be appointed. In 1984, Masahisa Takenaka was named the fourth kumicho, but his assassination in 1985 triggered a brutal gang war known as the Yama-Ichi War, plunging the organization into further turmoil.

Kazuo Taoka is remembered as one of the most influential and iconic figures in the history of the yakuza. His leadership transformed the Yamaguchi-gumi from a regional gang into a nationwide syndicate with vast economic and political influence. His methods of organization, expansion, and integration of legal business operations set a model that other yakuza groups would follow for decades.

Among the more unusual aspects of Taoka's legacy is his nickname, "The Bear," earned because of his large physical stature and his reported technique of gouging out opponents' eyes during combat. He also had a noted interest in Japan's entertainment scene, building relationships with celebrities and athletes to extend the Yamaguchi-gumi's reach into mainstream culture.

Yoshinori "Mr. Gorilla" Watanabe

Yoshinori Watanabe was born in the small town of Mibu in Tochigi Prefecture. After finishing high school, he moved to Tokyo, where he worked in a noodle shop before eventually settling in Kobe. There, he joined the Yamaken-gumi, a prominent faction within the Yamaguchi-gumi, Japan's largest yakuza syndicate. Watanabe's rise through the ranks was swift, and by 1982, he had become the leader of the Yamaken-gumi. His ascent came during a turbulent time marked by the Yama-Ichi War, a bloody conflict between rival factions sparked by a succession dispute. Following the war's resolution, Watanabe was appointed the fifth kumichō of the Yamaguchi-gumi in 1989, bringing a decade of internal strife to an end and ushering in a new era of stability and consolidation for the organization.

Under Watanabe's leadership, the Yamaguchi-gumi expanded its footprint across nearly all of Japan, operating in 43 of the country's 47 prefectures. The organization not only intensified its traditional criminal activities, such as drug trafficking, extortion, and illegal gambling, but also expanded deeply into legitimate businesses and public infrastructure projects. One of Watanabe's most notable innovations was the introduction of corporate-style management practices. He established a pension system for retired members and began structuring the organization more like a business conglomerate than a street gang. These changes allowed the syndicate to manage its resources more efficiently and further legitimize its public-facing operations.

Watanabe was known for his understated demeanor and meticulous, strategic mindset. Unlike flamboyant yakuza bosses of earlier generations, he kept a low public profile and communicated authority through discipline and order, emphasizing a tight code of loyalty and internal regulation. His focus on control and subtlety became a hallmark of his tenure and helped redefine the syndicate's modern identity.

In 1995, following the catastrophic Great Hanshin Earthquake, Watanabe drew national attention by ordering his members to participate in relief efforts. The Yamaguchi-gumi distributed food, water, and supplies to victims, an act that was met with mixed interpretations. While some viewed the gesture as humanitarian, others saw it as a calculated move to improve the organization's public image and strengthen local influence. In a separate controversy, Watanabe made legal history in 2004 when Japan's Supreme Court held him financially responsible for a murder committed by one of his subordinates in 1995. The ruling was a landmark case in Japanese law enforcement's efforts to hold top crime bosses accountable for the actions of their underlings.

During Watanabe's reign, the Yamaguchi-gumi saw an explosion in both membership and financial power. By 2004, the organization was reportedly collecting close to $25 million annually in membership dues alone. The syndicate's investments in real estate, construction, and entertainment industries further augmented its revenue streams, solidifying its place as one of the wealthiest criminal enterprises in the world.

Although no direct evidence of political collusion was ever confirmed, the Yamaguchi-gumi's longevity and reach during Watanabe's leadership suggest deep-rooted influence within certain sectors of law enforcement and local government. The group's ability to win public contracts and operate semi-openly points to a degree of protection or tolerance from powerful institutional allies.

In a rare and unexpected move for a yakuza boss, Watanabe voluntarily stepped down from his position in

2005, reportedly due to ill health. He was succeeded by Kenichi Shinoda, known within the underworld as Shinobu Tsukasa. His retirement marked a significant moment, as most kumichō serve until death. Watanabe's decision to relinquish power was seen by many as both pragmatic and unprecedented in the rigid world of yakuza hierarchy.

Watanabe died on December 1, 2012, at the age of 71. He was found collapsed in his Kobe residence, and his death was confirmed later that day. His passing closed the chapter on one of the most transformative periods in the Yamaguchi-gumi's history, a time defined by expansion, modernization, and the subtle integration of corporate strategies into organized crime.

Watanabe's legacy is that of a reformer and consolidator. He transformed the Yamaguchi-gumi from a violent, regional crime syndicate into a nationwide enterprise with bureaucratic efficiency and corporate infrastructure. His influence reshaped the way the Japanese public and even rival factions viewed the yakuza. Whether seen as a criminal mastermind or a cunning executive in underworld garb, his impact on Japanese organized crime is indelible.

Among those who knew him, on both sides of the law, Watanabe earned the nickname "Mr. Gorilla," a not-so-subtle reference to his slightly simian facial features. Despite the mockery, the name was used with a mix of fear and familiarity. He was also known for introducing internal pension plans and other business-like policies within the syndicate, reflecting his belief that organized crime could and should operate like a modern corporation. This blend of tradition and innovation made him a unique figure in the history of Japan's underworld.

Kenichi "Shinobu Tsukasa" Shinoda

Kenichi Shinoda began his career in the yakuza in 1962, joining the Hirota-gumi, a Nagoya-based affiliate of the powerful Yamaguchi-gumi syndicate. After the Hirota-gumi disbanded, he co-founded the Kodo-kai in 1984 alongside Kiyoshi Takayama. The Kodo-kai quickly evolved into a dominant faction within the Yamaguchi-gumi, aggressively expanding its reach across Japan. By establishing branches in 18 prefectures, including the traditionally off-limits Kanto region, Shinoda demonstrated a bold departure from the organization's Kansai-centric past. His strategic ambition culminated on July 29, 2005, when he was named the sixth kumichō of the Yamaguchi-gumi, the first leader in the group's history to come from outside the Kansai region. His rise marked a turning point for the organization and set the tone for a new era of national and international expansion.

Under Shinoda's command, the Yamaguchi-gumi diversified and amplified its criminal activities. The syndicate expanded operations in drug trafficking, extortion, illegal gambling, money laundering, and the infiltration of legitimate businesses. Not content to dominate domestically, the organization also extended its footprint abroad, forming connections and operations in multiple countries. With a hand in both illicit enterprises and real industries like real estate and construction, Shinoda ensured the Yamaguchi-gumi remained one of the wealthiest and most powerful criminal organizations in the world.

Shinoda has long been known for his low-key persona and calculated leadership. Despite the scale of his operations, he maintained a traditionalist's reverence for the yakuza code of honor, emphasizing discipline, loyalty, and internal unity. At the same time, he proved remarkably pragmatic, adjusting the organization's tactics to suit evolving legal and economic landscapes. His leadership style combined old-school principles with modern strategic thinking, allowing the Yamaguchi-gumi to thrive in an increasingly globalized criminal environment.

One of the most dramatic episodes in Shinoda's criminal history occurred in the 1970s, when he was sentenced to 13 years in prison for killing a rival gang member with a samurai sword, a brutal act that cemented his reputation for ruthlessness. Years later, in December 2005, just months after ascending to leadership, Shinoda was sentenced to six years in prison for firearms violations. He served this sentence quietly and was released in April 2011. Despite these legal setbacks, his grip on the organization remained unshaken.

During his tenure, the Yamaguchi-gumi reached unprecedented levels of financial success. With revenues estimated in the billions, the group profited from a diverse portfolio of income sources, ranging from drug trafficking and extortion to gambling and investment in legitimate business sectors. The group's wealth not only funded its criminal operations but also facilitated its expansion and influence across Japan and beyond.

Though precise evidence remains elusive, the Yamaguchi-gumi's longstanding ability to operate openly has long suggested the presence of political and law enforcement connections. Their involvement in public contracts and infrastructure projects implies a level of integration with institutional powers, and the group's survival through decades of anti-gang crackdowns points to deep-rooted systems of protection or collusion within official ranks.

However, Shinoda's aggressive expansion strategy was not without consequences. His push into Tokyo and the

Kanto region, traditionally off-limits for the Yamaguchi-gumi, sparked internal divisions. In 2015, these tensions erupted into a full-blown schism when a major faction split off to form the Kobe Yamaguchi-gumi. The resulting turf wars and violent incidents marked a period of instability and fractured the syndicate's once-monolithic control.

As of April 2025, Shinoda remains at the helm of the Yamaguchi-gumi. In a surprising move, top executives under his leadership submitted a pledge to the Hyogo prefectural police, declaring their intention to end hostilities with splinter groups. This public declaration suggests a possible shift in strategy, one aimed at consolidating power through diplomacy rather than conflict, and perhaps an acknowledgment of the changing landscape of organized crime in Japan.

Shinoda's legacy is defined by his transformative impact on the Yamaguchi-gumi. He oversaw its transition from a Kansai-based syndicate to a nationwide and international powerhouse. His blend of traditional values and strategic modernization left a lasting imprint on the organization's structure and operations. Whether remembered for his discipline, innovation, or the internecine battles his rise provoked, Shinoda remains a defining figure in the history of Japanese organized crime.

Known within the underworld by his yakuza name, Shinobu Tsukasa, Shinoda represents the archetype of the modern mob boss, quiet, disciplined, and fiercely intelligent. Under his leadership, the Yamaguchi-gumi also sought to manage its public image, participating in community relief efforts following national disasters. The group even began publishing internal newsletters to boost morale, with Shinoda reportedly contributing editorials. These unexpected gestures added complexity to his profile, blurring the line between criminal leader and institutional patriarch.

Tadamasa "John Gotti of Japan" Goto

Tadamasa Goto was born in Ebara, Tokyo, and relocated to Fujinomiya, Shizuoka Prefecture, during World War II. He began his yakuza career in 1972 when he joined a local affiliate of the Yamaguchi-gumi, Japan's largest and most powerful crime syndicate. In 1985, he founded the Goto-gumi, which quickly became a dominant force within the Yamaguchi-gumi hierarchy, especially in Tokyo and the surrounding Kantō region, an area traditionally outside Yamaguchi-gumi's sphere of influence. At its peak, the Goto-gumi boasted nearly 950 members and played a key role in expanding the syndicate's operations into new urban territories.

Under Goto's leadership, the Goto-gumi engaged in a wide array of criminal enterprises, including prostitution rings, protection rackets, white-collar crime, and real estate fraud. The group was notorious for its involvement in high-profile violent incidents, most infamously the 1992 assault on filmmaker Juzo Itami, who had portrayed the yakuza unfavorably in his films. Although Goto denied direct involvement, the attack sent a chilling message to critics and sparked national outrage. Beyond traditional rackets, Goto strategically expanded into legitimate business sectors, blurring the line between crime and commerce.

Goto cultivated a public image that mixed flamboyance with menace. He was often compared to American mob boss John Gotti, earning him the nickname "John Gotti of Japan." He socialized with celebrities, appeared in glossy magazines, and maintained connections with politicians and business elites. Despite his criminal background, Goto projected a charismatic persona, embodying a modernized version of yakuza authority that fused street power with corporate sophistication.

In one of the most controversial episodes of his life, Goto struck a secret deal with the FBI in 2001 to receive a liver transplant in the United States. He donated $100,000 to UCLA Medical Center and offered limited intelligence on Yamaguchi-gumi activities in exchange for a special visa. The deal was later exposed by journalist Jake Adelstein, triggering a wave of backlash. Adelstein received death threats, and the story cast international scrutiny on Goto's operations. The transplant episode remains one of the most infamous examples of a criminal boss leveraging global institutions for personal gain.

Goto's criminal empire brought him immense wealth. He reportedly controlled more than a hundred front companies, and estimates of his total assets reached into the billions. His reach extended into banking, real estate, and even aviation, with rumors, later disputed, that he held a significant stake in Japan Airlines. Regardless of the exact figures, Goto stood as one of the wealthiest and most influential yakuza leaders of his era.

Goto's ability to operate on such a grand scale pointed to extensive connections in both political and law enforcement circles. He was allegedly involved in political campaign financing and was known to have ties with several prominent politicians. His ability to secure a U.S. visa through an FBI deal underscored his skill at manipulating both domestic and international institutions to protect his interests.

Despite his success, Goto's unchecked ambition and increasingly public lifestyle eventually led to his downfall. In 2008, he was expelled from the Yamaguchi-gumi amid growing disapproval of his behavior, particularly the controversy surrounding his liver transplant and his ostentatious displays of wealth. His expulsion fragmented the Goto-gumi and severely weakened his standing within the yakuza world.

Following his expulsion, Goto shocked the nation by announcing his retirement from organized crime and entering the Buddhist priesthood. In 2009, he adopted the name "Chuei" and began training at a temple in Kanagawa Prefecture. His ordination, held on April 8, Buddha's birthday in Japan, marked an unexpected turn in the life of one of Japan's most notorious mob bosses.

Goto's legacy remains polarizing. He is remembered both as a ruthless enforcer and as a figure who tried, in his own way, to navigate the boundaries between tradition, power, and modernity. His memoir, *Habakarinagara* ("With All Due Respect"), offered rare insight into the inner workings of the yakuza and his own complex worldview. His controversial transformation from feared crime boss to Buddhist monk has sparked debate about redemption and the blurred lines between sin and salvation in Japan's underworld.

Among the more surprising facts about Goto is his portrayal in media. He served as a key inspiration for the character Shinzo Tozawa in the HBO series *Tokyo Vice*. His memoir provided a firsthand account of life inside the yakuza, and his highly publicized Buddhist ordination added a surreal epilogue to a life defined by violence, charisma, and contradiction. Whether seen as a master manipulator, a media-savvy boss, or a man seeking spiritual absolution, Goto remains one of the most enigmatic figures in modern organized crime history.

Du Yuesheng

Du Yuesheng, born on August 22, 1888, in Gaoqiao near Shanghai, endured a harrowing childhood. By age nine, he had lost his entire immediate family, his mother died in childbirth, his sister was sold into slavery, his father passed away, and his stepmother disappeared. In 1902, he returned to Shanghai and found work at a fruit stall in the French Concession but was fired for theft. After a period of drifting, he took a job as a bodyguard in a brothel, where he became acquainted with the Green Gang. By the age of 16, he had joined the gang, setting the stage for his rise to power.

Du became a central figure in expanding the Green Gang's influence throughout Shanghai. He came to control much of the city's gambling dens, prostitution, and protection rackets. With the tacit approval of local police and colonial authorities, he also ran the opium trade in the French Concession. Ironically, he became addicted to the very drug that helped build his empire, a detail that underscores the contradictions of his complex life.

Ambitious and calculating, Du Yuesheng saw himself not just as a criminal overlord but as a political actor. He presented himself as a patriot who supported Chinese unification, and he masterfully blended underworld power with political influence. His strategic navigation of both spheres gave him a unique place in Chinese society, where he was both feared and revered.

One of the most infamous events linked to Du occurred in April 1927. Alongside fellow gang leaders Huang Jinrong and Zhang Xiaolin, he created the Society for Common Progress, essentially a front group for arming thousands of thugs to suppress strikes organized by communists. On April 12, the crackdown began, quickly bolstered by

Kuomintang troops, and resulted in the deaths of thousands. Du then assumed control over the remaining communist-dominated unions in Shanghai, cementing his grip on the city.

Du's wealth during the height of his reign was staggering. Estimated to be in the hundreds of millions, his fortune came from his dominance over Shanghai's criminal enterprises and his deep entanglement with the Nationalist political machine. His influence extended beyond organized crime and into the heart of China's political and economic centers.

He maintained strong political ties, particularly with Chiang Kai-shek and the Kuomintang. For his role in massacring communist supporters, he was awarded the rank of general in the Nationalist army. In a further twist of hypocrisy, he was made head of the Opium Suppression Bureau, a position he used to confiscate rival supplies of opium for resale through his own syndicate.

As the Chinese Civil War came to a close and Shanghai was about to fall in 1949, Du fled to British Hong Kong. Despite overtures from both the Communists and the Kuomintang, he chose exile. His health declined due to asthma, and he died in Hong Kong on August 16, 1951. There are conflicting accounts of his burial; one story claims his body was taken to Taiwan by one of his wives and buried in Xizhi District, New Taipei, though doubts remain about whether his tomb truly holds his remains. A statue erected by Taiwanese authorities honors him with inscriptions praising his "loyalty" and "personal integrity."

Du Yuesheng's legacy is layered with contradictions. He is remembered both as a ruthless gang boss and a powerful political figure. Some consider him a symbol of the fusion between organized crime and state power in 20th-century

China, while others see him as a staunch nationalist. His life continues to be analyzed in both scholarly and popular circles for its unique intersections of vice, politics, and influence.

Du's personality was laced with superstition—he famously had three small monkey heads sewn into the back of his clothing, specially imported from Hong Kong. He had five wives and numerous concubines, fathering eight sons and three daughters who went on to pursue careers ranging from diplomacy to business. His larger-than-life persona has been portrayed in media, most notably in the 2012 film *The Last Tycoon*, which is loosely based on his life.

Chang "White Wolf" An-lo

Chang An-lo, born on March 13, 1948, in Nanjing, China, was shaped by upheaval from the start. His family fled to Taiwan during the Chinese Civil War, where he eventually joined the Bamboo Union, Taiwan's largest and most powerful triad organization. Known as a sharp strategist, Chang rapidly climbed the ranks. He later moved to the United States, where he earned multiple degrees, including from Stanford University, while simultaneously expanding the Bamboo Union's reach into California and Las Vegas. His ability to blend street-level influence with international reach marked the beginning of his complex dual identity as both a criminal and a political figure.

Throughout his career, Chang was involved in drug trafficking, extortion, and kidnapping. In 1986, he was convicted in the United States for drug smuggling and served ten years in prison. While incarcerated, Chang began cooperating with the FBI, offering intelligence on the Bamboo Union's operations and its ties to Taiwanese military intelligence. This collaboration raised eyebrows, as it revealed the deep entanglements between criminal groups and state actors in Taiwan.

Charismatic and politically ambitious, Chang used his platform to promote Chinese nationalism and the goal of cross-strait unification. He founded the Chinese Unification Promotion Party (CUPP) in 2004 while in China, advocating for Taiwan's reunification with the mainland under the "one country, two systems" model. His persona as a nationalist leader blurred the line between organized crime and political activism. While some saw him as a patriot, many viewed him as a frontman for Beijing-aligned criminal influence.

One of the most controversial episodes in Chang's life came in 1996 when he fled to Shenzhen, China, to escape prosecution in Taiwan. After nearly two decades in self-imposed exile, he returned to Taiwan in 2013 and was immediately arrested, though he was later released on bail. His return stirred public outrage and renewed concerns about the government's handling of high-profile underworld figures. In 2019, he was arrested again, this time on charges of accepting illegal political donations, embezzlement, and tax evasion, further reinforcing fears about the intersection of crime and politics in Taiwan.

Despite the criminal charges and continuous legal scrutiny, Chang remains alive and active as of May 2025. He continues to spark controversy in Taiwanese political circles, particularly for his CUPP party's alleged ties to Chinese funding and organized crime networks.

Chang's legacy is deeply polarizing. For some, he embodies the dangerous convergence of organized crime and political ideology in East Asia. For others, he is a provocative nationalist championing Chinese reunification. His life, steeped in both crime and politics, continues to be the subject of debate and investigation.

Amid his notorious career, there are also surprising personal twists. While serving time in U.S. prison, Chang earned two additional bachelor's degrees in psychology and sociology. In 2015, during a visit to Okinawa, he made headlines by voicing support for Ryukyu independence from Japan, claiming it was his duty as a Chinese patriot. In another bizarre moment, he stumbled into a prop coffin during a 2019 protest, an act meant to symbolize Taiwanese casualties in a war with China, that drew widespread media attention and served as a reminder of his flair for the theatrical.

Tujie Lai

Tujie Lai's rise within the Shui Fong triad is not extensively documented, but he is believed to have held a key leadership position in Macau's criminal underworld. Between 2004 and 2018, Lai allegedly oversaw a series of violent acts linked to the enforcement of casino junket debts. These included kidnappings, extortion attempts, and physical assaults, all tied to Macau's booming gambling industry. While the inner workings of the triad and Lai's exact rank remain somewhat obscure, available evidence suggests he was a central figure in coordinating operations tied to illicit gambling enforcement.

Lai is accused of leading a criminal syndicate involved in a wide range of illegal activities. Among the most serious allegations are his role in violent enforcement tactics, particularly surrounding gambling debts. Victims were reportedly kidnapped, assaulted, or threatened as part of the triad's effort to maintain control and ensure repayment within the junket system. These methods were typical of Macau's underground enforcement culture during the height of triad influence in the casino world.

Beyond physical intimidation, Lai's operations extended into large-scale financial crime. He is suspected of laundering millions of dollars through British Columbia casinos, exploiting systemic vulnerabilities in Canada's financial oversight. One common method involved purchasing significant amounts of casino chips, engaging in minimal gambling, and then cashing the chips out, effectively turning "dirty" money into "clean" casino payouts. These activities went largely unnoticed for years, allowing vast sums to circulate freely across borders.

Despite his alleged criminal activities, Lai maintained a notably low profile. He presented himself as a self-employed individual and avoided drawing attention to his background. This discretion, however, was juxtaposed with his apparent financial activities, which included high-stakes gambling and the movement of large sums through Canadian financial institutions. His behavior eventually drew the attention of regulatory agencies and law enforcement, triggering deeper investigations into his background and transactions.

One of the more telling incidents occurred in July 2017, when Lai reportedly purchased CAD $250,000 in casino chips and redeemed CAD $610,000 shortly after. This suspicious transaction raised red flags among investigators and became a focal point in money laundering probes. In 2024, Lai attempted to seal court documents that detailed his financial activities, citing personal safety concerns. This legal maneuver, though unsuccessful, underscored the sensitive nature of his operations and the potential risks tied to public exposure.

Investigations into Lai and his wife revealed a substantial flow of funds from Asia into Canada. Between Macau, Hong Kong, and Canadian accounts, the couple transferred approximately CAD $12 million. They also claimed to possess around CAD $100 million in assets based in China. These figures reflected not only significant personal wealth, but also the scale of operations allegedly under Lai's control. His ability to move large amounts across jurisdictions with minimal scrutiny illustrated the challenges of tracking and intercepting international financial crimes.

Although no direct political or law enforcement ties have been publicly established, Lai's ability to operate across borders and conduct high-value transactions suggests a level of sophistication in evading detection. The apparent success of his laundering techniques and his use of legal systems to attempt to shield records from public view further emphasize his understanding of both criminal and bureaucratic systems.

Lai's downfall began in October 2019 when he was apprehended by U.S. Border Patrol for illegally crossing into the United States. He was subsequently transferred to Canadian authorities, leading to a cascade of legal challenges. Among these was a civil forfeiture case targeting CAD $880,000 in bond money, as authorities sought to prevent his assets from being reclaimed without accountability. His capture marked a turning point in the investigation and brought increased scrutiny to casino-linked laundering schemes in Canada.

As of the latest available information, Tujie Lai is alive and residing in Canada. He remains entangled in legal proceedings related to his alleged criminal activities, though current details about his case and whereabouts are limited. His case continues to unfold quietly, reflective of the discreet persona he maintained for years.

Lai's legacy lies in the spotlight his case has placed on the vulnerabilities within Canadian financial and immigration systems. His use of casinos for laundering and the ease with which he transferred funds have become central talking points in discussions about transnational crime and regulatory reform. His story illustrates how organized crime can operate behind a veil of respectability, taking advantage of lax enforcement and delayed oversight.

One particularly revealing aspect of Lai's operations was his methodical use of casino chips to launder money. By purchasing large amounts of chips, gambling minimally, and then cashing out, he created a cycle that transformed illicit funds into seemingly legitimate winnings. His 2024 attempt to seal court documents further highlighted the lengths to which he was willing to go to protect his identity and operations, an act that, in itself, revealed just how much he had to hide.

Tse "Brother No. 3" Chi Lop

Tse Chi Lop was born in Guangzhou, China, and immigrated to Canada in 1988, eventually settling in Toronto. His entry into organized crime began through his involvement with the Big Circle Gang, a group with origins in China and known for its ties to international drug trafficking. In the late 1990s, Tse was arrested and convicted in the United States for heroin trafficking. He served a nine-year prison sentence and, upon release, reportedly shifted his focus to the burgeoning synthetic drug market. Recognizing the growing demand for substances like methamphetamine across the Asia-Pacific region, Tse began laying the groundwork for what would become one of the world's largest and most sophisticated drug trafficking operations.

Tse is alleged to have led the Sam Gor syndicate, a powerful conglomerate of multiple triad organizations. The group was known for its industrial-scale trafficking of methamphetamine, heroin, ketamine, and other synthetic drugs. With operations stretching across Asia, Australia, and New Zealand, Sam Gor quickly became a dominant force in the region's illicit drug trade. At its peak, the syndicate was estimated to control a significant portion of the Asia-Pacific meth market, generating between $8 billion and $17.7 billion annually in revenue. The scale and efficiency of the operation drew comparisons to Latin American cartels, and international law enforcement agencies began to take serious notice.

Despite the vast scope of his criminal enterprise, Tse maintained a relatively low profile. Unlike many other crime bosses who embraced public displays of power, he preferred discretion, keeping his name out of headlines for years. Nonetheless, he lived a life of considerable luxury, reportedly spending time at upscale resorts and gambling in some of the world's most famous casinos. His success in the underworld was largely attributed to his strategic mind and his talent for forging alliances across cultural and organizational lines. He managed to unify disparate criminal networks under a common business model, giving the Sam Gor syndicate a unique and dangerous cohesion.

Tse's criminal operations drew intensified international attention in the 2010s, leading to a decade-long multinational investigation spearheaded by Australian authorities. The breakthrough came in January 2021, when Tse was arrested at Schiphol Airport in Amsterdam while attempting to board a flight. His capture, carried out at the request of the Australian Federal Police, marked a turning point in the battle against Asia-Pacific drug syndicates. After spending nearly two years in custody in the Netherlands, Tse was extradited to Australia in December 2022 to face charges related to drug trafficking. His arrest and extradition were hailed as major victories in the ongoing global fight against transnational crime.

Although his personal net worth remains uncertain, the financial impact of the Sam Gor syndicate was staggering. The group's operations extended across multiple continents and deeply affected the drug markets in countries including Australia, Thailand, Myanmar, and Japan. Tse's ability to create a vertically integrated supply chain, spanning production, distribution, and money laundering, allowed his organization to operate with a level of sophistication rarely seen in the synthetic drug trade.

There have been allegations that Tse's success was partly enabled by corruption and weak law enforcement in certain jurisdictions. While concrete evidence about specific political or law enforcement connections remains scarce in public records, it is widely believed that such factors played a role in enabling the syndicate's activities for so long without disruption.

Tse's downfall began with the coordinated efforts of international law enforcement agencies. The Australian Federal Police led the charge, issuing an Interpol red notice and coordinating with other governments to track his movements. His eventual capture and extradition to Australia signaled a major disruption to the Sam Gor operation, although the full extent of the syndicate's collapse, or survival, remains unclear.

As of the latest available information, Tse Chi Lop is alive and in custody in Australia, awaiting trial. His case is ongoing, and the outcome remains to be seen. Regardless of the final verdict, his rise and fall have already left a profound impact on law enforcement strategy and international drug policy in the Asia-Pacific region.

Tse's legacy is tied to his leadership of what many consider the most powerful drug trafficking network in Asia. His organization's reach and profitability reshaped the regional narcotics landscape and highlighted the challenges of combating modern, globalized crime. He became known by the aliases "Brother No. 3" and "Sam Gor," meaning "Third Brother" in Cantonese, nicknames that masked the scale of his true influence.

One particularly striking detail about Tse was his reported gambling habit; he allegedly lost millions in a single night at a Macau casino, a reflection of both his wealth and his high-risk lifestyle. His life and operations were chronicled in the Discovery Channel documentary *The World's Biggest Druglord – Tse Chi Lop*, which examined how a quiet, strategic figure came to dominate the synthetic drug trade on a global scale.

Cheung "Big Spender" Tze-keung

Cheung Tze-keung, born on April 7, 1955, in Yulin, Guangxi, China, moved to Hong Kong with his family at the age of four. Initially trained as a tailor, he eventually gravitated toward the criminal world. In the 1980s and early 1990s, Cheung joined forces with infamous gangster Yip Kai-foon, participating in a series of high-profile armed robberies, including a 1990 heist at Kai Tak Airport that netted HK$30 million in Rolex watches. His criminal portfolio expanded further with a 1991 armored car robbery that brought in HK$167 million. Although arrested and sentenced to 18 years in prison, he was released in 1995 after the court found inconsistencies in the prosecution's evidence.

Cheung's criminal activities escalated significantly following his release. He masterminded two of the most lucrative kidnappings in history: the 1996 abduction of Victor Li Tzar-kuoi, son of business magnate Li Ka-shing, and the 1997 kidnapping of Walter Kwok, chairman of Sun Hung Kai Properties. The ransoms paid, reportedly HK$1.038 billion for Li and HK$600 million for Kwok, cemented Cheung's place as one of the most successful criminals in Hong Kong's history. His operations extended beyond kidnapping to include armed robbery, arms smuggling, and the acquisition of explosives, making him a central figure in the region's organized crime scene.

Nicknamed "Big Spender" Cheung was as flamboyant as he was feared. He cultivated a reputation for extravagant generosity and charisma, frequently handing out large tips, indulging in fine food and drink, and giving lavish gifts to friends and strangers alike. Even while incarcerated, he was known to request luxury items, including bird's nest soup, maintaining his opulent tastes regardless of circumstance.

Among the most audacious incidents in Cheung's criminal career was a failed plot in 1998 to kidnap Anson Chan, Hong Kong's Chief Secretary for Administration. Intended as revenge for the imprisonment of his associate Yip Kai-foon, the attempt highlighted Cheung's boldness and disregard for political boundaries. That same year, he reportedly acquired nearly a ton of explosives, intending to bomb government buildings, a plot that was ultimately foiled before it could be executed.

Cheung's criminal empire brought him an estimated fortune exceeding HK$2 billion. His wealth afforded him a lavish lifestyle and enabled him to bribe officials, evade capture, and sustain a loyal network of operatives. His notoriety and influence reached across borders, further complicating efforts to bring him to justice.

His downfall came in August 1998, when he was arrested by authorities in Mainland China after fleeing there to avoid prosecution in Hong Kong. He and 35 members of his gang were charged with kidnapping, arms smuggling, and illegal possession of explosives. The trial began in Guangzhou on October 8, 1998. On the first day, Cheung made a full confession. A month later, on November 12, 1998, he was sentenced to death by firing squad.

Cheung Tze-keung was executed on December 5, 1998, in Guangzhou. His death closed the chapter on one of the most notorious criminal figures in modern Hong Kong history, though his legacy lives on in popular culture.

Cheung's larger-than-life persona and criminal exploits have been dramatized in several films, including *Operation Billionaires* (1998), *Big Spender* (1999), *Trivisa* (2016), and *Chasing the Dragon II: Wild Wild Bunch* (2019). His story remains a fixture in Hong Kong's collective memory, emblematic of a unique era of criminal audacity.

One of the more bizarre footnotes of his life came after the ransom for Victor Li's release, Cheung reportedly phoned Li Ka-shing to ask for advice on how to invest the money. He was also remembered for spontaneous acts of generosity, such as giving tens of thousands of dollars to a young street painter in Bangkok, reinforcing his image as a paradoxical figure: a brutal criminal with an extravagant, eccentric charm.

Lai Tong Sang

Lai Tong Sang emerged as a prominent figure within the Shui Fong triad, a criminal syndicate founded in the 1930s in Hong Kong. By the 1990s, Lai had reportedly become the leader of the group's Macau faction. His rise coincided with a turbulent era in Macau, where rival triads engaged in violent turf wars for control over the city's booming casino industry. Among the most notorious of these rivalries was the feud between Shui Fong and the 14K triad, led by the infamous Wan Kuok-koi, better known as "Broken Tooth." Lai's leadership during this period placed him at the center of one of the bloodiest chapters in Macau's underworld history.

Under Lai's alleged command, the Shui Fong triad became deeply entrenched in a broad range of criminal enterprises. These included illegal gambling, extortion, loan sharking, drug trafficking, and money laundering. The organization maintained control over a network of nightclubs, mahjong parlors, and massage parlors throughout Hong Kong and Macau, using these establishments both for profit and as fronts for more covert operations. When Lai later relocated to Canada, authorities there would link him to multimillion-dollar money laundering schemes, suggesting that his criminal reach extended far beyond Asia.

Despite his reputed status within one of Asia's most powerful triads, Lai kept a deliberately low profile. He avoided media attention and maintained an outward image of respectability. In 1996, he successfully immigrated to Canada under a permanent resident visa and settled into a $750,000 luxury home in Vancouver. At the time, his past remained largely hidden, and his immigration approval sparked no immediate red flags. This quiet transition to suburban life was characteristic of

Lai's calculated efforts to distance himself from the violence and chaos that marked his earlier years.

However, Lai's past soon caught up with him. In July 1997, just a year after his arrival in Canada, his Vancouver home was the target of a drive-by shooting. Canadian authorities later linked the attack to the ongoing feud between the Shui Fong and the 14K triad. Wiretap recordings revealed conversations discussing a HK$1 million bounty on Lai's life, providing investigators with tangible evidence of his high-ranking position within the triad. The assassination attempt marked a turning point, prompting Canadian law enforcement to take a deeper interest in Lai's background.

Though the full extent of his wealth remains unclear, Lai's financial activities raised further suspicion. Between 2002 and 2006, investigators tracked 49 separate electronic funds transfers totaling approximately CAD $2.1 million and USD $140,000. These transactions pointed to extensive money laundering operations and provided further indication of his influence and financial capacity. The combination of luxury real estate, sizable bank transfers, and suspected criminal connections painted a clear picture of Lai's standing in the international underworld.

One of the most controversial aspects of Lai's case was his ability to enter and live in Canada for years without detection. His successful immigration, despite longstanding triad ties, raised serious concerns about the effectiveness of background checks and the sharing of intelligence between international law enforcement agencies. It wasn't until over a decade later that Canadian immigration officials were granted access to police wiretap evidence linking Lai to organized crime, giving them the legal foundation to act.

Lai's downfall came after years of quiet observation and mounting evidence. In August 2013, following extensive investigations and legal proceedings, the Immigration and Refugee Board of Canada ordered his deportation on the grounds of his affiliation with the Shui Fong triad and his involvement in organized crime. The ruling brought an end to Lai's long tenure in Canada, though by then he had already spent seventeen years living in the country undisturbed.

As of the latest available information, Lai Tong Sang is still alive. Following the deportation order, his current location and activities have remained largely unknown, in keeping with his long-standing tendency to operate in the shadows. No public record confirms whether he returned to Macau, Hong Kong, or relocated elsewhere.

Lai's story has left a lasting mark on immigration and law enforcement policies in Canada. His prolonged presence in the country, despite well-documented criminal associations, underscored the limitations of immigration vetting procedures and the need for improved international cooperation. The case served as a wake-up call to authorities on the importance of timely access to intelligence and the dangers posed by high-ranking organized crime figures operating behind a veil of legitimacy.

One of the more surprising details of Lai's time in Canada was how easily he had entered the country. His 1996 immigration application was approved without a thorough background check, granting him entry and residency without suspicion. Ironically, it was a wiretap related to a separate car-smuggling investigation that eventually exposed a plot to assassinate him, leading authorities to discover his true identity and past affiliations. It took Canadian law enforcement nearly two decades to uncover the full scope of Lai Tong Sang's ties to the Shui Fong triad and to act decisively on the information.

Raymond "Shrimp Boy" Chow

Raymond "Shrimp Boy" Chow, born Kwok Cheung Chow on December 31, 1959, in Hong Kong, immigrated to San Francisco with his family in the 1970s. His grandmother nicknamed him "Ha Jai" (Cantonese for "Shrimp Boy") due to his small stature, a traditional Chinese practice believed to ward off evil spirits. Chow became involved with the Hop Sing Boys gang in San Francisco's Chinatown and quickly rose through the ranks through his participation in various criminal activities. He was present during the notorious 1977 Golden Dragon Massacre, a pivotal moment in Chinatown's gang wars that shifted the balance of power among Asian street gangs.

Throughout the 1980s and 1990s, Chow built an extensive criminal portfolio that included armed robbery, extortion, drug trafficking, and racketeering. He served prison time in the 1980s for armed robbery and was later convicted of assault with a deadly weapon. By the 1990s, Chow had aligned himself with the Wo Hop To triad, a Hong Kong-based organization that sought to unify Asian gangs across the United States under a singular, powerful syndicate. This move elevated his status further within organized crime, and he eventually became a key figure in San Francisco's criminal underworld. His operations earned him additional convictions related to firearms trafficking and organized racketeering.

Chow was known for his flamboyant appearance and charismatic personality. Often seen in sharply tailored suits, he projected an image of confidence and community leadership. In public, he presented himself as a reformed gangster who had turned a new leaf, engaging in youth mentorship programs, giving public speeches, and participating in community events. However, law enforcement remained skeptical, viewing his transformation as a calculated disguise to continue illicit operations under the radar.

One of the most shocking episodes in Chow's life occurred in 2006, when he allegedly arranged the murder of Allen Leung, the sitting leader of the Chee Kung Tong, a Chinese fraternal organization with a long and controversial history in Chinatown. The killing was believed to be part of a larger power grab, as Chow subsequently took over Leung's leadership position. In 2014, a sweeping FBI sting operation exposed Chow's extensive criminal network and led to his arrest. The investigation, which also ensnared California State Senator Leland Yee, revealed bribery, weapons trafficking, and plots to traffic drugs and even supply arms to terrorist groups. The case shocked both the public and political institutions.

Chow's rise through the ranks of the Chee Kung Tong, combined with his connections to multiple criminal enterprises, suggested a high level of wealth and influence. Though precise financial figures were never publicly confirmed, his role at the helm of organized crime in Chinatown and his ability to walk freely among politicians and business leaders indicated deep-rooted power. His dual presence in both legitimate and illicit spheres made him a uniquely dangerous figure in San Francisco's complex sociopolitical landscape.

The case also cast a spotlight on potential political and law enforcement vulnerabilities. Chow's association with Senator Leland Yee, as well as the controversial rehiring of a San Francisco sheriff's deputy with known ties to Chow, raised serious concerns about corruption, oversight, and the reach of organized crime into public institutions.

Chow's downfall began with the years-long federal investigation that culminated in his arrest in 2014. The subsequent trial exposed the full extent of his criminal operations and debunked his claims of reformation. In 2016, he was convicted on 162 counts, including racketeering and murder, and was sentenced to life imprisonment without the possibility of parole.

Today, Raymond "Shrimp Boy" Chow is incarcerated at the United States Penitentiary in Terre Haute, Indiana. His appeals have been denied, and he remains behind bars for the rest of his life.

Chow's life story remains a complex narrative of ambition, reinvention, and deception. Once heralded as a reformed community leader, he ultimately proved to be a master manipulator who used public goodwill as a smokescreen for ongoing criminal activity. His rise and fall serve as a cautionary tale about the blurred line between redemption and deception in the world of organized crime.

Despite the seriousness of his offenses, Chow's story is full of surprising twists. After receiving civic recognition and awards for his supposed transformation, he was revealed to be a continuing criminal mastermind. His grandmother's nickname, "Shrimp Boy," originally intended as spiritual protection, would follow him into infamy as one of the most colorful and controversial figures in American organized crime history.

Wan "Broken Tooth" Kuok-koi

Wan Kuok-koi was born on July 29, 1955, in Portuguese Macau. Raised in the slums, he became involved in street fighting at a young age, a background that would shape his rise through the ranks of organized crime and earn him his nickname, "Broken Tooth," after having one of his front teeth knocked out in a fight. He joined the 14K Triad, one of the largest Chinese criminal organizations, and quickly advanced by engaging in violent turf wars and eliminating rivals. His ruthlessness and strategic cunning cemented his role as a key figure in Macau's underworld.

As the head of the 14K Triad's Macau branch, Wan oversaw a wide array of criminal operations, including illegal gambling, loan sharking, racketeering, and drug trafficking. His influence extended well beyond Macau, impacting criminal networks throughout Southeast Asia. His control over illicit enterprises made him one of the most feared and powerful figures in the region.

Unlike most triad leaders, Wan embraced the spotlight. Known for his flamboyant demeanor and media appearances, he became a celebrity of sorts. His public persona and ostentatious style became emblematic of Macau's criminal underworld in the 1990s.

Wan's criminal career reached a turning point in 1998 when he was arrested and later convicted on multiple charges, including illegal gambling, loan sharking, and criminal association. His 15-year prison sentence coincided with a broader effort to curb organized crime in anticipation of Macau's handover from Portuguese to Chinese control. His conviction marked a significant victory for law enforcement.

At the height of his power, Wan wielded immense control over Macau's gambling industry and amassed substantial wealth through his criminal enterprises. His influence was unparalleled, and he was widely regarded as one of the most powerful triad bosses in Asia.

Following his release from prison in 2012, Wan attempted to reinvent himself as a legitimate businessman and cultural figure. He founded the World Hongmen History and Culture Association, an organization that claimed to promote Chinese heritage but was later alleged by the U.S. Treasury to be a cover for illicit activities. Wan was also reportedly affiliated with the Chinese People's Political Consultative Conference, though this has been officially denied by Chinese authorities.

Wan's rebranding did not shield him from international scrutiny. In December 2020, the U.S. Department of the Treasury sanctioned him under the Global Magnitsky Act for his role in corruption and transnational organized crime. These sanctions targeted both Wan and his affiliated organizations, including the World Hongmen History and Culture Association and the Dongmei Group, highlighting ongoing concerns about his activities.

As of May 2025, Wan Kuok-koi is alive. While his exact location is unclear, he has reportedly been seen in several Southeast Asian countries, including Malaysia and Cambodia. He remains a figure of interest to international law enforcement due to his suspected continued involvement in criminal enterprises.

Wan's legacy is one of notoriety and infamy. He is remembered as one of the most iconic triad leaders in Macau's history, a figure whose life story has been dramatized in media such as the 1998 film *Casino*, which featured a character inspired by him. His career illustrates the deep entanglement of organized crime with political and business interests in the region.

Khun Sa

Khun Sa, born Sai Sa on February 17, 1934, in Loi Maw, British Burma, was of mixed Shan and Chinese heritage. Orphaned young, he was raised by his Han Chinese grandfather and received military training in the early 1950s from remnants of the Kuomintang forces who had retreated into Burma after their defeat in China. By the age of sixteen, he had already formed his own militia, laying the foundation for what would become one of the most formidable forces in Southeast Asia's criminal landscape.

Rising through the ranks of the Golden Triangle's illicit economy, Khun Sa became one of the dominant figures in global narcotics trafficking. At the peak of his power during the 1980s, he controlled a substantial portion of the world's heroin production, with some estimates suggesting he was responsible for up to 70% of the heroin entering the United States. His criminal empire leveraged the geography of the Myanmar-Laos-Thailand borderlands to sustain and expand its operations with ruthless efficiency.

Nicknamed the "Opium King," Khun Sa blended military leadership with political ambition. He publicly positioned himself as a Shan nationalist and freedom fighter, advocating for the independence and autonomy of the Shan people. His operations were conducted with a combination of guerrilla warfare tactics and political maneuvering, allowing him to both defy and negotiate with regional powers as it suited his agenda.

One of the most infamous episodes of his career came in 1989, when a U.S. federal court indicted him for attempting to import 1,000 tons of heroin. In a bold, controversial move, he offered to sell his entire opium crop directly to the U.S. government in an effort to control its distribution, a proposal that was ultimately rejected. The offer underscored his complex role as both a drug lord and self-styled political actor.

Khun Sa's immense wealth, derived from the opium trade, was not only used to fuel his operations but also invested back into his territories. He financed infrastructure development, including the construction of roads, schools, and hospitals, winning the loyalty of local populations and further entrenching his control over the region. His wealth and local power base made him one of the most influential criminal figures in Asia.

Throughout his reign, Khun Sa maintained intricate and often contradictory relationships with various government entities. At different times, he collaborated with the Burmese military and Thai authorities, exploiting these alliances to shield his empire from crackdowns and to outmaneuver his rivals. These connections played a key role in sustaining his criminal enterprise well beyond the reach of international law enforcement.

By the 1990s, however, Khun Sa's dominance began to decline. Increasing pressure from rival groups, intensified international scrutiny, and changing regional politics weakened his hold. In 1996, he negotiated a surrender with the Burmese government under the condition that he would not be extradited. His militia was disbanded, and he formally retired from the drug trade, effectively ending one of the most notorious narcotics empires of the 20th century.

Khun Sa died on October 26, 2007, in Yangon, Myanmar, at the age of 73. The cause of death was never officially disclosed, though reports cited his long-standing health issues, including heart disease and diabetes. His quiet death stood in sharp contrast to his violent, high-profile career.

To this day, Khun Sa remains a divisive figure. Some remember him as a criminal kingpin who flooded global markets with heroin and devastated communities, while others regard him as a Shan nationalist who used his power to pursue regional autonomy. His life has continued to inspire books, documentaries, and academic analysis, marking him as one of the most consequential drug traffickers in modern history.

Among the more unusual details of his life is his proposal to the U.S. government to purchase his entire opium crop, an unprecedented move in the world of organized crime. After stepping away from the narcotics trade, he invested in legitimate industries, including mining and construction, and lived relatively openly in Yangon for the remainder of his life.

Lo Hsing Han

Lo Hsing Han was born on September 25, 1935, in Kokang, Shan State, Myanmar. His rise began when he became the leader of a local militia called the Ka Kwe Ye (KKY), a force created with the backing of General Ne Win to combat communist insurgents. This role gave Lo control over opium production and trafficking in the region, marking the beginning of his ascent in the Southeast Asian drug world.

During the 1960s and 1970s, Lo became a prominent figure in the international heroin trade, especially known for trafficking high-purity "China white" heroin. His operations were rooted in the Golden Triangle, an area infamous for being one of the world's major opium-producing zones. His influence grew rapidly, making him one of the most notorious drug lords in the region.

Lo was adept at navigating volatile political environments, forming strategic alliances to preserve and expand his power. His ability to shift roles, from a militia commander to a legitimate businessman, demonstrated his pragmatic and calculating nature. He parlayed his underworld connections into a legitimate fortune, establishing a sprawling business empire.

In 1973, Lo's trajectory took a dramatic turn when he was arrested in Thailand and extradited to Myanmar. He was sentenced to death for treason due to a brief alliance with the insurgent Shan State Army. The sentence was later commuted to life imprisonment, and he was released in 1980 as part of a general amnesty. This chapter only temporarily slowed his rise.

Following his release, Lo re-established his narcotics empire and diversified into legitimate ventures. In 1992, he founded Asia World Company, which grew into one of

Myanmar's most powerful conglomerates, operating in construction, energy, and infrastructure. The company served as a vehicle for both influence and wealth, reflecting Lo's deep-rooted power.

His political connections ran deep. Lo maintained strong ties with Myanmar's military junta, which enabled him to secure lucrative government contracts for Asia World. His son, Steven Law, who is married to Singaporean national Cecilia Ng, took over the management of the company, solidifying the family's dynastic hold on economic and political influence in Myanmar.

While Lo evaded substantial legal consequences later in life, international pressure mounted. In 2008, the U.S. Treasury Department imposed sanctions on him, his son, and their companies for involvement in illicit activities and support of Myanmar's military regime. These sanctions exposed the ongoing intertwining of Lo's criminal past with his business empire.

Lo Hsing Han died on July 6, 2013, in Yangon, Myanmar, at the age of 80. His funeral was attended by many high-ranking figures, a testament to the prominence he maintained until his final days. His death marked the end of a complex and controversial life.

The legacy of Lo Hsing Han remains sharply divided. Some regard him as a savvy entrepreneur who contributed to Myanmar's development through infrastructure projects and investment. Others condemn his deep involvement in the heroin trade and the systemic corruption he helped entrench. His life serves as a case study in how criminality and legitimacy can blur within certain political systems.

Lo's transformation was so complete that he was tasked with organizing the lavish 2006 wedding of the daughter of Myanmar's then-dictator, Than Shwe. Despite being under international sanctions, his company Asia World continued to win contracts for major infrastructure projects, including ports and highways, proof that the reach of his influence extended well beyond his lifetime.

Dawood Ibrahim

Dawood Ibrahim Kaskar was born on December 26, 1955, in Khed, Maharashtra, India. His father worked as a police constable. In the 1970s, Dawood and his brother Shabir became involved in petty crimes and smuggling operations in Mumbai. Their criminal activities gradually escalated, and together they established the D-Company, which would go on to become one of the most powerful criminal syndicates in South Asia. After Shabir's death in 1981, Dawood assumed full control of the organization, expanding its reach and establishing strongholds in Dubai and other international hubs. He forged key alliances with other underworld groups, securing D-Company's place in the global criminal ecosystem.

Under Dawood's leadership, D-Company engaged in a wide range of illicit activities, including drug trafficking, extortion, smuggling, contract killings, and even terrorism. The organization built a transnational network spanning South Asia, the Middle East, and beyond. One of the most infamous events associated with Dawood was his alleged orchestration of the 1993 Mumbai bombings, a coordinated series of attacks that killed 257 people and injured over 700, shocking the nation and the world.

Dawood Ibrahim is known for his strategic thinking and ability to operate from the shadows while maintaining control over a vast and sophisticated criminal empire. He has been described as both ruthless and charismatic, with a talent for forging alliances and managing diverse operations. His criminal ventures are often supported by legitimate businesses, providing a front for laundering money and reinforcing the illusion of legality.

Beyond the 1993 bombings, Dawood has been embroiled in several high-profile scandals. He has been linked to match-fixing schemes in international cricket and maintains alleged connections to Bollywood, raising suspicions about the extent of his influence in India's entertainment industry. More controversially, he has been tied to terrorist organizations such as al-Qaeda and Lashkar-e-Taiba, a factor that has drawn widespread condemnation and attention from global intelligence communities.

Dawood Ibrahim has amassed immense wealth over the years, with estimates placing his net worth in the billions. His revenue streams span drug trafficking, extortion, and various investments in both illegal and legitimate enterprises. He has been featured on Forbes' list of the world's most wanted fugitives and is widely considered one of the most powerful and elusive crime figures in the world.

Reports suggest that Dawood enjoys protection from Pakistan's Inter-Services Intelligence (ISI), which has allegedly provided him with shelter and support. These connections have made it difficult for international agencies to apprehend him. Although Pakistan officially denies his presence within its borders, various reports continue to claim otherwise, complicating efforts to bring him to justice.

Despite being designated a global terrorist by the United Nations and the United States, Dawood Ibrahim has remained at large for decades. International sanctions have targeted his finances, and several of his known properties have been seized or auctioned off by government agencies. Yet he continues to elude capture, adapting his operations and maintaining his empire from the shadows.

As of now, Dawood Ibrahim is believed to be alive and residing in Pakistan. Though reports occasionally emerge regarding his health or possible movements, none have been conclusively verified. His continued evasion of law enforcement remains one of the most significant failures in international crime-fighting efforts.

Dawood Ibrahim's impact on organized crime in South Asia is unparalleled. He transformed D-Company from a small-time smuggling outfit into a global criminal enterprise, creating a model that has been emulated by numerous syndicates. His life has inspired countless books, movies, and documentaries, solidifying his image as one of the most notorious underworld figures of the modern era.

Among the more surprising aspects of his life is his family's connection to high society: Dawood's daughter, Mahrukh, is married to Junaid Miandad, the son of famed Pakistani cricketer Javed Miandad. Despite his criminal past, Dawood has also invested in legitimate ventures, including real estate and the film industry, further blurring the line between legality and crime in his far-reaching empire.

Closing Note

The individuals profiled in this book were not just criminals, they were architects of vast underground empires that reshaped economies, destabilized governments, and left an enduring impact on modern history. Their legacies are marked by violence, corruption, and the manipulation of power, often hidden in plain sight. While their stories can be fascinating, they are not meant to glorify, but to reveal the inner workings of a global underworld that continues to operate in shadows.

Organized crime is not a phenomenon confined to the past. It adapts, modernizes, and thrives where oversight is weakest and desperation is greatest. By understanding how these figures rose to power, and the systems that enabled them, we gain not only historical perspective, but also the tools to recognize and challenge similar forces in the present.

This book is just one step in a broader effort to document and examine the dark undercurrents that shape our world.

Enjoyed the Book?

If you found this book compelling or informative, please consider leaving a review. It helps other readers discover the work and makes a big difference.

I have more books on true crime coming soon, along with new titles across a wide range of genres including history, psychology, fringe culture, and more. Be sure to follow my author page and check out the "More from This Author" section to stay updated.

Thank you for reading.

More From This Author

Coming Soon: (final title names may change slightly)

- *50 of the Most Powerful Criminal Organizations in History*
- *The Most Brutal Wars Between Criminal Organizations*
- *The History of the Most Profitable Illegal Trades in the World*

Browse all current and upcoming titles here:
amazon.com/author/alexandergambino

If you enjoyed this book, **please consider leaving a review.** It helps others discover it and helps me to continue releasing more.

Made in United States
North Haven, CT
17 July 2025

70767068R00186